APL and bilingual le

Assessment ... learning systems are now widely
used in colleges to open up access for potential students by harnessing
their prior learning, knowledge and skills. But one major issue, language
... our education
... rs of English.
... oaching these
... systems, and
... tructures. The
... ssessing prior
... qualifications,
... here is a strong
... nples are used
... its.

... ge of Further

Further education: the assessment and accreditation of prior learning series

Also available in this series:

Introducing APEL
Maggie Challis

APL
Developing more flexible colleges
Michael Field

APL
Equal opportunities for all
Cecilia McKelvey and Helen Peters

APL and bilingual learners

Meena Wood

London and New York

To my daughters Shakira and Devika Rani

First published 1995
by Routledge
11 New Fetter Lane, London EC4P 4EE

Simultaneously published in the USA and Canada
by Routledge
29 West 35th Street, New York, NY 10001

© 1995 Meena Wood

Typeset in Palatino by
Florencetype Ltd, Stoodleigh, Devon

Printed and bound in Great Britain by
T. J. Press (Padstow) Ltd, Padstow, Cornwall

British Library Cataloguing in Publication Data
A catalogue record for this book is available from the British Library

Library of Congress Cataloging in Publication Data
A catalogue record for this book has been requested

ISBN 0–415–10421–1

Contents

Illustrations

Acronyms and abbreviations

AAT:	Assistant Accountant Trainee
ALBSU:	Adult Learning and Basic Skills Unit
APEL:	Assessment and Accreditation of Prior Experiential Learning
APL:	Accreditation of Prior Learning Systems
APLA:	Assessing Prior Linguistic Ability
BTEC:	Business and Technology Education Council
CAL:	Computer Assisted Learning
CEDEFOP:	European Centre for the Development of Vocational Training
CEREQ:	Research Centre for Occupational Training Analysis
CGLI:	City and Guilds London Institute
CLAIT:	Computer Literacy and Information Technology
DTI:	Department of Trade and Industry
ESF:	European Social Fund
ESOL:	English for Speakers of Other Languages
EVB:	External Validating Body
EUROFORM:	ESF Scheme
FE:	further education
FEFC:	Further Education Funding Councils
FEU:	Further Education Unit
FORCE:	EC vocational scheme
GA:	guidance advocate
GNVQ:	General National Vocational Qualifications
HE:	higher education
HORIZON:	ESF scheme for unemployed
JES:	Joint Efficiency Study
LASER:	London and South East Region
LEA:	local education authority
NARIC:	National Academic Recognition Information Centre
NCC:	National Curriculum Council
NCVQ:	National Council for Vocational Qualifications

NIACE:	National Institute of Adult and Continuing Education
NNEB:	Nursery Nurses Examining Board
NOW:	New Opportunities for Women (ESF scheme)
NRA:	National Record of Achievement
NVQ:	National Vocational Qualifications
PETRA:	EC vocational scheme
PGCE:	Post Graduate Certificate in Education
ROA:	record of achievement
RSA:	Royal Society of Arts
RTEC:	Refugee Training Education Council
SATS:	School Assessment Tests
SEM:	Single European Market (Act)
TDLB:	Training Development Lead Body
TEC:	Training and Enterprise Council
TEED:	Training Enterprise Employment Directorate
UDACE:	Unit for the Development of Adult and Continuing Education
VET:	vocational education and training
WRFE:	work-related further education

Foreword to the series

In Britain, the assessment and accreditation of prior learning (APL) began with the assessment of prior experiential learning (APEL). When discussion first began about APEL and further education, accreditation of anything other than examined outcomes was hardly on the map. Partly this was because APEL was seen as an additional way of widening access. But also it was because self-assessment stood out as one of the richest dividends for individuals from APEL. Accreditation might follow, but that was a separate issue. Over time, and that means from the early 1980s, the term APL has come to refer to all previously acquired learning, which necessarily includes experiential learning. So whereas APEL refers specifically to uncertificated learning, APL refers to that as well as to previous learning that has been formally certificated through some recognised examining body. Both are vital. So often the one can lead to the other and both can serve as approach routes to additional formal learning. Throughout the books in this series, this distinction needs to be borne in mind. Perhaps the easiest way is to think of APEL as a subset of APL. And now, of course, accreditation is a lively issue for both.

Discussions about introducing the assessment of prior experiential learning to formal education in Britain began with higher education in the early 1980s. About two years later, further education entered the arena in two ways. Jack Mansell, then Chief Officer of the Further Education Unit, commissioned a project which resulted in the publication in 1984 of *Curriculum Opportunity: a map pf experiential learning in entry requirements to higher and further education award-bearing courses*. Alun Davies, then the Chief Inspector for Higher and Further Education in the Inner London Education Authority, recognised the potential of APEL for further education as an influence on curriculum reform, staff development and for assisting colleges to prepare for a future that was going to be different from the past and present. So he gave a brief to a succession of enthusiastic and energetic staff in the Curriculum Development Unit to promote APEL activities in colleges wherever they could.

As some staff moved on to other posts inside and outside London,

APEL activities spread so that by the time the National Council for Vocational Qualifications was established in 1986, there were staff in a number of further education colleges who had gone some way towards developing schemes for APEL, some of them promoted by the FEU, some of them connected with REPLAN projects for the unemployed. The Unit for the Development of Adult and Continuing Education took a hand through its programme of work on Access. And as Open College Federations and Networks worked at ways of awarding official recognition to non-institutional, off-campus learning, so they added yet another strand to APEL activities. As the benefits of progression and credit accumulation began to be more widely appreciated, both APL and APEL became an increasingly important dimension to Access, while NCVQ gave a strong lead in that direction through its own version of Prior Learning Achievements

Now colleges face a different and uncertain future. It seems that to remain effective as incorporated institutions, they have to find ways of supplementing their funding from the FEFC, while pursuing policies designed to increase and widen participation. That means evolving imaginative forms of collaboration with industry and commerce. It means finding viable ways of handling Vocational Qualifications. And it all poses difficult organisational issues for a college that sets out to meet that range of requirements. So APL and APEL have become deadly serious considerations, so much so that it would be hard work to walk into any college without finding people who were talking about both. And often at the heart of those discussions there is the tension between using both APL and APEL for personal development and as a component of liberal education and seeing them as part of the provision for Vocational Qualifications.

In the real world of day-to-day activity in colleges, however, there is more talk than action. This is not surprising. Incorporating APL as a mainstream activity rather than seeing it as something rather fancy at the margins, touches issues from the top to the bottom of any institution. Overall management, academic organisation, the curriculum, modes of learning, teaching styles and delivery, admissions, student guidance and support systems, assessment procedures, relations with awarding bodies and NCVQ and, more recently, with higher education through franchising and associated status, all come into the reckoning. And since, as the books in this series imply, flexibility needs to be the hallmark of successful colleges in the future, and the effective introduction of APL requires flexibility, the message is clear. Colleges need APL to be flexible, effectively. APL requires flexibility to be successful within an institution.

This series of books on Further Education: the Assessment and Accreditation of Prior Learning, is a contribution towards encouraging colleges to incorporate APL schemes as mainstream provision. Moreover, we hope that because each of these books is written by men and women who know what they are talking about from their direct professional experience in the theory and practice of APL and APEL, whatever the particular focus of their writing, they will be of practical help to colleges and college staff wishing to develop schemes of their own.

Norman Evans, Director, Learning from Experience Trust
Michèle Bailleux, Deputy Director, Learning from Experience Trust
London

Acknowledgements

The author would like to thank the following people for their professional help and for their contribution of material: Inder Geer/Harminder Geer (language consultants); Jean Cook (Business Management and Humanities, Newham College of Further Education); Denise Clarke (Student Learning Support, Newham College of Further Education); Pieter Gebrundy (NCVQ); and Europe Singh/Luke Finn (BBC Education Unit).

The author would also like to thank the following people for their sustained support, encouragement and personal help in producing this book: Rob Wood, Sita Bhatia, Linda Hanmore, Chris Cook and Rakesh Banot.

Introduction

Assessment and accreditation of prior learning systems (APL) are now widespread. By assessing the prior learning, knowledge and skills of potential students, colleges of further education can open up access to a wide range of courses, including National Vocational Qualifications.

To date, however, APL frameworks do not seem to have taken account of the issue of language and literacy, a crucial facet of the learning process. This creates special problems for non-native speakers of English, and people with qualifications, experience and skills gained overseas. It is all too easy to view bilingual learners as deficit models, and their linguistic ability, past qualifications and experience views as irrelevant within an APL framework geared mainly towards a white, English-speaking majority.

This book focuses on ways of setting up practical and proactive systems to address these issues, within the context of vocational training, work-based learning and educational developments in Europe. It also looks at the implications for staff development, and the TDLB APL assessor and adviser award.

Chapter 1 provides a background to the area and offers a working definition of the term 'bilingual learner'. APL is proposed as a potential access point to a system of education which currently holds many barriers for non-native speakers of English. Chapter 1 also discusses potential resourcing models for APL systems, looking at the roles of the Further Education Funding Council, the Training and Enterprise Councils, and employers.

Chapter 2 looks at the role of the guidance advocate worker, as an integral part of the model of threshold services, which is put forward potentially as an example of good practice for all learners – bilingual, monolingual and learners with special needs. It looks in particular at barriers in assessing prior linguistic ability (APLA) and evidence gained from overseas qualifications, skills and experience. It proposes strategies for lowering cross-cultural barriers in assessment systems.

Chapter 3 looks at the critical process of drawing up a holistic learner profile, including diagnostic assessment, in relation to core skills and language skills. It also identifies issues around work-based assessment. Chapter 4 shows the importance of detailed assessment and evaluation of prior learning styles, particularly for those learners with experiences of overseas education systems.

Chapter 4 outlines a 'Learning to Learn' APL induction module which gives learners the opportunity to:

- develop their portfolio of evidence still further;
- develop training and assessment of their 'core skills' and language;
- familiarise themselves with new forms of learning methodology, for instance, task- and assignment-based learning; and
- recall past learning styles and linguistic abilities, and acknowledge the transferability of skills across two or more cultures.

Chapter 5 uses a case study to illustrate more graphically the potential barriers within current APL systems, and proposes models which could enhance the chances of success for bilingual learners.

Chapter 7 focuses on developments within Europe as a result of the post-1992 single market and the increased mobility between the member states. It examines the implications for further education colleges of Europeans coming to Britain to study on vocational, academic and linguistic courses. In particular, it looks at the potential transparency of European qualifications and experience, as proposed by an EC Directive, which would have repercussions for National Vocational Qualifications and current systems of APL.

Chapter 8 identifies two specific features of European educational and work-based practice with relevance to APL and suggests possibilities for pro-active partnerships between colleges of further education, the TECs, business and industry.

Chapter 1

The background

INTRODUCTION

APL is becoming a feature of education as a result of four main developments. First, there is greater pressure on colleges of FE and colleges of HE to widen access and increase progression rates, particularly for bilingual learners on account of funding guidelines outlined by the Further Education Funding Council (FEFC). Second, organisational and structural changes have taken place in colleges of FE coupled with the development of Further Education Funding Councils, who have set a national target of 8 per cent increase over the next three years in student participation in colleges of FE, thus aligning funding with the need to incur expenditure. This has necessitated a change in ethos, with colleges unwilling to exclude potentially lower achieving students from vocational/academic courses along with a reinforced focus on learning and achievement.

Third, employers are facing increasing pressure to create a flexible work-force through retraining and updating skills. Fourth, in line with the other three developments, colleges of FE are needing to implement demand-led and flexible curriculums. At the heart of this is the need to increase the range and volume of student-managed learning, to develop more effective teaching and learning strategies and to provide 'core' curricula which would be appropriate for all learners.

The four factors outlined above combine to set a context for the implementation of an APL service which would aim to harness existing potential in the British population by retraining and/or up-skilling in reduced time. Much has been written about an APL framework for use within colleges of FE; however, the specific needs of bilingual learners – and more generally, of language and literacy – do not feature as part of that framework. Consequently, bilingual learners come to colleges of FE with a variety of prior experiences and qualifications which are largely unrecognised and unaccredited. The present APL system needs to address crucial issues, such as communication and language assessment, coupled with recognition of overseas qualifications. It should also concentrate on the process of 'core' skills recognition and prior learning strategies so that it builds confidence and self-awareness and increases opportunity, not only for bilingual learners, but by implication for all learners. This and subsequent chapters propose the implementation of APLA (Assessment and Accreditation of Prior Linguistic Ability) as part of the APL framework. The Further Education Funding Council has forwarded guidelines which have specific funding implications. These will be explored within this chapter, together with a focus on curriculum entitlement for bilingual learners.   This is essential for a true under-standing of why radical changes need to take place and how they may be implemented within the current APL framework. This needs to happen in the interests of *equality, equity* and *effectiveness*. Currently, the onus to improve participation and attainment in colleges of FE is inescapable.

A responsive and quality framework for an APL system as part of the *guidance and admissions* activities at point of entry would promote the key to equality, equity and effectiveness. In other words, how well a programme of study matches a learner's needs will determine its worth to the learner and its value to the public purse. The barriers inherent within this 'matching process' for bilingual learners are explored within the context of curriculum entitlement.

Definition of bilingual learner

A working definition of bilingual learner as used in this volume would encompass a potential student with linguistic ability of varying levels in the four skills of reading, writing, listening and speaking in two or more languages.   Fluency and accuracy in English would need to be Level 3 and above, so that a learner may follow a course of vocational study with varying forms of learner language support. A recognition of this fact is crucial to a radical transformation of the APEL (Assessment and Accreditation of Prior Experiential Learning) process as currently undertaken in colleges of FE.

APLA

APLA will underpin the areas of discussion in this work in relation to language assessment as part of the APL process. In the absence of nation-ally validated descriptors of levels for language assessment, reference will be made to the following:

- the Languages Lead Body framework for language assessment;
- the author's summary 'descriptors' of language levels with reference to the ALBSU (Adult Learning and Basic Skills Unit) language standards and GNVQ (General National Vocational Qualifications).

An important point which needs to be stressed here is that even if colleges of FE are currently using any of the above 'descriptors' or other guidelines, the methods of diagnostic assessment employed to match an applicant's language aptitude, capabilities and skills to the levels are not nationally devised. There are, therefore, wide-ranging discrepancies in the quality, relevance and appropriateness of assessments used within a single college and from college to college.

Anomalies occur whereby a bilingual learner, or, for that matter a native speaker, may be refused entry to a vocational course within one department of a college on the basis of 'inadequate English' and at the same time be following a GCSE English programme quite successfully.

If the systems in place at point of entry for initial screening and diagnostic assessment of an applicant's language and literacy skills are not *valid* or *reliable*, then applicants are not benefiting from curriculum entitlement. They will also be less likely to progress to vocational/ academic courses of study, or to attain successful learner outcomes in the form of accreditation.

APL is the process of focusing on assessing and accrediting a person's competences, i.e. knowledge, skills and prior experience, by whichever route they have been acquired. An integral part of this process needs to be APLA specifically for bilingual learners, but more generally, for all learners, leading to the identification of gaps in language and communication skills. In addition to this, there needs to be a central focus on the assessment of 'core skills' as part of the APL evidence presented. These skills would cover areas such as general communication, problem-solving and personal skills (i.e. working with others and working independently). It is essential that valid and reliable methods of assessment do not confuse issues of language assessment with the more generic 'core skills'. Methods of assessment should create a profile of an applicant's potential aptitude and ability in both areas, which are mutually exclusive and interdependent at the same time.

The difficulties faced by bilingual learners are compounded by the absence of a nationally recognised NVQ (National Vocational Qualifications) framework of language accreditation for English and/or other languages. Bilingual learners are thus unable to gain accreditation for their language skills. There does not appear to be any examining and validating body that offers *bilingual certification* in Gujarati, Urdu, Bengali, Turkish, Punjabi, French, Spanish or any of the other non-European or European languages in which people in Britain do business – working as retailers and shopkeepers, publishing newspapers, running radio stations, advertising, practising medicine as *'hakims'* (Asian traditional healers), running community groups, creches, catering projects and much more. NVQ will offer a Certificate in Business Language Competence in French, German, Spanish and Italian but not in any of the other languages spoken in communities in Britain, nor in any other occupational field to date.

As part of the APL process, APLA needs to be embedded in the wider context of the 'student journey' throughout the college. At the pre-entry stage, learners will have access to the building-up of a portfolio that outlines their previous experience, knowledge, skills and linguistic ability. This portfolio is part of a continuum whereby learners can include further information on qualifications gained and progress in language acquisition at appropriate intervals.

The rationale for devising a system of curriculum access via an APL framework will be argued in the next section, which focuses on curriculum entitlement for all learners and explores the barriers to access and progression for bilingual learners in particular.

AN APL SERVICE FOR BILINGUAL LEARNERS AS PART OF CURRICULUM ENTITLEMENT

Accumulated evidence suggests strongly that bilingual learners do not progress and gain access in college and, therefore, cannot lay claim to curriculum entitlement. Curriculum essential entitlements or elements would imply those that a college is prepared to provide for all students. These would be outlined in the college's strategic plan and mission statement. Individual assessment of needs and a demand-led and flexible curriculum would usually be at the core of a college's strategic plan. All students, for example, should be entitled to a well-planned quality curriculum. The lack of such a curriculum would affect the quality of teaching and learning assessment, performance criteria, the provision of technology and materials and would create barriers for access and progression. A guidance and admissions process needs to incorporate a well-developed APL service which could analyse learner need and thus inform curriculum development. As part of the curriculum entitlement there are currently two main aspects:

1 the *common necessary variants* which are elements, facilities and services that *reflect* the nature of the population served and provide for common variations in course requirements and facilities (i.e. essential entitlements such as guidance and admissions procedures); and
2 the *specific necessary variants* which are elements, specific facilities and services that *support* the education and training of certain individuals and particular groups, for example, bilingual learner support, essential skills, disability learner support or childcare facilities.

The APL process would be part of the *essential entitlement for individual assessment*, i.e. 'appropriate procedures for recognising and accrediting prior learning'. Within this should be a recognition of overseas qualifications and experience. By promoting this as an integral part of the service, there would be an effort to equalise opportunities and a sincere recognition of the worth of bilingual learners, not simply tokenistic lip service.

In the model put forward by FEU, *Supporting Learning – Promoting Equity and Participation*, ESOL (English for Speakers of Other Languages) is still seen as a specific necessary variant on a par with childcare, support for specific learning difficulties and so on. If bilingual learners are to achieve true equal parity with other student groups within the college, and in an effort to equalise opportunities for bilingual learners so that they are entitled to access and progress through the curriculum, a reworking of the essential entitlements needs to take place. A different perspective on the notion of *learning support* for bilingual learners is clearly needed. What is being argued for here is the notion that without appropriate assessment and learner support, many learners – both bilingual and monolingual – cannot succeed on vocational courses and as such, their need for learning support has to be recognised as an essential entitlement by colleges. The notion of 'Appropriate Opportunities to participate in the delivery process of a vocational subject with language development support' (FEU 1992), i.e. English, European languages and British community languages (e.g. Urdu and Hindi) should become part of the *Common Necessary Variants – Essential Entitlements* (FEU 1992), and be a service for all students. This would enable bilingual learners to participate fully in the curriculum, using their linguistic expertise as appropriate, and to build upon specific areas that require improvement and learner support. The colleges of FE need to lay down a 'threshold level' – a minimum requisite of English language levels which is necessary for access into the full vocational curriculum. By adding the element of 'accelerated language development' as part of the *Common Necessary Variants – Essential Entitlements*, this allows bilingual learners to follow courses of intensive English which would bring them up to this threshold level, i.e. minimum requisites to enable access to vocational courses. This also means that all learners are offered the opportunities to further the acquisition of at least one language in which they have some grounding. By reworking this model, it is possible to argue the case for developing *bilingualism* as an integral part of the curriculum offer, and as part of the APL process.

STUDENT CHARTER OF RIGHTS

An APL process that is embedded into this model of curriculum entitlement makes a statement concerning the status of bilingual learners as pro-active learners who are in need of 'enabling', in order to access and progress. They are not then perceived as a deficit cohort of learners who enter the college with a 'negative' linguistic profile, unable to access the vocational/academic curriculum by remaining marginalised in the ESOL classes. By incorporating these changes to the model, offered by the FEU, in line with current developments on APL, colleges can confer a genuine parity of esteem for individual learners. Currently, most colleges perpetuate a system with an in-built differential valuation of different client groups, based on somewhat arbitrary selection processes.

In keeping with curriculum entitlement, a student charter of rights should therefore give students the right to be assessed on their personal portfolio, to access, to progress and to be proactive in their learning. An APL process which incorporated assessment of language would automatically afford bilingual learners the opportunity to access such a system and to feel valued.

This would link in directly to one of the major challenges facing further and higher education in the 1990s, which is, 'to raise the level of competence of individuals, whether or not they are in employment, through the provision of open and flexible opportunities for "life-long" learning' (Confederation of British Industry, 1992).

In order to respond to a student's charter of rights, a college of FE needs to promote accessibility, flexible ways of learning and individual personal achievements at the forefront of their work. It is the responsibility of colleges to develop into dynamic, responsive institutions with an in-built potential for metamorphosis, moving through phases of growth, decline and development as student and staff populations change. Accordingly, it is essential to appreciate the recent changes that have taken place with the traditional client groups of bilingual learners from overseas, particularly in London colleges over the last five years.

CLIENT GROUPS OF BILINGUAL LEARNERS

Bilingual learners attracted to colleges for English language acquisition and/or vocational/academic training can be divided largely into three culturally homogeneous groups – very generally speaking:

- Group 1 consists of students from the new Commonwealth countries such as India, Pakistan, Bangladesh and non-Commonweath Asian countries such as Vietnam, either recently arrived or who have been resident in the UK for more than two years;
- Group 2 consists of recently arrived students from African non-Commonwealth countries who are usually political refugees and/or asylum-seekers, countries such as Angola, Somalia, Zaire, Eritrea – the Horn of Africa;
- Group 3 consists of students from Eastern Europe who are political refugees and/or asylum-seekers, countries such as Bulgaria and the former Yugoslavia and USSR. Added to this group are non-refugee

students from Western Europe (France, Spain) and from South America (Colombia, Venezuela, Brazil).

The arrival in this country of the second and third groups has meant a shift in the focus of learner needs and aspirations and client satisfaction with the 'system'. Formerly, many bilingual learners arriving from the subcontinent of Asia, including Vietnam and Hong Kong, were from sometimes illiterate rural peasant and/or fishing communities. These students were, arguably, content to stay in the ESOL classes, where they were told they needed to stay for years at a time in order to improve their English. Nowadays, a number of students from the subcontinent who have been resident in this country for several years are no longer happy to perpetuate the myth of chasing the elusive chimera of 'perfect English'. A number of them have been in paid or unpaid employment and have skills and experience gained in this country. They are now at the stage where they can benefit from a well-organised APL system which would recognise their true worth and progress them through the system. They have realised the long-term inadequacies of studying English and working for five years or much more in this country but, on the other hand of not achieving credible employment, noteworthy qualifications and training. The more recent group of bilingual learners who have arrived in Britain, largely asylum-seekers and refugees, are highly skilled, experienced and motivated, and come from Eastern European and African countries with European languages such as French, Spanish, Italian, Polish and Russian. They would not be able to claim effective 'client satisfaction' either, if they are limited to learning only 'performance English', and are not able to capitalise on their previous experience and qualifications.

Overwhelming evidence exists in the survey of numbers of black adults with professional qualifications gained overseas produced by NIACE/TEED (1992), in which Stella Dadzie points out that the data highlight a vast waste of human resources. Considerable numbers of highly qualified black adults were found to be unemployed. She also states the examples of individuals whose work experience bore no apparent relationship to the qualifications held or to individual skills and competences – an architect from Bombay doing unskilled manual labour and an accountant from Chittagong in casual low-paid work. Ten per cent of the overseas qualified adults in the sample were in employment and almost 50 per cent of the whole sample were registered unemployed with one in three actively undertaking education and training.

To reiterate the point made earlier, sadly, true curriculum entitlement does not take place for these groups of adults, should they wish to return to college. There is no national system of recognition for many overseas qualifications and, as a result, colleges and higher education institutions are approached by adults – notably bilingual adults – who cannot get official recognition of the value of their qualification.

PERFORMANCE INDICATORS IN COLLEGES OF FE AND HOW THESE APPLY TO BILINGUAL LEARNERS

More recent work on the effectiveness of work-related further education (WRFE) has led to lists of key indicators which extend those presented by Joint Efficiency Study (JES) to include, for example:

- non-LEA (local education authority) income as a percentage of gross expenditure on WRFE
- proportion of enrolled students aged over 19
- number of courses which prepared students for assessment for National Vocational Qualifications (NVQs)
- proportion of students who receive a Record of Achievement (ROA) on completion of their studies
- number of September and post-September enrolments

(Training Agency 1990)

Her Majesty's Inspectors of Schools (Scotland) (1990) have advocated the following key indicators for FE colleges:

- student success ratio
- post-course success ratio
- quality of learning and teaching profile
- unit costs profile

Arguably, it is not possible to assess many of the ESOL students successfully against some of the above performance indicators. Leaving aside the availability of NVQ English language qualifications and an ROA, 'client satisfaction' is difficult to evaluate and quantify. It is true to say that many bilingual learners feel frustrated and anxious at the lack of opportunities for access and progression to main vocational study and training. This is because English qualifications such as Pitmans and Cambridge First, for example, may concentrate on the acquisition of English language skills to the exclusion of other transferable 'core' skills, i.e. problem-solving, working with others. Moreover, in the absence of competence-based language learning for those students not following an RSA Profiles Objectives in ESOL or WORDPOWER, Communication Skills 3793 CGLI, some may be unable to see clear progress being made in the wider field of adapting to new ways of 'learning'. At present, in colleges of FE, the attendance of bilingual learners demonstrates a pattern of low retention rates in some ESOL classes and vocational courses. This is on account of dissatisfaction with the lack of visible progression within ESOL classes, vocational and academic courses. The low retention rate does not correlate with the bilingual student profile (i.e. highly skilled, experienced and motivated). What is needed then is resourcing of different delivery modes to provide a quality *learning support* framework. This in turn should entail a greater proportion of student success.

In terms of measurement for curriculum wide progress, indicators such as 'post-course success ratio' could guarantee access to a recognised and appropriate NVQ ESOL course completer qualification. Moreover, adding the notion of 'value-added' and measurement of student progress in the broader area of communication skills would tremendously benefit a student's self-perception and self-confidence.

The 'quality of teaching and learning profile' needs to take into account the prior learning experiences of bilingual students and for tutors to deliver teaching styles which are generally accessible.

The inclusion of a key indicator on a 'student language profile' can legitimise this vital area of student self-development within the college curriculum.

THE NOTION OF 'VALUE-ADDED' AS A PERFORMANCE INDICATOR AND BILINGUAL LEARNERS

It is assumed that colleges would want to provide for the education needs of as wide a cross-section of the local adult population as possible. In order to achieve this, colleges need to implement policies that facilitate admission to programmes based on entry criteria and do not exclude large sectors of the community. Learners should not be required to produce evidence of achievements not easily acquired by some individuals or client groups at the initial stage of assessment. Moreover, further education for bilingual learners should not be narrowly conceived around the acquisition of the English language.

The college is in a position to take a broad approach to the assessment of prior learning and should have in place flexible systems for managing and supporting learning. However, the major step forward will be the underpinning notion that all bilingual learners start from differentials in levels of language and prior experience, but that it is the *progress* or 'value-added' made by learners that is the real indicator of quality, as measured through 'ipasative assessment', i.e. learner progress. Colleges may assess outcomes through the achievement of high academic standards and, therefore, implement covert selection procedures or adopt an overtly elitist approach by excluding bilingual learners who are assumed incapable of attaining qualifications. Students in such a college may make little actual progress but their accreditation achievements may be perceived as better than the bilingual students who are starting from lower levels of attainment but who are in a position to make considerable progress, given the correct levels of support.

The measurement of 'value-added'

The key to measuring 'value-added' lies in identifying/negotiating and recording individual student and teacher expectations, and establishing assessment systems which reflect those. There needs to be a degree of impartiality attached to the setting up of these systems which involves both local and college national consensus and verification. If this is not carried out, tutors may confer criteria for assessment which does not enable the lowest common denominator of needs and expectations to be met. This is because unless required to, tutors have been working within a framework which may have actually excluded bilingual learners as they have low expectations of these learners' capabilities and achievements. Developing 'profiling' systems to enable learners to monitor and review their progress over a period of time can only add to the process of self-awareness and confidence building.

Any system of measurement that values only achievement of specific external targets will favour those who are most able and highly motivated, and more importantly, those without special needs, and/or learning difficulties/disabilities, who do not require learner support. Random evidence in colleges of FE suggests that bilingual learners with relatively well-developed communication skills in two or more languages are consistently excluded from mainstream provision at entry/admissions stage, but are channelled into traditional ESOL classes. Fluency and/or native speaker standard in Community or European languages are not considered as desirable criteria for admission to these courses. It is, sadly, a myopic strategy, in view of the fact that many bilingual learners are already in employment using Community and/or European languages, and already interacting with members of other ethnic communities. Moreover, detailed language acquisition research has demonstrated that learners who have mastered two or more languages are much more aware of the acquisition of linguistic technicalities of communications skills and knowledge, having more developed transferable skills. Added to this, many bilingual learners have informally demonstrated initiative, 'survival skills' and day-to-day learner strategies, through adaptation to life in Britain. Consequently, indicators for measuring 'success on learner outcomes' as matched against funding resources need to examine closely the notion of 'value-added'. The 'credit' framework developed by FEU and described as a 'multi-purpose instrument' defines credits for all levels and types of qualifications from GCSE to degree, in terms of the notional amount of *study time* required for a learner to achieve outcomes. It would be possible to measure an institution for performance and quality in terms of credits, e.g. for a single module in a modular A level or a single NVQ unit, as well as offering more flexible credit accumulation and transfer opportunities.

The use of a credit framework might lead to the sensitive measurement of performance based on the illusive concept of 'value-added', or the amount of progress made by a student rather than simply the outcome of a course.

ADVANTAGES OF AN APEL SERVICE FOR BILINGUAL LEARNERS

An APEL service enables bilingual learners to put together a portfolio which charts their achievements, capabilities and linguistic abilities and highlights potential learning routes to vocational training and/or employment.

Learning support profile

Negative attitudes prevalent amongst some vocational and academic staff can be very damaging for the morale and motivation of bilingual learners, as illustrated by the following examples. One senior lecturer in a large community college referred to a GCSE course with language support as 'a Noddy course, not a real course, where students are wasting their time'. Another lecturer, a bilingual speaker himself – delivering a learner-supported City and Guilds Information Technology 4242 to a group of bilingual learners, frequently shouted at learners when they failed to understand his instructions and when asked by students to repeat information from previous lessons, told them that he had already explained the information once and that it was the student's problem if he/she had not understood. Although these attitudes in part reflect examples of bad teaching practice, nevertheless there are issues concerning the low status of learner-supported courses combined with the lack of curriculum entitlement for bilingual learners, i.e. the importance of access and progression and quality of 'client satisfaction'.

In outlining the 'quality of teaching and learning profiles', it is vital to take into account the needs of bilingual learners who need a greater or lesser degree of support. It is feasible to design courses in-built with units that are expensive to deliver which would be offset by courses with units that are cheap to deliver. In other words, providing support through team teaching in the classroom with a language support tutor working alongside a vocational tutor is a more expensive way of delivery than designing for learning support needs to be met in Open Learning resource-based workshops. Units of achievement such as, for example, the achievement of a specific series of units from an NVQ course, can be related to different delivery modes for costing purposes, which will provide a more cost-effective learner-support service than is presently the case in many colleges. Flexible models of learner support delivery are very beneficial for many bilingual learners, allowing both access and progression to desired vocational and academic college programmes. The implications for the APL process is that the type of support and mode of delivery would need to be assessed at the initial stage of guidance and built into the student's portfolio, thus forming an integral part of a tutoring system, continuously reappraised at various intervals. The ideal flexible model of support over a period of time would be intensive teacher input in the initial phase with ever-diminishing levels of support in an Open Learning situation in the latter part of the course. It is suggested that learners eventually become more autonomous and are able to work in an Open Learning resource-based environment with tutors as facilitators, as illustrated in Chapter 5.

The following statement is taken from the Croydon LEA Strategic Plan 1990–1993:

> Provision should be available in as many delivery and learning modes as possible to ensure maximum flexibility and accessibility for clients. The strategy will require the development of support services including guidance, initial assessment and tutoring.
>
> (Croydon LEA 1990)

Flexible models of learning support, which relate positively to performance indicators of responsiveness, high retention rates and outcomes in terms of achievement, could also provide the basis for a system of efficiency indicators.

Statistical data collected from this exercise could be used to inform programme areas on:

- levels of learner support required for achievement;
- most efficient modes of delivery for learner support and achievement;
- most cost-effective modes of delivery for learner support and achievement; and
- most client-centred modes of delivery for learner support and achievement.

Integrated learner support in the curriculum as a vital part of delivery will shift current thinking on meeting bilingual learner needs in a more systematic and effective way. The feedback from the APL and other curriculum staff on the quality and quantity issues around learner support will inform modifications to the system.

Meeting bilingual learner needs

How responsive is the college service to the real needs of bilingual learners? Research into defining an 'adequate' education and training service for adults has stressed the role of 'needs identification and the provision of a range of learning opportunities which respond appropriately to those needs' (FEU, 1992).

Ironically, contrary to a popular assertion concerning adult education that 'the system itself has failed to be relevant and attractive to a large proportion of the adult population', ESOL as a long-term palliative continues to attract large numbers of bilingual learners who are unable to secure vocational education and training, and are constantly being told:

1 their English is not good enough for admittance on vocational/ academic courses;
2 that their skills, knowledge, experience and qualifications are not recognised for equivalence in this country.

This current situation needs to be posited against a real crisis in some vocational areas which may be suffering from underenrolment and a failure to recruit the 'right sort of student who fits the programme', i.e. entrants with minimum learner-support needs, who have a substantial chance of leaving with good qualifications. This system of recruitment, therefore, fails to address the relevance of the provision for those who are not being assessed as suitable to participate.

The large waiting lists for ESOL classes are perceived as 'unmet demand; and frequently interpreted (especially for the purposes of Section II funding) as a positive indication that the college is providing a relevant service, albeit unable – because of budgetary constraints – to respond as fully as it would like to the needs of all potential students.

But what are the needs of the potential students? Sufficient evidence in both the NIACE/TEED research on 'Black Adults' and in the British Council's 'Research on Refugees' can testify to the desire of bilingual learners for British qualifications, training and recognition of their prior learning. Apart from assessing and accrediting a learner's portfolio based on the student's prior experience, knowledge and skills, the following should be included to enable student progression to vocational/academic courses:

• induction and diagnosis of needs of students;
• formative assessment of language and communications skills; and
• diagnosis of delivery mode of learning support.

APL AS A MEANS OF MEETING THE NEEDS OF A BILINGUAL WORKFORCE

APL in this context is a means of:

1 offering opportunities of recognising the skills, abilities and past experiences of their employees for the purposes of promotion;
2 offering opportunities of recognising the skills, abilities and past experiences of their employees for the purposes of retraining in cases of redundancy and redeployment;
3 creating a structured framework with a two-way process with feedback from the training establishment in order to identify further potential training needs within the local community;

4 offering an overall strategy for the improvement of the deployment of human resources;
5 offering a means of assessing work experience on a voluntary, unpaid or community work scheme, with an aim of providing a programme of training leading to credible National vocational qualifications.

The 1991 White Paper 'Education and Training for the 21st Century' emphasises the importance of good quality education for adults 'to help them improve their qualifications, update their skills and seek advancement in their present career or in a new career' (Department of Education and Science, 1991).

The ability to speak more than one language needs urgently to be recognised as a skill in itself which also facilitates the acquisition of further languages. This is currently the case in European countries where bilingualism/multilingualism is prestigious and leads to favourable bias for candidates when seeking jobs. Workers have the opportunities in many European countries – notably France, Germany, Spain and the Netherlands – to build upon and accredit linguistic skills already acquired as a means of entering an appropriate and satisfying occupation.

Only 33 per cent of workers in Britain currently hold a vocational qualification compared to 64 per cent and 40 per cent of the work-force respectively in Germany and France. In part, this is attributable to the low status accorded to technical, vocational and linguistic skills possessed by British and ethnic minority workers resident in the UK. They may currently be unable to have access to quality assessment and accreditation systems with individualised programmes of work-based training as compared to Holland and Germany. Nevertheless, if Britain is to compete with other countries in terms of world markets, then enabling individuals within the population to fulfil potential in the area of languages and occupational skills is essential so that British manufacturers become more adaptable to the new world order of short and specialised production runs.

An investigation into purchasing and marketing in 1980 revealed:

Both in marketing and purchasing, British overseas customers were agreed that inadequacy in languages was one of the UK companies major deficiencies and these deficiencies led to poor feel for the market, difficulty in establishing firm relationships and a failure to benefit fully from suppliers technical expertise.

(Liston and Reeves 1985)

The most recent survey, 'Languages in British Business' by Steve Hagen (1988) contains data collected between 1984 and 1987. It identified a gap of alarming proportions between the foreign language skills needed by industry and the in-house skills available. More importantly, 'the overwhelming message of (the) study . . . is that British companies are losing trading opportunities for the lack of the right languages, many without realising it'. One of the conclusions of the survey was that for many years the overwhelming message from the majority of employers/companies has been that, whatever research may prove and whatever foreigners may think, 'foreign languages are really just not that important to business success'.

The Department of Trade and Industry (DTI) launched its major campaign 'Europe – Open for Business' to publicise the likely effects of the Single European Market (SEM) Act, and included in its 1992 information pack a factsheet on Language Skills (No 331) which states:

> There is clear evidence of a direct link between export performance and proficiency in foreign languages. Language training is an investment.

The emphasis from all quarters is primarily on a strategy for training largely monolingual British native speakers with little or no knowledge of a European language. In any strategy paper that reflects on options to help bridge the language skills gap (cf FEU, 1989) no mention is made of harnessing a potential human resource in the form of bilingual, highly qualified, motivated and experienced persons from overseas who may be locked into ESOL programmes and largely segregated from vocational areas of study.

Although investment in language training for British monolingual native speakers is an imperative, nevertheless, recognition of the cosmopolitan profile of the British nation in terms of investment for language, vocational and professional training is an equally urgent issue.

RESOURCING APL SYSTEMS

Further Education Funding Council's resourcing guidelines

Targets for efficiency and effectiveness relate to an element of achievement in the form of number of completions, drop-out rates, examination successes and student destinations. The present Secretary of State for Education has placed a special new emphasis on further education with a commitment to a 25 per cent increase in student numbers over the next three years. A strong argument lies therein for harnessing the potential of bilingual learners in order to increase student numbers and to access and progress these students to appropriate learning outcomes. Coupled with this is the CBI National Education and Training Targets (1991, first published as 'World Class Targets'). One of the foundation learning targets is 'education and training provision to develop breadth, self-reliance and flexibility'.

In order to institute an accessible system, a college needs to become sufficiently responsive in resourcing and pricing. Bilingual learner support can gain high status and kudos by incorporating it at the APL stage of assessment and admissions. Bilingual learner support as an essential entitlement becomes an integral part of service delivery and results in the internal delegation of budgets to programme areas. Allocation of resources to these programme areas, on the basis of target numbers of unit credits will act as a powerful incentive to 'unitise the curriculum and thus increase flexibility'. The Further Education Funding Council's ethos of achievement-led resourcing would favour the funding of ESOL leading to vocational learning outcomes and give greater weighting to those vocational courses earmarked for learning support. Thus, additional units of learner support added on to programme areas for students attract additional funding. This in itself acts as a powerful incentive for colleges to develop effective screening and diagnostic systems at the admissions and APL stage.

The Further Education Funding Council has opted for funding on achievement-led resourcing, which, at this stage will be within all learning programmes at: 'entry', 'on programme' and 'exit' stages. (See Table 1.1.)

Table 1.1 Elements of FEFC funding learning programmes

Learning programme	Funding (%)
Entry	
Marketing, including outreach*	
Diagnostic assessment including APL*	
Guidance and counselling*	
Registration and induction*	8
On programme	
Learning programme	
Assessing and recording progress	
Guidance and counselling*	
Support services*	
Establishing an ethos*	
Exit	
Assessment and recording of achievement	10 for NTETS qualifications
including final examinations	8 for other qualifications
Guidance and counselling*	

Source: FEFC 1992.
Note: * – areas of special funding significance for bilingual learners.

The 'Entry' and 'On Programme' areas are of greater consequence because of the funding significance. In keeping with this, it is essential for colleges to institute systems which would maintain *auditable evidence of activity* at all three stages, such as student records, portfolio, tutorial action plans and so on.

Relating funding to the three elements of learning programmes 'entry', 'on programme' and 'exit' effectively 'reinforces the focus on learning and achievements' and 'aligns funding with the need to incur expenditure' (FEFC Funding Learning document). Funding is very much linked to pre-entry programmes and learning aims, i.e. courses of study. However, it needs to be noted that the funding programme elements allow different types of payment to be made, reflecting the different types of activity in each programme element:

- Entry: a single payment, the same for most students
- On Programme: time variable payments related to the cost of the programme
- Exit: an incentive payment, at a flat rate or a percentage of the total programme cost.

(FEFC guidelines)

If these funding programme elements are taken in conjunction with the suggested changes in the entitlement curriculum the following recommendations for funding may be made:

On Entry

It is envisaged that bilingual learners would need a greater element of action planning and assessment of prior linguistic ability (APLA) with built-in learner support from the guidance advocate (GA), in which case the costings are higher in terms of staff costs and time than for a student with less support needs.

A 'menu' pricing system, which allows candidates variety and flexibility, would cater for their unique learning needs and allow for individualised or group assessments/counselling/guidance with access to evidence pin-pointing workshops.

Vouchers or 'training credits' provide learners with real choices and would allow the FEFC to assign the rates of funding.

On Programme

Embedding an APEL module into various programme areas of the curriculum creates a link between 'Entry' and 'On Programme', an essential part of the programme elements with a 'value-added' element. Monitoring learning outcomes and student achievements within such a module has implications at both stages of programme elements, 'On Entry' and 'On Programme'. Consequently, funding elements attached to both learning programme areas need to be adjusted accordingly to allow for this. A greater degree of learning support built into the module and generally into 'on programme' delivery needs to be reflected in the weightings of the programme area, but not in the cost to the student, which should not be prohibitive.

Implications of resourcing APL for bilingual learners

Let us consider the issues of resourcing the provision of an APL service, particularly in relation to bilingual learners. The issues for *all* learners are as follows:

- the charge to be made;
- the location and time to be taken;
- the type of staff to be employed; and
- the organisational problems involved in providing this service on demand.

For bilingual learners, an added dimension is necessary as follows:

- investment in translation/interpretation facilities and outreach for marketing the APL system to community groups;
- a specific focus on recruiting bilingual staff;
- a cost-effective, valid and reliable assessment of linguistic ability and the 'core skills';
- a guidance advocate worker for initial counselling, equivalence of overseas qualifications, preparation of portfolio and learner support;
- a framework of nationally recognised equivalented overseas qualifications linked to National Vocational Qualification levels;
- a nationally recognised NVQ language accreditation framework.

The costs involved in providing a system to deal with APL are very similar to those incurred for assessment. It is difficult to apply a 'fixed rate charge', as it is widely acknowledged that the time taken to accredit prior learning varies, depending on the complexity of the competence to be tested and the ability of the individual. Obviously, this has repercussions for costs, specifically in the area of the time expended and the type of staff to be employed. Nevertheless, funders of an APL system need to recognise that by pump-priming resources into the system, i.e. by initial investment of funds to create a user-friendly and financially attractive service for bilingual learners, they would reap the dividends in the long term. That is to say, there would be a general increase in the retention and progression rates for bilingual learners.

The FEU Project (1992) carried out by the London Borough of Croydon and Croydon College estimated that the cost of providing APL on a one-to-one basis and on demand, amounted to as much as 15 per cent of the cost of delivering the actual unit. Delivering APL on a group basis and within college premises is by far the more cost-effective way. A 'menu' pricing system achieves simplicity of operation by offering dual rates.

In this context, the dual rates could take into account whether the accreditation was being carried out at the institution or, for instance, at the applicant's place of work, and also takes into account increased cost of travel and lecturer time required for the provision of off-site APL.

BARRIERS TO ACCESS AND PROGRESSION IN COLLEGES OF FE

Recognition of overseas qualifications

At a training session in Birmingham in 1987, run by the Training Unit of the Refugee Council, a group of refugees from a wide variety of countries listed their skills as: selling, typing, office skills, counselling, catering, scientific, organisational, lumbering, painting and decorating, bartending and teaching. They also listed amongst their personal qualities: commitment, readiness to learn, ambition, a fresh approach to looking at things, an ability to understand other cultures.

Overall policy and methods for assessing prior/experimental learning should encourage and favour those potential students with skills and abilities from other cultural and linguistic grounds. Moreover, at the implementation stage within colleges, the emerging perspective focuses around the area of

> the assessment of experiential learning . . . updating and retraining. It relates to progression and competences. By laying out what people know, and can do, it displays the foundations for building further competence and study. The assessment of experiential learning, therefore, is based on the practical implications, of the development of people as learners.
>
> (CNAA 1989, NCVQ 1988)

Recently, a clear distinction was formulated by the NCVQ between *learning* as a process and the output of such learning, which is described as *achievement*: 'Accreditation is based upon evidence of achievement not learning' (NCVQ 1986b).

Authentication/verification of evidence

This has direct implications for bilingual learners. Many of the potential students from the client groups from Europe, Africa, Asia and South America will have evidence of achievement from their countries in the form of certificates. Until 1991, National Academic Recognition Information Centre (NARIC) of the British Council provided a service for individuals whereby they could write in with copies and translation

of their certificates with a view to being informed of how their qualifications related to British qualifications, having clarified to applicants
that:

> there is no *official equivalence* of overseas and British qualifications in
> Britain. British educational and professional institutions are autono-
> mous and as such, reserve the right to make their own decisions
> on the acceptability and recognition to be accorded to any overseas
> qualification.

(NARIC 1991)

This is in sharp contrast with other European countries where there
are developed and properly funded qualification recognition services. In
the French system 'homologation' or equivalency occurs according to
stipulated criteria and guidelines laid down by the Ministère de Titres
et de Diplômes. For instance, a Zairois would be able to, in theory, have
his or her qualifications recognised by French Institutes since the system
of education in Zaire is recognised and validated by the French Ministry
of Education. Ironically, the same qualification would not necessarily
qualify for recognition or validation in Britain.

Two further examples are cited by NIACE in the 'Survey of Number
of Black Adults with Professional Qualifications Gained Overseas',
(Dadzie 1993), which also support this. A woman whose initial educational qualifications were gained in Aruba cannot gain recognition
in Britain, yet her qualifications are recognised towards nursing training
in the Netherlands. A woman with an engineering degree from Pakistan
asked a Midlands university for advice on the equivalence of her degree
and whether she could have advanced standing on a British engineering
degree. She approached Leicestershire's community education service
for help after being told to acquire two A levels.

The caution of awarding bodies can be understood in part, in relation
to developing or Third World countries in Africa or Asia with disruptions
to normal educational activity resulting from political unrest or war.
However, the irony of the situation is that examples can also be found
whereby adults with qualifications from European countries – Spain,
Portugal and France – are faced with barriers, vis-à-vis recognition of the
value of their qualifications in colleges of further education and higher
education.

The following example illustrates the situation very well. A woman
from Portugal (with a degree and MA in history) arrived at an FE college
wanting English classes. After counselling and assessment of English it
emerged that she wanted to teach and undertake a PGCE (Post Graduate
Certificate in Education). She was advised to go to the local university
where, without formal assessment, she was told that her certificates from
Portugal were not equivalent to GCSE Maths, and that her English (on

the basis of an interview) was not good enough to undertake a degree. She came back to the college of FE where she told the adviser that the certificate from Portugal did include mathematics to GCSE level and that she would ask her sister in Portugal to send the certificate. She returned to the university with the relevant certificate and was told she could apply for a degree course in the following academic year.

This example focuses on the following issues:

- a need for an equitable system of qualifications recognition nationally, which would move towards harmonisation of qualifications gained in the EC and in other countries; and
- a need for an APL system which would enable potential learners to *demonstrate* their competence, experience and knowledge without needing to produce certificates.

The woman in the above example was fortunate in so far as she was articulate and persistent in her efforts to gain a teaching qualification and was encouraged by the FE adviser not simply to join English classes. She also had the good fortune to be able to obtain her certificate, unlike many refugees who may leave homes at short notice without formal proof of study and qualification and may not be in a position to seek verification from their country of origin.

Invalid certificates

Of particular concern for bilingual learners is the extent to which achievements acquired at some point in the past – possibly some considerable time before, beyond two years – have 'decayed' or fallen out of currency because of changes in work systems/practices/technology. In this case, the assessment procedures that form part of the APL process – the methods for the collection and presentation of evidence of achievement – need to be focused very clearly in order that the systems devised provide individual learners with an *assessment map*. An assessment map is traditionally used 'in respect of a learning programme for an individual or simply for examining the way in which his/her achievements are brought together in formal or informal certification or accreditation processes' (FESC, 1989). With bilingual learners especially, this could prove to be an invaluable way of gathering information or evidence, as sources would vary and learning would have taken place in different locations or modes. In situations where a student does not have suitable 'evidence' in this country, gaps in training and up-skilling would be identified. Moreover, the assessment map would be able to record the equivalences or absence of equivalences, for overseas qualifications and to identify possibilities for providing evidence for achievement in *workplace assessment*.

Barriers in the 'student journey'

A typical student journey for bilingual learners involves three stages:

1 access and placement;
2 adjusting and learning; and
3 achieving and progressing.

If the issues of access and placement are not addressed in relation to the other two issues in terms of assessment of prior learning and future learning needs, a learner would have to contend with many obstacles towards effective quality learning, invariably lessening his/her chances of success. There are many identifiable barriers to access and placement for bilingual learners, involving areas of student self-perception, confidence and marketing. Some of the following examples in the solutions taken from colleges of FE have been culled from the FEU publication 'The Flexible Colleges' (1990–1) and are acknowledged where they occur. The barriers identified below are followed by example solutions and a commentary making a general statement about these solutions and others.

Barrier

Sources of information and advice provided within a college may not be accessible to many potential client groups because of the location of the college or because of the format/style/marketing of the information.

Solutions

Hall Green College provides a high street 'shop' where pre-entry diagnostic counselling is well developed and where services can assist prospective learners in crossing the college threshold or even service their learning needs completely. The idea of curious enquirers looking in through the shop window and watching their peers using computers and other learning resources has been traditionally used to great effect in adult community centres, to draw in clients. A good South London example of this is the Charlton Community Centre – which attracts good-sized groups of Asian women for ESOL classes, knitting, sewing and socialising.

Commentary

The attraction of this type of provision is for a targeted group of clients where the assumption is that they would be 'put off' or inhibited by their perception of educational institutions as threatening. Examples are often cited of Muslim women who are timid or tentative and would be wary of venturing into 'traditionally designed' colleges of FE, especially those with grandiose entrances. Whilst it is true to say that in some parts of communities all over Britain, both black and white women are discouraged from entering employment and/or formal education and training on account of traditional perceptions of education and cultural and societal mores, nevertheless, it needs to be recognised by educationalists that the majority of bilingual learners with formal education experiences from overseas, i.e. Africa and Asia, are used to highly formal, prescriptive and traditional teaching methods. This means that far from finding the grandiose architectural designs of colleges a negative and threatening factor, on the contrary, they will be impressed, and respect the education institution as representative of formal educational values. On the other hand, groups of bilingual learners who find local adult community drop-in centres more comfortable and accessible, tend to be a client group searching for a social nexus where they are able to acquire some basic communication skills in an informal and friendly gathering. This in itself would mirror the rural adult education programmes currently widely developed and systemised in Africa and Asia.

It is clear then, that it is suspect to formulate policy concerning access for bilingual learners at the college threshold based on a set of cultural assumptions. Evidence in the FE classrooms demonstrates that some of the most forward and educationally advanced students in terms of motivation, initiative taking and desire for progression are Muslim Somali women, clad in traditional 'purdah'. In order to fulfil their potential and to enable them to benefit from vocational and academic training, it would be a total disservice to situate them in off-site community centres with 'drip-feed doses of ESOL', i.e. a few hours a week over a long period of time.

Conversely, developing more positive access routes for students via the APL framework means offering bilingual clients the opportunity to make informed choices about their education and training. With a centralised admissions system, appropriate counselling and guidance, this can be a feasible reality. Bilingual learners can *choose* any of these options: to enrol in intensive English literacy or numeracy courses, to form a social club or self-help group, to learn on an Open Learning or Distance Learning basis in a resource-based workshop, to enrol for a number of chosen modules on a vocational course to top up their own experience and qualifications or develop a personal portfolio with an APL adviser to reassess further options concerning possible training and employment.

Barrier

Some people from ethnic minorities – particularly first and second generation – may feel unable to cross a college threshold because of *language* and *culture* barriers.

Solutions

Many colleges, such as Rotherham College, employ an outreach worker/community worker/community liaison officer and so on, to assist in attracting people from minority groups into the college either through outreach centres or off-site provision or through the main centres. A variety of other strategies include:

- translation of college publicity into target languages
- visiting temples, mosques, gurdwaras (Sikh temples) and community centres
- holding regular sessions of open learning and/or counselling in local community voluntary groups and schools.

Commentary

In terms of most effective strategies, once again, what needs to be developed is familiarity with the local client group whose needs vary enormously from community to community, and within communities themselves. Basically, colleges need to recognise that more important than language and culture as barriers, are the twin barriers of *class* and *educational history*. In other words, a bilingual learner who has not benefited from formal education would not know what college has to offer. By the same token, a bilingual learner with formal educational experience could take advantage of the British system in a very assertive way. One of the most economical and effective means of attracting potential client groups is to provide publicity in translation, in combination with sessions of counselling. This approach provides detailed information about the college APL service, and more importantly, detailed case studies of local bilingual learners' student maps with information on the following:

1 background of student and linguistic profile;
2 educational history, especially overseas;
3 work qualifications and experience, paid and unpaid, overseas and Britain;
4 map of student's progression route via APL service through to 'units of learning' in college with work-based learning;
5 stages of assessment
   - formative
   - continuous
   - summative; and
6 details of summative certification gained and future aspirations.

These case studies, or student maps, can be made available in computer software and situated in Open Learning centres for self-access by potential students. Bilingual learners who can actually talk through their own personal experiences, achievements and profile in community and religious centres have greater impact as 'active' role models with potential client groups than 'static' written publicity. Examples of case studies are only effective in so far as potential client groups can identify with them. If the people depicted are always young, upwardly mobile, white, Anglo-Saxon, Asian or Afro-Caribbean, then this has disastrous results as a marketing exercise towards breaking down barriers for other client groups.

What is more realistic is for colleges to focus on a blueprint of a potential client group, for instance a group of Gujarati elderly women who live with their families, have never followed formal education beyond the age of 15 in India, and have lived in Britain for more than 10 years. This is a typically representative group, which to date has either by and large never been recruited at college on vocational training courses or has remained in outreach ESOL classes which have a heavy element of socialising. For them, the socialising and not the English has then become the focal point for being in the class.

It is not always necessary to pick on examples of students with huge success stories in order to make the point. The main thrust of the case study is to demonstrate to other potential learners that the college can offer services that can capitalise on all students' skills, expertise and qualifications and that the access point is via a responsive APL service.

ADDITIONAL BARRIERS

Other major barriers, which can be identified specific to access and progression for bilingual learners, relate to language, culture, discrimination and bias in the following areas:

1 absence of APLA process coupled with non-recognition of overseas qualifications;
2 hierarchy of recognisable merit attached to European and overseas qualifications, i.e. greater value attached to European qualifications;
3 process of assessment may involve:
    (a) some groups of candidates who are not familiar with some forms of presentation
    (b) different techniques are easier for some groups of candidates to use
    (c) activities are required which cannot be performed by all candidates;
4 process of assessment involves interview which gives rise to bias in the form of stereotyping, prejudice, assumption-making;
5 process of assessment involves inadequate and inaccurate judgements on linguistic achievements of student;

6 poor or non-existent mechanism for skills audit;

7 absence of objective procedures and infrastructure for evidence gathering linked to core competence and for demonstration of core skills and language. Consequently, bilingual learners are prey to the whims and fancies of individual advisers/assessors. For instance, a Somali-speaking student is informed by an APL adviser that he cannot apply for accreditation of a typing unit, if he can only type in Arabic, but then finds out from another adviser who has checked with the assessor that this is possible, and can proceed with a credit for the unit.

8 absence of, or inadequate quality assurance mechanisms needed to monitor progress and actual learning outcomes for bilingual learners.

As can be seen by the above pointers, bilingual learners are by and large impeded from entry, access and progression on to vocational and academic courses in colleges of further education and higher education. Cheshire LEA asserts that the Authority will secure:

> adequate facilities [to] ensure that adults learn in ways which offer opportunities for progression 'upwards' to higher level courses, 'laterally' to develop wider interests and 'outwards' to opportunities where the benefits of learning may be applied.
>
> (Cheshire LEA 1989)

CONCLUSION

It is vital then that in view of the above, criteria drawn up for the recognition of any particular skill or ability should avoid ethnocentricity and recognise the experience of people from different communities. In addition – and even more importantly – by devolving power to advisers and assessors to make all-important decisions about the viability of a candidate's evidence, it is essential that they have the opportunity to experience appropriate cultural and linguistic awareness training as part of human resources development in order that they may play a vital role in maintaining and improving upon the quality of the APL service.

Further education is positioned on the edge of a new era in which flexibility of response, open access, the provision of 'lifelong' learning opportunities, and the continuing pressure to pursue 'value for money' will be key issues for college managers. Up to now, the use of current resources for bilingual learners such as European Social Fund and Section 11 have been largely aimed at the development of ESOL teaching. If lecturing and learning support staff are to take an effective part in the threshold services of FE colleges, there is an urgent need for up-skilling, reskilling and reorientating of these staff. By and large, traditional ESOL staff have substantial experience of working with bilingual learners, but in a highly specialised capacity, i.e. by relating only to the students' linguistic development in the English language. It is essential for a fundamental shift in attitude to take place alongside retraining, so that staff assess students' needs and abilities holistically. Paramount in this would be staff's ability to assess a learner's communication skills and 'core' skills such as problem-solving, managing own learning, numeracy, working in a team, information technology and relating to others.

An infrastructure that includes an effective and efficient APL process facilitates the mapping of the crossover of skills, integrated and individualised learning support programmes and utilises existing resources towards other forms of service delivery – i.e. a variety of teaching and learning styles such as Open and Flexible Learning, Distance Learning and Work-based Learning. The ethos of such a framework centres around capitalising on client's experience, knowledge and skills.

In relation to National Vocational Qualifications and General National Vocational Qualifications, such a comprehensive framework can enable a variety of client groups other than bilingual learners, (i.e. those from traditional basic skills course areas and those with special needs) to access on to these accredited courses and to gain credit for their learning and experience.

APPENDIX 1.1: STANDARDS FOR LANGUAGES (LANGUAGES LEAD BODY)

Level Descriptors Used in the Language Standards Framework

Level 1   Competence in a range of routine and predictable simple language tasks.

Level 2   Competence in a range of varied language tasks, performed in varied everyday work and social contexts. Some of these tasks are non-routine, and the individual is expected to use a limited range of language to meet the needs of differing but familiar situations and topics.

Level 3   Competence in a broad range of factual, persuasive and expressive language tasks performed in a variety of contexts. Most language tasks require decision making to select appropriate language; and the individual is expected to be able to combine and recombine language elements to accomplish key work tasks.

Level 4   Competence in a broad range of complex or technical language tasks, performed in a wide variety of contexts and with a substantial requirement to select and adapt appropriate language strategies. The individual is expected to make and respond to a wide range of spontaneous foreign language interventions and to infer or express implicit and multiple meaning for a wide variety of work and social purposes.

Level 5   Competence in a broad range of complex and non-routine tasks across a wide and often unpredictable variety of contexts; and which involves the application of a significant range of language strategies selected from an extensive repertoire, which the individual continuously updates to meet changing requirements.

LANGUAGE COMPETENCE

Definition   The ability to use a *modern* language for personal, social and occupational purposes

Performance statements   In contexts involving increasing linguistic demands, being able to:

1   • respond to a limited range of language in familiar situations
     • convey simple information and ideas, requiring limited repertoires, language structures and vocabulary

2   • respond confidently to a range of language within mostly familiar situations, applying known linguistic concepts
     • maintain communication by adapting and applying language to mainly familiar situations

3   • respond confidently and independently to a wide range of language in a variety of familiar and unfamiliar contexts
     • initiate and maintain communication, selecting and applying language from a known repertoire in response to familiar and unfamiliar demands

4   • respond to complex language, applying an understanding of cultural and linguistic factors to infer meaning when it is not clear
     • communicate fluently and sensitively, selecting and adapting language to meet unpredictable demands

APPENDIX 1.1 *cont.*

	Purpose of the language act	Autonomy in using foreign languages	
		Flexibility (Structure)	Appropriateness of language (Vocabulary)
I	To interact with people in familiar roles, establish relationships and exchange limited routine oral and written information on familiar and routine operational matters within one's occupational role.	Limited to the structures of a fixed repertoire of prepared materials and rehearsed information. Repertoire limited to simple sentences; mainly the present aspect; subject pronouns.	Vocabulary sufficient to express terms for everyday objects and events, and to conduct routine, everyday transactions with people in familiar roles.
II	To interact with people in familiar roles, maintain relationships and exchange routine oral and written information on familiar routine and non-routine matters within one's occupational role.	Repertoire extends to use of the future aspect; some object pronouns; the reporting function is limited to recounting events. Performance is based on the use of prepared materials/ rehearsed information. Makes simple combinations to vary the communication according to the subject matter and context.	Vocabulary includes everyday alternative words and expressions for familiar objects and events, and for people in familiar roles. Vocabulary is sufficient to cope with changes from one familiar topic to another.
III	To interact with individuals and groups, sustain and foster relationships and exchange oral and written information and advice on a broad range of routine and non-routine matters related to one's occupational role.	Combines, recombines and extends repertoire to deal with the full range of familiar, and a limited range of unfamiliar, communication tasks. Repertoire includes some complex sentences, including simple relative and causal/explanatory clauses; full reporting function; conditional states; subject and object pronouns.	Vocabulary is sufficient to achieve a broad range of factual and expressive tasks. Vocabulary includes alternative expressions for use in speaking or writing mode. Vocabulary is sufficient to cope with changes from familiar to some unfamiliar topics.
IV	To interact with individuals and groups, maintain relationships, and exchange information and advice on the full range of matters related to one's occupational role.	Combines and recombines a wide range of complex sentences, pronouns, tenses and aspects to deal with familiar and all but extremely unfamiliar matters. Expresses factual, descriptive, comparative and evaluative information independently.	Vocabulary sufficient and appropriate to a wide range of oral and written communication tasks. Recognises accurately current colloquialisms and different writing conventions for business and social purposes. Identifies and extends repertoire to deal with unfamiliar matters and situations.
V	To deal with complex interactions, extend relationships and exchange complex information and advice for specialised purposes.	Combines, recombines and extends a repertoire sufficiently extensive to deal with complex tasks, including unusual and highly specialised language tasks.	Vocabulary includes highly specialised terms and expressions required for one's role. Identifies appropriate substitutes for expressions and terms for which there is no equivalent in the alternative language.

Autonomy in using foreign languages / Cultural adaptation (Register)	Contexts - recipients and environments	Need for evaluation
Uses everyday polite forms of address and social conventions.	Interacts with people familiar with the content of what is written/ said and in frequent contact with the individual. Interactions are highly predictable. Environments are familiar and relatively stable.	The meaning of key points in matters raised by others is checked, using stock phrases. Recipients' understanding of the language used is checked. Repetition is used to clarify meaning.
Uses a variety of everyday polite forms of address and social conventions; including simple expressions of gratitude, regret and apology.	Interacts with people familiar with the content of the communication, who include those in infrequent contact as well as those in frequent contact with the individual. Interactions are simple – one to one and one to a group member. Environments are familiar, routine and relatively stable.	The meaning of key points in matters raised by other people is checked, using stock phrases. Recipients' understanding of the language used is checked. A limited repertoire of alternative expressions is identified to redress misunderstandings.
Uses appropriate language to interact at work and socially with a range of people in different types of formal and informal roles and relationships.	Interacts with people familiar and unfamiliar with the content of the communication, and in frequent or infrequent contact. Interactions are planned and include multiple interactions within small groups.	The individual confirms understanding (own and others) of what is written or said and uses emphasis or alternative vocabulary/ structures to clarify misunderstanding. Appropriate sources of assistance are accessed promptly.
Uses appropriate language to interact spontaneously with people in familiar and unfamiliar work and social roles and relationships and cultural settings. Varies register to match the tone, status and emotive content of the setting.	Interacts spontaneously with people familiar or unfamiliar with the content of the communication and in simple and complex inter-personal group settings.	Additional information to clarify, amplify or explain key points made by the individual or others is provided when necessary. Ambiguities of expression are identified accurately and appropriate action taken to clarify meaning – including recourse to third parties or other sources.
Adapts language to interact with people in a variety of formal and informal settings, including those in which people may be considerably stressed.	Interacts with and on behalf of people familiar and unfamiliar with the content of the communication in complex interpersonal and group settings.	Additional information to clarify, amplify or explain key points made by the individual or others is provided when necessary. The nature, scope and con-sequences of misunderstand-ings are accurately identified and remedial action taken.

APPENDIX 1.2

Table 1.2 The entitlement curriculum

	Entry	On Programme	Exit
Learning programme	Guidance/ Action Plan	Guidance Review	Guidance/Action Plan
Learning resources	APL Induction Module	Teaching/Learning Strategies and Additional Units for Learner support/Core Skills	Summative Statement – Student
Learning outcomes	Diagnostic Assess/APLA	Assessment & Recording	Summative Statement – College

Chapter 2

The role of guidance advocate within the APL process

INTRODUCTION

A focus on APL as part of the threshold services is particularly relevant in view of the developments towards flexible, modular-based courses. It is essential to develop a quality-control approach whereby APL advisers and then tutors help students formulate their own objectives, expectations and achievements at various stages in the course. These can be continuously reviewed and recorded, i.e. at the formative, halfway stage and summative stage of the course. This is paramount with all learners, but in the case of bilingual learners, students are having to review their objectives and progress, not only in terms of the vocational area, but equally importantly, in terms of the language profile. It is suggested, therefore, that the APL process incorporate a guidance advocate worker at Stage 1, whose role would be akin to that of the APL adviser but would be more specialised in the areas of guidance, counselling and assessment of language and 'core' skills. A more detailed focus on actual assessment methods will be outlined in subsequent chapters. Generally speaking, the guidance advocate has an enabling and enhancing role vis-à-vis bilingual candidates at all stages of the model outlined in Table 2.1.

THE PRE-ENTRY STAGE OF APL

During the pre-entry stages of APL, it is the responsibility of FE colleges to disseminate information to attract potential candidates. This involves extensive marketing and in relation to bilingual learners, special strategies involving accessible publicity in English and other languages. Pre-entry activities include distributing brochures, producing press releases, meeting with groups of employers, community groups, local tenant groups, promotional events within local businesses and the community, or any of a whole range of other strategies that are used to market services and products and disseminate information. Locating the Guidance Advocate worker in an educational APL workshop is one part of the overall

Table 2.1 The traditional APL process

Stages of quality control approach		
Candidate profiling	Pre-entry counselling and guidance and student profile	Stage 1
Gathering of evidence	Formative stage of assessment	Stage 2
Assessment	Review of objectives/ achievements	Stage 3
Accreditation	Summative stage of achievements	Stage 4
Post-assessment guidance	Exit counselling and update on student profile	Stage 5

Source: Simoko 1990

marketing strategy which can be particularly effective in recruiting bilingual learners to a process that is unfamiliar and innovative.

PROVIDING A COST-EFFECTIVE APL SERVICE FOR GROUPS OF BILINGUAL LEARNERS

It is viable to identify various groups of bilingual learners with homogeneous backgrounds, experience and needs, and to provide APL to these students on a group basis. Moreover, if instituting a cost-effective service implies cutting down on staff time, trained bilingual APL advisers and assessors could facilitate the process of English language assessment and development much faster, for the following reasons:

1 They could use the person's own language to help distinguish between what are English language training needs in the professional area and what are purely professional training needs.
2 Bi- or multilingual advisers are needed in specific areas on the basis of known patterns of demand in vocational areas coupled with the background and expertise of students from other cultures who wish to build on their experience in these areas.
3 These advisers, having worked with bilingual students from a specific culture and background sharing virtually the same patterns of expertise and need, can then go on to formulate 'student maps', that is to say a blueprint profile which maps out the specific background, qualifications and experience of a homogeneous group of learners. In practice, this means that the adviser's job would become easier and quicker as he/she becomes more familiar with the candidate's prior experience and is able to work with groups of candidates on a more cost-effective basis. For instance, here is one specific example of a profile of a recently arrived homogeneous group of students with

a shared need: Zairean French-speaking, highly motivated and ambitious individuals with a background in business administration. They wish to capitalise on this prior experience by following NVQ Business Administration Levels 2 and 3 – or a Business and Technology Education Council (BTEC) GNVQ Level 2 – depending on their level of English and past experience.

4 In building up the 'student map' the bi- or multilingual APL advisers and assessors are more likely to have an understanding of the person's country of origin and the professional practices in that country. Even if they are not familiar, they are possibly more likely to have empathy and understanding with the candidates. Bilingual learners would be more likely to volunteer the range of their experiences, precisely because they feel that their experiences would be recognised and valued by the bi- and multilingual APL advisers. This can surely speed up the APL process by forming the basis of a positive interaction, between adviser and client.

In conclusion, there are powerful arguments for identifying target groups of bilingual learners in terms of shared linguistic cultural background and expertise, and to employ APL advisers who share similar experiences for the purposes of assessment and building of portfolios. These groups of bilingual learners may – through Community and voluntary groups – apply for and receive funding from the Training and Enterprise Councils (TECs), European Social Fund (ESF) and so on, and would be in a position to buy APL services from colleges of FE. One way of empowering bilingual learners, especially refugees and asylum-seekers, is to set up an APEL service locally within the community group so that not only do candidates have access to assessment, but also to advice on reorientation of skills in relation to the job market. This could form an essential link with the local college services and could replace current college outreach ESOL provision which may not be so cost-effective and may not be funded under the new FEFC guidelines. On the other hand, it would be possible to incorporate just such an APL service as a necessary adjunct to outreach ESOL community classes, which currently form an effective access point for bilingual learners into the college.

Another way forward is to utilise the potential for APL bilingual advisers to be found in the local target communities. Bilingual individuals with training, teaching, counselling and guidance experience from their own countries are surely capable of undertaking the Training Development Lead Body (TDLB) APL advisers training. They could then advertise their services on a paid basis to colleges and local community groups. TECs or colleges could, for example, sponsor the training of bilingual individuals and subsequently offer employment to them on a voluntary basis initially, to recoup the cost of the training. Some 80 per cent of inner-city respondents in the Leicestershire Education Authority Highfields Impact Survey (Dadzie, 1993) said they would use an educational/vocational guidance service if one was available. Guidance advocate workers recruited from the local ethnic communities would enhance the quality of the service for bilingual candidates. At this point in the historical development of APL, it is highly unlikely that many colleges have access to the necessary bilingual skills on their staff to service the needs of bilingual learners cost effectively, as outlined above. A combination of imaginative and creative thinking (through partnership between colleges, TECs and the community groups) could result in a very useful package of reorientation of skills training for bilingual learners and provide the human resources with specialist skills much needed by colleges.

SKILLS AND ABILITIES OF GUIDANCE ADVOCATE WORKER: COUNSELLING AND ADVOCACY

It would be possible to recruit suitably qualified and experienced workers from local communities recently settled in this country with teaching, advocacy, guidance or counselling backgrounds. What is suggested is to offer training to these individuals, standardised to a quality format, for instance, along the UDACE plan (1987) currently used in counselling. There is a need, however, to recognise the cultural appropriateness and relevance of the UDACE training plan and to balance this alongside the skills and culturally specific experience which the GA worker would be bringing to the APL process. The process of giving guidance and advice is culturally specific. What would be deemed 'politically correct' in one culture as the way to implement the process would be discouraged in another culture as being inappropriate to the culturally specific communication discourse skills of that society. John Gumperz's research (1982b) on ethnic differences in counselling interviews suggests that for example, in Asian–Asian counselling interviews, the counsellor does a great deal of inferring of fact and opinion, and then checks with the client. This is in contrast to white British interviews where the clients make a lot of evaluative comments about their situation without much prompting from the counsellor.

Enabling the bilingual candidate to outline accomplishments is a major step on account of language difficulties and nervousness over talking about past experiences which may have been traumatic if, for instance, the candidate is a refugee fleeing from persecution. This requires sensitive but directed questioning. Contrary to the popular usage of open-ended questioning as opposed to 'closed questions' in counselling, experience has borne out with many bilingual learners that the best response is elicited from using both types of questions, on account of language difficulties. Initial directed questions, which confirm details, can allow a bilingual candidate a space in which to develop confidence in self-expression. This can then be fanned out to more open-ended questions, such as 'Tell me about . . . ?'.

Guidance advocates and APL advisers need to receive awareness training on different models of delivery for guidance and advocacy work and for discussions to take place around the most appropriate and sensitive ways to implement flexible varying styles to match culturally different case-studies.

With reference to the UDACE 'Seven Activities of Guidance', there is a need to adapt and modify this model to incorporate the specialist role of the GA worker within the APL process, as outlined in the table below.

The cornerstone of the entire relationship between the GA worker and the bilingual candidate is a confidence-building process which offers support, unbiased information and guidance to the bilingual learner.

The role of the APL adviser is very clearly specifically around the area of candidate profiling and the gathering of evidence. However, it is during contact with the guidance advocate and with the APL adviser that candidates can clarify their expectations in seeking recognition of their learning and equate what they know and can do with the standards of learning outcomes of a particular programme or qualification. The portfolio becomes much more specialised in its applicability during the interview between the APL adviser and the candidate.

The initial staged interview with the APL adviser is split into two parts, with both the Guidance Advocate worker and the APL adviser taking responsibility for each part.

The role of the Guidance Advocate and the APL adviser is to 'lift the canopy from candidates' often limited self-perceptions and self-appraisals'. This is even more pertinent in the case of bilingual learners. Both workers must have the skills and abilities to:

- encourage candidates to clarify goals, identify obstacles or issues and to develop strategies for overcoming them;
- help candidates reflect on their past experiences and identify their strengths and accomplishments;
- help candidates to develop a strong personal profile which is linked to the standards or courses against which the person wishes to be assessed;
- provide correct and adequate information which will enable candidates to make sound decisions;
- help candidates develop their portfolios of evidence and prepare for assessment;
- actively listen to candidates and provide appropriate feedback throughout the process;
- liaise with APL assessors and others on the APL team; and
- maintain accurate records at the summative stage of assessment when the bilingual candidate needs further guidance and counselling on training and/or employment.

It may be appropriate in some situations, particularly with bilingual

Table 2.2   The role of guidance advocate within the threshold services

Role	Definition	Examples of activities
Informing	Providing range of options without recommending one in particular Providing details of practical considerations, e.g. cost of APL procedure, cost of course, mode and pattern of delivery, childcare, special needs Providing information on process of APL	• Videos produced locally in college of past bilingual candidates involved in APL process charting student journey – pre-entry stage to summative stage • Computer software which allows candidate access to information concerning equivalence of European and overseas qualification and details of evidence required for specific courses, in different languages, giving a range of options
Advising/enabling	Personalised or group discussions to help candidates interpret information and to choose initially the most appropriate options through discussing merits of each Providing guidance on application to particular courses Supporting the candidate in dealing with the demands of education/employment or training Advising candidate of different routes to accreditation to recognised professional status and to professional employment in the three vocational areas	• Discussions in English and other languages • Suggesting visits to meet students in college/ workplace • Following up queries • Arranging for interviews with vocational/ academic members of staff if necessary • Arranging for candidate to participate in: – accelerated/intensive English course module – study skills module – oral skills module – computing/IT module • Practising communication skills • Arranging for candidates to participate in APL modules (modules of 4–10 weeks)
Advising	Supporting candidates throughout the APEL process	• Advising candidate of referral points within educational system

Counselling	Working with candidates to help them discover, clarify and understand their needs and find ways of meeting them	• Providing structure • Reflecting back • Clarifying • Using peer group discussion and pair work in focusing on language and negative experience to develop positive pro-active communication skills and attitudes
	Working with bilingual candidates in ways suitable and appropriate to them	
	Working with bilingual candidates to build up confidence and self-esteem in language and negative past experience	
	Working with bilingual candidates to overcome their inhibitions about themselves and the educational system, so that effective counselling can take place	• Talking through barriers and discrimination candidates have faced in the past in Britain and in the educational system Talking through 'working solutions' and pooling together a set of strategies with candidates individually and in small groups
Assessing	Helping the client define current levels of skills, knowledge and experience using appropriate methods	• Using a variety of assessment methods which focus on: – language skills – candidate's overseas qualifications – candidate's past experience and vocational/academic skills – candidate's core skills
	Liaising with APEL adviser	
	Assisting candidates in setting their own goals and objectives	
	Assisting candidates in familiarising themselves with relatively new concepts in teaching and learning methodology in Britain	• Introducing candidate to concepts and skills: – self-evaluation – self-assessment – assessment of teaching and learning – record-keeping National Record of Achievement (NRA)
	Assisting candidates in a developing a pro-active role in assessment process	• Assisting action planning/evaluation
	Assisting candidates in identifying their competences and evidence, alongside discussions with the APL adviser	• Assisting candidate in putting together an initial portfolio (to be devised by APEL adviser) and an NRA

- Helping bilingual candidate in initial portfolio preparation, to include an initial curriculum vitae, general profile of learning achievements, work experience and linguistic profile

- Assessing language and common learning outcomes 'core' skills of candidate

- Facilitating 'screening assessments' and diagnostic assessments of a candidate's linguistic aptitude for joining vocational/academic courses

- Helping candidates establish equivalency of their overseas qualifications and to advise candidates of the currency value of their qualifications within the NVQ framework

- Working with candidates on a range of exercises designed to assess aptitude in the area of reflection and analysis of learning experience

- Giving candidates the confidence and practice in communication and core skills for the interviews with APL adviser/assessor or when demonstrating evidence for claimed competences

Assisting candidates with editing evidence to be presented. Providing English language support and help with rehearsals for oral and written assessment task

- Familiarising himself/herself with appropriateness of evidence to competence, familiarising himself/herself with technical jargon of assessment

		• Advising candidate on specific routes available to collate evidence and to progress with chosen qualifications
		• Helping candidate reassess initial individual action/assessment plan
		• Supporting candidate through self-assessment process using checklists of NVQ units, elements and performance criteria – developing work initiated by Guidance Advocate worker
		• Supporting and advising candidate to collect suitable evidence of competence drawn from prior learning achievements and compile final portfolio of evidence to support competence claims, e.g. portfolio preparation workshops
		• Liaising with APL assessors about evidence requirements, registration with awarding body, assessment contract and evaluation of portfolio
Advocating	Negotiating directly with the agencies/institutions on admissions and/or modifications to courses	• Networking
		• Lobbying
	Negotiating with local TEC, local authorities economic development units, local voluntary and community groups to gain local information on businesses and employers with multilingual needs	• Researching
		• Producing reports and publicity
		• Approaching academic staff within the college
		• Approaching other training providers in borough, nationally and in Europe to develop partnerships

	Negotiating with voluntary sector umbrella organisations who are working closely with ethnic minorities	
	Negotiating with the LEA's Community Education service which provides a wide range of formal and informal education opportunities for bilingual adults through its network of community centres and community	
Feeding Back	Gathering information on needs which are unmet, inappropriately met and encouraging providers to respond	• Monitoring • Suggesting changes • Providing material evidence
	Liaising with APL assessor within college	• Making concrete proposals
	Evaluating effectiveness and efficacy of candidates participating in APL process and feedback of results to Institution alongside APL adviser	• Being pro-active • Suggesting changes in assessment procedures if appropriate
	Implementing a quality control model through monitoring and review of service with feedback	

candidates who find the initial process with the guidance advocate worker confidence-boosting and reassuring, to return to the model of working in small groups to develop their individual profiles, using the evidence pin-pointing workshops.

ADVANTAGES OF SHARED COMMUNICATION STYLES AND CULTURAL BACKGROUND

Use of a shared language, other than English, either verbal or written, would be invaluable for the explanation of new concepts such as competence, core competence, units of learning, record-keeping, NVQ, GNVQ assessment procedures such as performance criteria, range, statements, performance evidence and so on. The bilingual candidate would be able to take in and discuss the new concepts using the language that was most comfortable for him/her. This would have the desired effect of generating greater self-confidence which would eventually unblock inhibitions and low self-esteem and would have an enabling effect on the acquisition of English.

In terms of costing, a guidance advocate worker may be seen at first glance to be somewhat of a 'luxury item', non-cost-effective, or super-fluous as part of the Threshold Services. Nevertheless, the role of such a worker in relation to bilingual learners and other learners in need of support systems, is an essential one. It is a role that provides support and access for the learner to the APL system and explores the training options and relevant evidence available. In one sense, such a worker may also be used in a similar way to the Community Education Development workers, whose brief traditionally includes disseminating information, publicity and access to courses for adults within the community.

The guidance advocate worker would be in a position to provide valuable information to enable the potential learner to make informed choices concerning educational decisions for his/her future develop-ment, and would be a crucial referral point in the system. By pump-prim-ing resources into this area, it would be financially viable to realise two main functions as follows – first, initial screening and second, rebuilding the candidate's self-esteem and confidence.

Initial screening: individually and in groups

All bilingual and monolingual learners entering the system could be 'screened' initially, and given initial counselling and information concerning their personal profile aspirations and different accreditation options. The GA assists the learner in assembling a curriculum vitae, an initial generalised portfolio not as yet linked into any specific evidence-related competence, unit or level. The GA can familiarise the learner with interview techniques, verbal and written assessment techniques which he/she will meet at the stage of APEL adviser/assessor. This is vital for building up confidence, especially for bilingual learners. The reality of the situation is that these students have a good command of the English language but are underconfident and nervous of their linguistic ability when confronted by assessors. The problems of underconfidence and underachievement are exacerbated when bilingual speakers are faced with monolingual assessors. With the best of intentions and with the most sympathetic assessors, different expectations and cultural understandings can inhibit effective assessment and distort perceptions of linguistic ability. In these situations, learners do not express them-selves to the best of their abilities because they may need convincing that the assessor can relate to them and values their past experiences. The trust and confidence in the relationship between the bilingual student and the monolingual assessor may take longer to establish than that between bilingual learner and bilingual adviser.

The 'mapping process' of matching qualifications and experience to desired elements/units is more cost-effective if carried out with groups of homogeneous learners, i.e. learners who share a mother tongue and perhaps similar qualifications, skills and experiences. The GA could draw upon blueprint profiles of 'student maps' which would facilitate the process of officially equivalenting overseas qualifications and equivalenting evidence of overseas experience, knowledge and skills to NVQ units.

At the initial entry Stage 1, it is possible to use computer software to log a candidate's personal details, information concerning equivalences of overseas qualifications, past experience and skills and an outline from the candidate's portfolio with suggested competences and evidence available. As the candidate progresses to the APL adviser, he/she will have more substantial details included on the software as part of the portfolio. The candidate may not be in a position to move from the GA worker directly to the APL adviser because:

- he/she may enrol for an APL induction module
- he/she may have decided to enrol for a course in intensive English
- he/she may pursue a a vocational taster
- he/she may decide to pursue employment for a period of time.

In this case, the record of the candidate's portfolio will remain on software until some future date when he/she returns to the APEL process. The candidate may be advised to join an APEL module because he/she is not in a position to provide 'secondary' indirect evidence, i.e. testimonials and graphic evidence of skills, experience and knowledge. Therefore, participating in a module where he/she will have the opportunity to demonstrate expertise and to compile relevant evidence into a portfolio would appear to be the best option.

Rebuilding candidate's self-esteem and confidence

The main barriers facing bilingual candidates wishing to enter the field of education and training are as follows – lack of confidence in their own usage of English and low self-esteem in the area of English language acquisition which results in 'fossilisation' of language. That is to say, they are not motivated to progress any further with the acquisition of new language concepts, i.e. vocabulary/grammar, and skills remain 'fossilised' at a particular 'plateau' of level. By and large, the lack of confidence results from "others'" negative perceptions of their use of the English language, thus resulting in communication difficulties, which will eventually spiral downwards (Figure 2.1).

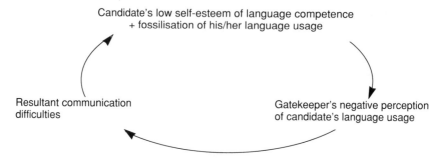

Candidate's low self-esteem of language competence
+ fossilisation of his/her language usage

Resultant communication
difficulties

Gatekeeper's negative perception
of candidate's language usage

Figure 2.1 The downward spiral of language skills

Advisers must recognise the needs of three types of candidate:

1 Candidates who have been through the educational system in their own country and have succeeded, will normally have high aspirations and ambitions concerning their own achievements and future potential. The role of the adviser is to deal tactfully and sensitively in order to help them realise their potential but to offer as much realistic feedback as possible on the feasibility of their ambitions in the current climate of the recession;

2 Candidates may have had negative past experiences of the British educational system as they may have been sequestered in ESOL classes for many years and therefore underestimate their potential. The adviser needs to build up their confidence and self-esteem, in some of the following ways:

(a) accelerated and intensive English language provision as opposed to 'drip feed' English tuition which incorporates wider 'core' communication skills and study skills, based on the GNVQ 'core' skills;

(b) enrolment in an intensive course of English which develops verbal confidence through intensive role-play, debate, discussion and presentation;

(c) counselling through the medium of the learner's first language either at the college or through enlisting the help of local community groups;

(d) encouraging learners with similar backgrounds to form peer groups and to work together on integrated task-based assignments – bilingually or monolingually. The outcome may then be presented to an APL adviser/assessor and assessed against a unit of competence for a particular programme. More importantly, the shared learning experience will create confidence and increased self-esteem. Encouraging learners to work together with dissimilar backgrounds sometimes also has a positive 'ripple effect', in so far as those with more confidence will encourage others through a process of 'modelling'.

3 Candidates who have come from a different background may be unfamiliar with the system and society as a whole in this country and need to undergo a sympathetic process of reorientation.

CROSS-CULTURAL ISSUES AROUND COLLATION AND ASSESSMENT OF EVIDENCE

In the bilingual workplace

The GA worker can prove to be very effective in working with bilingual candidates/employees in the workplace context. A good example of this was a group of guidance advocates who worked with an Asian Women's Centre for the assessment of management competences. Advantages included enabling candidates to gain in confidence through group activities, whilst being both time- and cost-effective. Moreover, the employer and the organisation found that the process of candidates identifying their management competences and matching them against the standards enhanced their own management skills and performance in the Women's Project.

A relevant general point which arose from this experience was that the standards which had been set in professional areas did not always include the range of competences required by the bilingual candidates in their work contexts. This was particularly true in management, where candidates felt there were a range of cross cultural skills and cultural and community development skills which were essential for them to carry out their management tasks. Yet there were no NVQ units which included these competences, for example, in the area of bilingual counselling and service delivery.

Reflection and analysis of experience

The ease with which individuals can analyse and reflect is related to linguistic and cultural backgrounds and a more specifically formal academic/vocational education which encourages that sort of creative and verbal reasoning. With bilingual candidates, there are two types of difficulties: first, he/she is able to analyse and reflect in his/her own language but not in English. Second, he/she may not have had prior experience of this specialised thought process and, therefore, finds great difficulty in analysing and reflecting in either their own language or in English.

Candidates need information, advice and support in practising the processes of analysis and reflection for the purposes of assessment and profiling. Experience has demonstrated that if candidates can work through this process with bilingual advisers and/or with their peer group, the process is more successful for all the reasons noted previously in connection with inter-ethnic communication styles.

The need for proficiency at a high level of reflection and analysis and translation of this into English can be a barrier to assessment for bilingual candidates. Difficulty in this process does not necessarily denote lack of competence because the process of articulating this evidence is a separate skill in itself. It is crucial that at the entry and formative assessment stages with the guidance advocate and the APL adviser, a bilingual candidate is made aware of the importance of this skill and is equipped with the necessary communication strategies to either develop and practise the skill or to look at alternative ways of presenting their evidence with the assessor.

There is no doubt that the questioning of candidates for underpinning knowledge and demonstration of transferability of competence to other unexpected situations, relies heavily on their ability to reflect, explain and infer other courses of action in a language (i.e. English) which may not be the one they are most able to think, reflect and analyse in. This process, however, is used in order to provide the assessor with a 'feel' for how someone operates in a professional and/or vocational role. It is, therefore, a standard technique used in assessing transferability of 'underpinning knowledge' and the ability to deal with unpredictable situations.

BIAS IN ASSESSMENT

It is clear that interviews between white assessors (gatekeepers) and bilingual learners can disadvantage clients on account of stereotyping, assumption-making and a quest for 'intelligible English'. This last criterion is open to wide and unsubstantiated interpretation by vocational assessors. Very often, students who wish to apply for entry to vocational courses are not given any formal language assessment to dovetail into a framework of stipulated language requirements for the specified course. For instance, a student's English may be fluent, if somewhat inaccurate or may be fluent and accurate but he/she commands a heavy ethnic accent. A student may lack the appropriate cultural *discourse skills* within the given assessment situation, that is to say, familiarity with the culturally appropriate sequence and presentation of thought and response in a given context – formal or informal. Then again, a student may be very nervous and underconfident of her/his ability in English, having been told on several occasions by language and vocational specialists that her/his 'language' is a stumbling block to personal progress. Nervousness can be a major barrier to fluency. Potential learners will risk failure to access a course of their choice because of the assertion by language and vocational staff that they do not meet the criteria for 'intelligible English'. This masks a *'hidden agenda'* as very often vocational staff do not have the expertise and training to accommodate learning support within a classroom situation or within an Open Learning situation and consequently lack the confidence to enrol students who may 'demand too much from them in terms of learning support'. Once again, this has implications for staff training with a focus on reassessing traditional teaching styles and modes of delivery which assume all learners have homogeneous needs and are culturally and educationally an ethnocentric group.

Another implication is the need to develop good practice by matching modes of assessment to individual bilingual learners and as a logical extension to all learners, in order that they are 'not being set up to fail' and are put into realistic assessment situations which furnish them with an opportunity to achieve their personal potential. A group of learners who would be potentially disadvantaged are those with Creole or patois dialects. Traditionally, these candidates have been channelled into an Adult and Basic Skills Education programme for help with reading and writing strategies. Redefining the APL framework entitles these student to a linguistic profile with an assessment map which charts strengths and areas of improvements plus prior learning experience and areas of support, as in the case of bilingual learners. In keeping with the ethos of APL, these candidates particularly benefit from a review of their informal and work-based learning. Consequently, a recognition of their existing skills enables them to take more flexible routes through training and education in reduced time.

POTENTIAL AREAS OF FAILURE FOR STUDENTS

Professor Alan Smithers' report 'All Our Futures' (1993), commissioned for the Channel 4 *Dispatches* programme, expressed the following reservations as areas of potential failure for NVQs and GNVQs:

- their schematic framework is largely derived from behavioural psychology;
- students' underpinning knowledge and theory are not separately tested – but inferred through bureaucratic procedures;
- there is often misunderstood jargon, no syllabus, no specified courses; and
- there are no compulsory examinations for NVQs.

Implementing a system that ensures fairness and lack of bias at point of assessment means training for APEL advisers and assessors so that they are aware of the various factors which could potentially discriminate against bilingual learners. For instance, if a candidate for a childcare qualification or hairdressing qualification cannot write very articulately in the academic sense, the assessment should be conducted orally or through an integrated assignment approach, which might involve discussion, group work, researching and collating information and then presenting it orally, thus utilising other skills. If writing is not the most important skill for successful competence 'on the job' and other skills such as oral interaction are, then there should be greater weighting for the latter. Equally important is the correct interpretation and use of the performance criteria. If an assessor is unwilling or unable to relate the interpretation of the performance criteria to the National Framework, this could well result in biased and subjective assessments.

For instance, candidates are competent at NVQ Level 1 if they can achieve competence criteria under supervision and in a restricted range of work conditions. At NVQ Level 2, a candidate would be required to work without supervision. A bilingual learner who is able to work at Level 2 in his/her own language but unable to do so yet in English will receive only Level 1 in Business Administration. This would mean that at a given point in the continuum of learning in this student's profile, he/she would be able to work with ease and confidence (on his/her own initiative) in an environment where the medium of instruction was that of his/her first language. If he/she could be given the opportunity with the BTEC units in language to be assessed in both languages, through work-based learning, both levels could then be stipulated in his/her ROA as a more realistic assessment of his/her capabilities.

Similarly, a student who undertakes a GNVQ Level 2 Health and Social Care and is able to demonstrate competence in his/her own language, would need to have this recorded in his/her ROA, especially if he/she is in an environment using his/her first language. It is worth noting that the Evidence Indicators for Element 1.1, 1.2 and 1.3 both maintain that:

> Standards might be demonstrated in the context of a project to explore the interests and life patterns of peer group members. The project would include individual and small group discussion.

Two points can be highlighted in connection with this:

1 Peer group may be interpreted as individuals sharing the same language and cultural background of the student, thus it would be valid for the student to provide evidence of these elements in these contexts, using his/her own language. The contexts could be advocacy counselling in a voluntary/community group, developing social interaction in drop-in sessions to encourage the formation of bonding and friendship of a peer group, advocacy/counselling for 'crisis' situations.

2 The performance criteria that would be used to measure the evidence, if operating in a cultural and linguistic setting other than English, would naturally be biased towards the chosen culture.

In this instance, it would be critical for an assessor to be well trained in the awareness of culturally biased guidance, counselling and interview techniques, especially in the projection of non-verbal messages/body language, active/reflective listening if judging the student with a client group that is not English. Moreover, it may be very relevant and appropriate for the student to be using his/her own culturally based discourse skills, with his/her client peer group, as this group of individuals would share a cultural specific framework for communication skills, both verbal and non-verbal. He/she would have more success in communicating with his/her client peer group in this way, than if he/she were to adopt 'English-specific' cultural norms.

It may be more appropriate to conduct the assessment in the language shared by the student and his/her client group. This raises questions around the acceptability and validity of GNVQ qualification in languages other than English and around training issues in languages for APL advisers and assessors. In some instances the ability to speak more than one language is a considerable asset for an occupation, as for a bilingual receptionist. In some cases it is essential for the success of the post as in counselling for ethnic minorities, yet there is no means of awarding credit for this particular skill.

VALID AND RELIABLE ASSESSMENT PROCEDURES

It is at the point of entry and access to vocational/academic courses that the bilingual learner's progress is impeded on the whole. Initial assessment and diagnosis may be regarded as a function of a central guidance service or it may be the responsibility of other staff with vocational specialisms. Where diagnostic tests and/or interview procedures are applied, there appears to be a variety of tests and interviewing styles with no consistency from one college to another nationally, and sometimes with little or no consistency within a college. Consequently, bilingual learners are excluded from admission on the basis of a system that lacks:

- validity;
- reliability; and
- utility.

In terms of general access to education or more specifically, access to a course of training – vocational and educational training (VET) – the concept of 'validity' needs to be thoroughly understood by those involved in direct assessment – and by extension, those who design skills proficiency/competency tests, write projects/assignments, or obtain evidence from learners' prior experience/achievement.

The starting point may well include the following definitions:

> Validity is a measure of the extent to which an assessment assesses that which it purports to assess . . . whether a test does what it was meant to.
>
> (Frith and Macintosh 1984)

> Validity is the extent to which a given test is an appropriate measure of what it was intended to measure.
>
> (Page and Thomas 1977)

From the point of view of bilingual learners, assessment tests at point of access (with few exceptions of good practice) have traditionally been skewed in favour of monolingual, Anglo-Saxon native speakers of English and have not necessarily passed the litmus test of validity if the question asked is:-

> Is the assessment procedure valid for *all* learners – to test their potential and their abilities for a chosen course/courses and to highlight areas of learner support?

In other words, assessment procedures should create validity by encompassing a wide range of student needs and accepting them for entry on courses with the proviso that the *learner support* will then be made available.

It is essential for the assessor to offer other forms of assessment. A one-off interview with a candidate or a single performance of a task may not provide a reliable indicator of a candidate's potential or aptitude for a chosen area of study. Similarly, a single source of information concerning qualifications – not from a nationally recognised and legitimised body (NARIC) – does not constitute a basis for a reliable decision concerning suitability. An unreliable and invalid system of assessment for access to a course permits the entry of students who ostensibly appear well matched to the yardstick of the model student but who do have real needs for learning support, which may not be identified. On the other hand, such a system impedes the entry of students who do not fit into the conventional pro forma, but have very credible abilities, skills, experience and real potential to succeed on a chosen course. It is thus essential that all those concerned with assessment recognise that an unreliable test is an unfair and biased test.

This is where *validity* and *reliability* factors are interdependent in assessment procedures. Reliability implies by definition that assessments be equivalent or consistent from one context to another.

For instance, potential Asian students for the City and Guilds Childcare 324.1 course in a college of FE were unable to secure places on the course on account of a standard question-and-answer interview procedure in English with questions such as 'What do you understand by the term equal opportunities?'. The result of the interview supposedly demonstrated their English as being inadequate for course requirements. At the time two of the four candidates were working in a voluntary or paid capacity in a creche and a special needs school. Shortly afterwards, the same students, with effective and individualised language learning programmes, were able to complete a task-based assignment in oral and written English, relating to their own work and domestic experience, which demonstrated awareness of underpinning knowledge. This exercise succeeded where the interview did not, at pre-entry stage, as it enabled the students to demonstrate their practical experience in a more graphic way. This was because they had greater time for analytical reflection of their experience which was carried out in their own language, Urdu, and then transferred to clear 'intelligible' English.

This example of a barrier to course entry highlights the need for clearly defined and stipulated minimum entry requirements located very firmly within an APEL framework where a variety of unbiased diagnostic assessments is available with learning support. This has strong implications for resourcing, staff development and training.

ASSESSMENT STRATEGIES FOR LOWERING CROSS-CULTURAL BARRIERS

Psychometric testing

The bilingual candidate could undergo especially designed appropriate and relevant forms of written psychometric testing in his/her own language to evaluate and determine his/her verbal analytical and reasoning powers. As the test's results are pitched against an appropriate group norm, then if they are designed with specific linguistic and cultural features in mind, and their content taken from the vocational context, their appropriateness, validity and reliability could be verified. Consequently, candidates may not be at a disadvantage by participating in the test. From the point of view of the advisers and assessors, as the tests are based on multiple choice answers, the marking would be relatively easy, but the results would give a *fair indication* of the reflective, verbal, analytical reasoning and creative thought processes of individual candidates in their own language. If these thought processes are indeed required to complete the vocational course, to acquire and demonstrate the underpinning knowledge and to demonstrate transferability of skills, then these tests may be one of a variety of ways of ascertaining the gaps in the candidate's learner profile. However, it should be not be used as a means of excluding candidates from the process, should the results demonstrate a limited ability in this area. Candidates may not be used to this form of testing and would need appropriate training in order to fulfil their potential. Psychometric tests are an objective measure of ability which can be used for diagnostic purposes to identify the type and level of support required. Therefore, if a candidate performs well in these tests he/she would be much more likely to be equally successful in English on the desired vocational course, given the correct learner support.

In the end result, the guiding rule should be, first, to access the candidate on to the desired qualifications and units through validation of past experience and qualifications. Second, it is necessary that the workers within the APEL process collectively make judgements about the assessment of evidence process for crediting claimed competences and whether these types of skills in the performance of the job for which the qualification is intended are actually needed.

Use of bilingualism

Advisers and assessors could consider providing oral questioning and written reports in the bilingual candidate's own language, once again, with a view to assessing proficiency at a high level of reflection and translation of this into English. Initially, as with the psychometric tests there would be a lot of work and cost involved in designing these assessments. Nevertheless, this resource, if available in major targeted languages, could be used in the long run to identify gaps in all bilingual candidates' learner profiles. The main drawback with providing oral questioning and written reports is the availability of resources, both in terms of multilingual advisers and assessors and financial resources for translated written reports in various languages.

Comparing the effectiveness in English and candidates' first language in both oral and written formats would require *bilingual* guidance advocate workers and APL advisers. Candidates who have a language in common can work in small groups with a bilingual adviser or guidance advocate.

Presentation of 'direct' evidence

For candidates who have a limited ability in demonstrating orally underpinning knowledge and transferability of competence to other unexpected situations, it would be much more useful to allow them the option of delivering this evidence in other ways. For example, by completing an integrated assignment, the candidate uses written and oral skills and is able to identify the competences within the unit by referring to his/her practical experience. In other words, an individual who has gained work experience in a particular context needs to have the focused help of the advocate or adviser to work though a self-assessment process relating this experience to checklists of NVQ units, elements and performance criteria. He/she needs to be able to understand the 'jargon' of competence, to be able to focus on a personal practical experience of work and to break it down into elements of occupational competence, conforming to performance criteria, thereby demonstrating 'underpinning' knowledge. An *integrated assignment* allows candidates to demonstrate a variety of language and 'core' skills such as problem-solving, working on your own, using initiative, communication, IT and so on. Candidates research relevant information and apply it in a specific context. For instance, applicants for a Childcare CGLI 324.1 can find out the procedural aspects of health and safety in the workplace and then design a suitable game/activity for children (users of the creche) in order to impart the information.

Once the candidate has completed the assignment, the next stage would be for the adviser/assessor to question the candidate on his/her work, using a variety of culturally appropriate techniques. Questions need to relate closely to the nature of the assignment. Candidates may be asked how they undertook the assignment and to outline stages of the process.

This technique can be used much more widely and to a much more effective degree with 'on-the-job' assessment, i.e. in the workplace where bilingual learners perhaps operate in their own language for most of the time, but need the underpinning knowledge, regarding for example, health and safety, psychology and needs of young children, good practice in business administration, basic food hygiene for caterers and so on. This is particularly relevant for candidates who come from local homogeneous communities where they have employment within the communities in areas such as catering, running playgroups, creches, hairdressing services, managing and running local businesses or local community groups. They have substantial experience but wish to translate or up-skill the experience into qualifications.

The role of the guidance advocate could be to work effectively with the candidate or groups of candidates in the workplace or workshop in the college to rehearse the assessment process and the 'language' of the concepts in English, so that the candidate is confident about the process, before the assessment.

Use of role-play or simulation

Similarly, it would be possible to enable the candidate to role-play a specific set of competences in a unit or to observe the candidate in workplace or simulated workplace context. Once the candidate has completed the exercise, he/she can then be asked to identify the full range of skills he/she has just demonstrated, by relating them to the specific occupational competences/performance criteria. Once again, questioning the candidates for 'underpinning' knowledge and demonstration of transferability of competence after they have developed a practical context from which to reflect and analyse, would be much more successful from the point of view of both adviser/assessor and the candidate. Both techniques rely on the basis of experimental learning for their effectiveness.

Use of video recordings

Candidates can be shown a video of a role-play or workplace simulation which demonstrates elements and performance criteria and are asked to discuss the relevant mapping over of occupational competences. They may then reflect on their own experiences in verbal and in written format. These methods constitute a form of learner support for bilingual candidates at the point of gathering evidence for the portfolio and assessment of evidence by allowing candidates to 'rehearse' or 'revise' ways of presenting evidence.

The Guidance Advocate worker could be responsible for implementing any of these methods or techniques. These allow the bilingual candidate sufficient practice in familiarising him/herself with reflecting on and matching work and learning achievements to competence standards. It is also crucial that the APL adviser is able to provide further practice for the candidate before he/she meets the assessor, as the assessor would want the candidate to demonstrate competently 'underpinning' knowledge and transferability of skills.

Use of a viewing and reviewing process

Simply allowing candidates access to anonymous portfolios does not ensure that the candidate:

(a) has developed a process of analysis and reflection,
(b) has understood the technical jargon and concepts,
(c) is able to apply them to his/her own context through a process of analysis and reflection, or
(d) can articulate his/her own experiences.

Therefore, it is essential to build into the 'viewing' process a diagnostic assessment procedure that requires candidates to analyse the information, either in writing or orally. This could be carried out in any of the following ways:

1 a gapped information exercise requiring candidates to provide the missing information on evidence or performance criteria, from a varied list;

2 a matching exercise requiring candidates to match the evidence needed for a particular performance criteria in a given 'range'; or

3 a predictive exercise requiring candidates to predict the evidence needed for a particular performance criteria in a given 'range'.

These exercises could be graded to allow the candidate to build up his/her confidence, knowledge and skills gradually, and familiarise him/her with the APL process of evidence gathering.

Use of computer software

Developing computer software allows the bilingual learner to access into practical real-life examples of evidence taken from anonymous bilingual learner portfolios and to match them up with relevant elements and performance as an option for those candidates who are computer literate. The software developed in different languages would enable the candidate to familiarise him/herself with the 'technical jargon' in English. Once again, candidates assessed either verbally or in writing would reveal the range of their abilities in analysing and reflecting on such material.

Quality assurance standards for language

As noted previously, there is a real danger of bias, as oral questioning by native-speaker assessors may inadvertently lead to assumptions about competence if candidates' responses are constrained by lack of colloquial language or relevant vocabulary. The stipulation of 'intelligible English' is open to wide interpretation by assessors. Some standards contain implicit prerequisites for communication skills, e.g. proficiency in written forms such as memos, reports or 'hidden values' about manner, personal style, relating to colleagues etc. 'Interpersonal skills' could be assessed according to assessors' own subjective judgements if external quality-control procedures are not stipulated.

Consequently, if real progress is to be made concerning the APL of bilingual learners, it would seem logical for further discussions to be held with professional bodies, industry lead bodies, NCVQ and other external validating bodies such as City and Guilds, the Royal Society of Arts and the BTEC, to establish more clearly the levels of proficiency required for spoken and written English, both explicitly and implicitly within the standards and in the requirements for vocational and professional employment. Developing national quality assurance standards for assessment of English language competence as part of NVQs/BTEC is identifiably an urgent need if the barriers for bilingual learners are to be lowered.

INTERVIEWING AS PART OF THE ASSESSMENT PROCESS AND FOR EVIDENCE GATHERING

Interviews of candidates during 'profiling' and 'gathering of evidence' wouid still be crucial in general assessment terms. Whether an interviewer is aiming to elicit broad-based information concerning a bilingual candidate's prior experience, knowledge and skills or is involved in matching evidence to elements/units of qualifications through oral question-and-answer techniques, the process itself risks potential failure and breakdown on account of various factors which might militate against successful cross-cultural communication.

At all stages of the admissions and assessment process of the student journey within the educational institution, the bilingual learner will be involved in interviews with 'gatekeepers'. 'Gatekeepers' is a term used by Frederick Erikson and Jeffrey Shultz (1982) to describe those officials in institutions who have control over certain resources, facilities and opportunities, and who decide who should be allowed to have them; in other words, who should be allowed through 'the gate'. In terms of an educational institution, the gatekeepers at the pre-entry/entry stage will be the guidance advocate and the APL adviser, and at the assessment/ accreditation stages the APL assessor and vocational course tutor, who might or might not be the same person as the APL assessor.

It is imperative that if interviewing is adopted as part of the assessment and selection procedure, then interviewers be given appropriate cross-cultural interview training which would include an emphasis on linguistic and cultural barriers. Historically , there has always been considerable emphasis placed on the delivery of cross-cultural training in colleges for so called 'gatekeepers' (cf FEU 1985). However, the development and implementation of such training as an integrated part of the TDLB, APL Adviser and Assessor awards, TDLB 32–35 is now an imperative and not a bolt-on 'equal opportunities staff development' option. If candidates are not able successfully to compile their learner profiles/portfolio for assessment, owing to breakdowns in communication with advisers/ assessors, overall recruitment of numbers of students to courses would be affected. Consequently, inappropriate APL guidance at pre-entry stage could adversely affect the retention patterns of students and progression routes. This, in turn, would affect funding resources.

The stark reality is if clients fail to get satisfaction from a system for which they are paying, they will not use the system. Furthermore, if APL is to become part of work-based learning for bilingual employees, then there needs to be a recognition by colleges of FE and other training providers that they are able to satisfy a different type of client group. The employer client group or corporate client is in a position to pick and choose its training consultants on the basis of demonstrably favourable outcomes, i.e. achievement of qualifications and customer satisfaction with the system.

CROSS-CULTURAL TRAINING FOR APL ASSESSMENT INTERVIEWS

Some assessment interviewers take for granted that the way they interview candidates and make decisions about them is the right and only way. The assumption is that if they give everyone (bilingual and native speaker) the same treatment, then everyone will be fairly treated and those candidates who do not 'pass' have not done so because they are not suited for the course and would fail if admitted to the course on the basis of inadequate language and communication skills. Other interviewers may express concern and good-will but they feel uncertain about the judgements they make in cross-cultural interviews. They do not know how to reconcile their commitment to equal opportunities with their feelings of uncertainty over assessing bilingual candidates. To date, the TDLB Assessor Awards do not offer substantial guidelines as part of the training for staff in the following area: cross-cultural and linguistic issues which arise during the interview process, as linked into Assessment of Prior Learning for Bilingual Learners.

There is an implicit assumption that staff applying for these awards would have assimilated sufficient underpinning knowledge and experience of counselling, guidance and interviewing skills in dealing with bilingual candidates and/or candidates with special needs. The questions which need to be addressed here are

- How accurately is a bilingual candidate judged on his/her prior experience, knowledge and skills?
- How far does the assessment of his/her competence in English 'interfere' with the unbiased assessment of the prior experience?
- Is the candidate given adequate and appropriate support in demonstrating evidence of prior learning?

It is essential that the two areas of assessment, i.e. linguistic and vocational/academic, remain mutually exclusive in so far as the former does not prejudice the latter area. That is to say, interviewers must not dismiss a candidate's experience as insufficient or inappropriate if he or she is judged communicatively inept by the interviewer on the basis of the APL interviewer alone. Furthermore, assessment of language and 'core' skills needs to be much more comprehensive, systematic and culturally unbiased. A readability analysis such as that included in ALBSU 'Basic Skills Screening Assessment' (1991) which aims to assess literacy levels, would consistently disadvantage bilingual learners on account of the culturally specific vocabulary and style of prose, which might be unfamiliar. In other words, this test would not necessarily fulfil the criteria of *validity* and *reliability*. In order to gain overall insight into the learner's holistic profile – language- and knowledge-based, it is essential to devise systems of assessment which would be valid, reliable and designed to assess a range of skills and competences, both communicative and vocational.

CROSS-CULTURAL AND LINGUISTIC ISSUES IN ASSESSMENT

Sharing a style of communication

The NVQ criteria for a minimum level of acceptability in English is defined as 'intelligible'. In order that a bilingual candidate be successful during an interview for entry on to a course, it would be necessary for him/her to demonstrate 'intelligible' English. During any assessment interview situation, the interviewer should be assessing three criteria: *effectiveness, relevance* and *intelligibility*. The extent to which a candidate is successful will depend on:

1 How far both sides share a style of communicating;
2 How far both sides share assumptions about the common goals and outcomes of the interview assessment procedure;
3 How comfortably both sides manage the interaction;
4 How far the interviewer appreciates the 'culturally bound' discourse skills of the bilingual candidate;
5 How far the interviewer appreciates the effects of the possible lack of confidence and past negative experiences endured by the bilingual candidate;
6 How far the bilingual candidate understands what is expected of him/her in the interview process;
7 How much of a linguistic stumbling block the candidate experiences on account of nervousness and lack of confidence.

Culture-specific styles of communicating affect the expectation both sides bring to an interview, and the way the interview is conducted and progressed. Both the bilingual candidate and the interviewer bring to the interview assumptions about the purpose of the assessment interview and about appropriate behaviour. But the outcome also depends on how both sides react to each other during the different stages of the encounter.

Sharing a style of communicating means sharing a tradition of what is considered appropriate and meaningful to say in context. People who share such a tradition are said to be members of the same 'speech community'. Not only do they share a language, but also the way of interpreting the speech and listening behaviour particular to their group. How communication creates social identity is described by John Gumperz (1982b).

In an unequal encounter like an assessment interview, candidates who do not share a style of communicating with interviewers will be at a disadvantage, particularly so if the interviewer is making assumptions and judgements about the level of 'intelligible' English during this encounter. Moreover, the bilingual candidate may be categorised as part of a group that triggers negative stereotypes for the interviewer. The interviewer and the candidate may also find misunderstandings or uncomfortable moments that occur, because each side misinterprets the other's intentions or because they lack shared assumptions about how the talk should be managed.

It has been demonstrated by John Gumperz and other socio-linguists that those 'speech communities' are not watertight compartments at all and that individuals are capable of switching consciously or unconsciously from one context to another. Therefore, the successful outcome of the assessment interview for the bilingual candidate will depend to a great extent on whether he/she and the interviewer are capable of adapting their styles in terms of 'communicative flexibility', a phrase employed by John Gumperz.

Assumptions affecting the communication process and management of the dialogue

The point to be made here is that in eliciting examples of evidence from bilingual candidates, the type of questioning employed by the interviewer (APEL adviser/assessor) will determine how much or how little information a candidate will give. As part of the training for the TDLB awards, no explicit recognition or due consideration is given to these issues.

Bilingual candidates will come to an interview process with stored past experiences of officials who may have put forward fact-finding questions interpreted by the candidate as questions to 'catch them out'. During an APL interview, the bilingual candidate's answers may appear defensive or terse coupled with the fact that they are already underconfident of their ability in the English language.

Let us consider the following example. A question in an admissions interview to a City and Guilds 324 Caring Course such as 'why do you think it is important to prepare all the work materials for the activities before the children start on the activity?' seems a simple enough one. Nevertheless, an Asian bilingual candidate may focus on the 'you' because of the particular *prosodic* features of the question and be unable to answer relevantly or even intelligibly as he/she would have missed the most important context of the question. The term '*prosody*' includes intonation, pausing, pitch, rhythm, voice quality and stress as perceived by the listener. Moreover, in terms of *high redundancy* and *low redundancy*, the question has a low redundancy. That is to say, it would not be possible to take out many of the words in the question and still leave the same contextual meaning. A sentence with high redundancy would mean that it would be possible to take out some words and still leave the contextual meaning intact. Therefore, a more meaningful way of rephrasing the question might be to say: 'The carers usually put out on the table all the things they need to carry out an activity with the children before the activity begins. Tell me why this is important/good practice. Give me an example of an activity which you carried out with children in your care.'

Generally speaking, because a candidate is feeling uncomfortable and is unwilling to disclose his/her discomfort or to reveal lack of confidence in his/her communication skills, she will rarely ask for clarification, nor will he/she give relevant feedback to the interviewer that he/she has not understood the question.

Thus an awkward moment in an interview occurs where the candidate attempts to answer the question irrelevantly. The interviewer will usually rephrase the question but still in a low redundancy style which means that the candidate's answers become shorter as he/she becomes more dispirited at not achieving the 'right' answer. The interviewer's questions may become longer but not necessarily clearer, thus resulting once more in a downward spiral (Table 2.3).

Table 2.3   Pattern of failure caused by low-redundancy interview technique

Interviewer	Candidate
Question	Irrelevant answer
Question rephrased	Shorter incomplete answer
Longer question rephrased	Minimal incomplete answer
Dissatisfaction + sense of failure	Dissatisfaction + sense of failure
And/or stereotype of linguistically incapable student proved correct	

The repetitive and *accumulative* effect of this during the course of an interview would have disastrous consequences: the candidate can lose his/her confidence and linguistic self-esteem still further, and the interviewer would have his/her stereotypes and assumptions about the candidate's inadequacies confirmed. If the interviewer assumes the candidate has not understood, then he/she has failed to pick up on the candidate's listening responses. By systematically repeating the same question or by repeating the same question in a louder tone of voice, the interviewer can make the candidate feel confused or insulted, as he/she may feel patronised.

For instance, this question was directed at an Asian candidate wishing to enrol for the City and Guilds 730 Teaching Adults Certificate, 'What would you consider to be the most important responsibility of a teacher in the classroom?' This particular candidate had had ten years' experience of teaching children in Pakistan, aged 5–11 years. The answer elicited from the candidate centred very specifically on her day-to-day responsibilities and duties as a teacher in Pakistan, and was not the exact answer the interviewer had in mind. The interviewer wanted her to give an evaluative generic answer based on her experiences which would demonstrate underpinning knowledge. Instead, she judged her to be rigid and inflexible, and did not grant her admission to the course. This illustrates the potential pitfalls of eliciting evidence of prior learning using an interview technique.

The identifiable issues which form part of *Cross-cultural Training* are as follows:

1 Clear lines of communication;
2 The use of hypothetical questions;
3 Shared discourse skills; and
4 Listening skills.

Clear lines of communication

The interviewer needs to be much more direct in his/her questioning – in other words, he/she needs to be very clear to the candidate as to the purpose of the question and the stated outcome that he/she would like. In the example above, the interviewer would need to prompt the candidate by saying 'Now that you have told me about your duties and responsibilities in Pakistan, can you describe which was the most important and why?' It is very enabling for bilingual candidates to hear the interviewer/assessor talk about his/her overseas experiences and qualifications in a positive way.

Few assessors, course tutors and 'gatekeepers' have considered systematically whether the specific communication skills required by the interview, to gain information and access to the candidates' linguistic ability and his/her past experience, skills and qualifications really will be needed on the course itself and/or in the workplace. Very often the communication skills demanded of a candidate in an interview are abstract and analytical, thus creating unnecessary barriers. Once again, it seems clear that assessment procedures in the form of a one-to-one interview need to be geared far more realistically to the linguistic demands of the course and the workplace.

Use of hypothetical questions

At present, one of the most common techniques in admissions interviews is the use of hypothetical questions, for instance 'What would you do if a

small child in your care in the creche/nursery were to have a tantrum?'
Hypothetical questions are difficult for all candidates to answer for the
obvious reason that at the pre-entry stage of admission to a course, it is not
necessarily evident that a candidate would be able to answer the question
from personal experience. In this situation, they are being asked to guess
how they might react in a situation they do not know or think about a
similar situation they may have experienced and to talk through the transferable skills. Bilingual candidates face an added disadvantage in so far
as their particular circumstances may mean that their work experience
or previous learning from overseas may result in answers to the questions
which are considered less obviously appropriate than their native-speaker
counterparts.

As far as possible, it is preferable to avoid the use of hypothetical questions. Such questions put unnecessary linguistic demands on candidates
who do not speak English as their mother tongue or who have not yet
acquired native-speaker standard English. For example, talking about
hypothetical situations requires speakers to set the imaginary scene and
to use conditional tenses. Assessors/interviewers expect an answer like
this – 'Depending on whether X or Y was the case, I would do . . .'
This may be a linguistic skill necessary at the formative (on course) and
summative stage of assessment and can be taught during the programme
as part of the core skills, i.e. problem-solving. The guiding criterion
should be how useful would this be in terms of 'on the job' competence.
In other words, how often would the candidate need to talk through a
hypothetical situation as part of his/her everyday work?

Hypothetical questions are often about how candidates would deal
with people. These questions are in line with recently formed western
concepts about psychology, about how to handle people in organisational
settings. They require candidates to explain how they would behave in the
context of a range of possible options or to make evaluative judgements.
Experience and behaviour have to be referred to or hypothesised about,
which puts enormous linguistic demands on all bilingual candidates.

Talking hypothetically as part of communication, in terms of transferable 'core' skills is indeed a necessary skill, so this could be included
in the area of guided learner support given by the Guidance Advocate to
the bilingual candidate at pre-entry stage. A candidate may be trained
to talk about his/her skills in another context whilst demonstrating his/
her 'underpinning' knowledge.

Shared discourse skills

Interviewers/assessors may judge candidates as lacking clarity in their
line of argument for three main reasons. First, if candidates do not know
the purpose of the question they may introduce points that are perceived

as irrelevant. Second, they may order and emphasise their points in a way that is unfamiliar to the interviewers as the discourse skills used are culture specific. For instance, some bilingual candidates may use a narrative style in which the argument is gradually built up through description and context, the main point of the argument coming at a later stage. As indicated in Table 2.4, British discourse skills very typically tend towards a style which focuses on the main point immediately and then digresses into subsidiary points which support the main thrust of the argument. Discourse skills are generally influenced by gender, culture and class.

Table 2.4   British and Asian discourse styles

British discourse style	*Asian discourse style*
Main point	Narrative build up
Subsidiary points	Main point

In terms of presenting information for the purposes of assessment and in terms of having his/her communication skills assessed, the bilingual candidate is at a disadvantage in an inter-ethnic exchange. Differences in the use of culturally determined discourse styles on both sides may lead the British native-speaker interviewer to lose patience with what he/she perceives as an irrelevant and rambling discourse, with the bilingual candidate simply not listening. This will result in information loss and misunderstanding and a poor appraisal of the candidates's communication skills by the interviewer.

Third, there is substantial evidence to suggest that during an 'interview' situation, there can be information loss on both sides if interviewers and candidates do not use prosodic features in the same way (Celia Roberts, 1985). Differences in the use of these features can mean that both sides may have difficulty in working out the connection between what was just said and what is being said now. Moreover, if information is ordered and sequenced in an unfamiliar way, both assessor and candidate may also have difficulty in picking up points of contrast and emphasis. Different uses of prosody, i.e. the use of intonation, stress, rhythm, may complicate matters where there are also grammatical or lexical confusions. It is not uncommon for people to understand 'every word' and yet not make sense of what the speaker said. Gumperz (1982a) has contrasted the use of prosody among native English speakers with the prosody used by speakers of English from an Asian background (Gumperz 1982b). Pausing, rise and falls in pitch levels and sequencing of information are used systematically in different ways by different groups. So, for instance, interviewers cannot assume that repeating a word with rising intonation is necessarily interpreted by the candidate as 'an encouraging noise' and an invitation to elaborate. The candidate may well interpret it as a signal that the interviewer has understood and perhaps agrees with what they have said, and thus say no more. In other words, the function of prosody and the nature of discourse skills deployed to convey meaning is crucial to communication. APL advisers, guidance advocates and APL assessors without awareness training and practical skills in this area could find themselves unconsciously excluding competent bilingual candidates on account of linguistic and cross-cultural misunderstanding.

Training issues around the area of communication skills and in particular, 'active' listening skills are not presently highlighted as being potentially crucial to the success of an APL interview.

Listening skills: a focus on models of 'non-empathetic listening' which can be culture specific

Active or empathy listening is especially important when the assessor and the bilingual candidate do not have the same style of communication. In order to focus on the most 'communicatively flexible' model of active listening, it is important to outline the types of 'non-empathetic' listening, which may be demonstrated by interviewer and candidate alike, with potentially negative consequences for communication.

Consider the following passage, recalling the experience of an Asian woman newly arrived in Britain, which perfectly illustrates the sort of cross-cultural misunderstanding which can take place:

> When I spoke to my landlady I would look down, I would never look her in the eye. It really reached a crisis and I might have been thrown out of the house. Then she asked me why?

> We discussed it all and I told her that in my culture we don't look anyone and particularly an older person , in the eye. She told me 'In our culture if you don't look into somebody's eyes that means you are telling a lie. It is a bad example for my children'.

> Her other complaint was that I was very rude, I didn't say thank you, didn't say please. So I explained the whole thing, I explained to her that in my culture it should be a pleasure for her that I don't say thank you because I have accepted her house as my home. If I was living there as a guest then I would say thank you and please. It was rude in my culture for friends of mine who came to my home to say thank you and please to my parents. Obviously, my culture does not apply in this country.

> ('Language and Culture' from Amrit Wilson 1985)

If this sort of cross-cultural mismatch takes place as part of an APL process and is allowed to prejudice the outcome of the assessment interview, the results could be disastrous for the bilingual candidate. The following example illustrates the sort of problems that can arise.

A Hungarian candidate with a university degree in computer programming from Budapest University was seeking entry to a BTEC National Diploma Computing Course in a college of FE. She gained grade A in GCSE English in the same college later that year – she was nevertheless perceived by the admissions tutor as uncommunicative. On the basis of this interview assessment, she was advised to join an NVQ Business Administration course or a BTEC first. In fact, the student was linguistically very adept but had greater confidence in writing than in speaking. Her spoken English and comprehension were excellent in terms of accuracy but her lack of self-confidence impaired her fluency.

A FOCUS ON THREE LEVELS OF 'NON-EMPATHETIC' LISTENING WHICH CAN BE CULTURE-SPECIFIC

Model A

The listener looks 'glazed', keeps looking away or looking down, gives some 'para-linguistic signals', e.g. nods or mumbles assent, but there is no eye contact. This type of listening would be perceived in Anglo-centric terms as being negative and the speaker would interpret the listener as being passive, disinterested or absent-minded. In fact, in some African and Asian cultures, it is considered rude and disrespectful to give eye contact to someone who is in a superior position of power, especially in an interview situation. The listener, if coming from such a culture, would be at pains to demonstrate politeness and discreet humility in the only way he or she knows. The listener may be having difficulties following the content and meaning of the speaker, in some of the ways outlined in the previous points on prosody and discourse skills. He/she does not feel confident enough to ask for clarification from the interviewer. However, in trying to juggle with the content of the speech, the listener may be trying to tune into the speaker's verbal and non-verbal feedback, thus displaying a blank stare.

Model B

The listener looks eager but interrupts and finishes ends of sentences for the speaker. This is referred to as 'empty/fake listening'. In an Anglo-centric interview situation, this is interpreted as the listener being more concerned with the impression that he/she is forming on the speaker than in 'listening'. Nevertheless, in many African, Asian and some southern European and South American cultures, to interrupt and finish ends of sentences is a sign of empathy, bonding and familiarity and is indicative that the listener is on the same wavelength as the speaker.

Model C

Once again, the listener listens to what he/she wants to hear. In this case he/she will focus on part of the superficial message (words) coming from the speaker as he/she is focusing on content, not emotion/feeling which is indicated through prosody, intonation, tone, stress, etc. This may be because the listener is unfamiliar with the culturally determined prosody being used. The speaker on the other hand, may be lulled into a false sense of being listened to and understood. It is dangerous as misunderstanding can arise leading to breakdown in communication.

ACTIVE/EMPATHETIC LISTENING

This is a crucial skill which needs to be developed in bilingual candidates. Through paraphrasing or rephrasing crucial parts of what someone says in the form of a statement and returning it to the speaker, misunderstandings and breakdown in communication can be avoided, for example 'so what you are saying is . . .', 'as I understand it, you want to . . .'. In an assessment interview situation, whether at the level of guidance advocate, APL adviser or APL assessor or simply for admission to a course, it is essential that bilingual candidates have the confidence coupled with the ability to check out and clarify understanding in this way. This is a skill which bilingual learners need in the classroom as part of their learning strategies and very often do not come to a learning environment equipped with the skills.

Assessors/interviewers need to possess this skill and it should not be taken for granted that they would automatically be equipped with active listening skills. More importantly, interviewers/assessors need to recognise that bilingual learners might be arriving without this skill in English. It is probable that 'active' listening skills, which form the basis of good counselling techniques, are not ones that most bilingual learners would necessarily possess or use in their own language and culture. It requires a certain degree of self-conscious analytical impartiality and 'suspension of belief' in order to be successful. In other words, most people, regardless of culture, let the 'interference' of critical, sympathetic, biased and analytical responses, emerge in those situations where they are not quite sure what somebody really means. These responses are least likely to create empathy nor do they probe for the real meaning of the content. Active listening skills need to be fostered through training.

CONCLUSION

An imperative is to train guidance advocates, APL advisers/APL assessors in all four areas as an integral part of the TDLB adviser/assessor awards, e.g. CGLI 7281/13. Equally importantly, bilingual learners need training in these skills. Once again, the role of the guidance advocate worker would be crucial in this, especially if this individual is someone with a teaching and/or counselling background with bilingual skills. He/she would be ideally placed to practice/rehearse the active listening, discourse and general communication skills needed in the assessment interview situation with the bilingual candidate at all stages of the APL process. This further element of training for the bilingual learner could well be included as part of an APL Induction module.

APPENDIX 2.1: ASSESSMENT OF PRIOR LEARNING ACHIEVEMENTS INTERVIEW PROCEDURE FOR BILINGUAL SPEAKERS

Process applicable to bilingual speakers	General process	Specific APLA process
• Identify Communication and Discourse Skills • Identify Linguistic Profile	• Guidance • Language Support	• Explanation of APLA process
• Facilitate candidate's CV • Recognise equivalent overseas qualifications • Recognise and value student's cultural experience and background	• Qualifications • Knowledge • Current + Prior Experience	• Recognise relevant experience • Identify relevant achievements
• APLA: recognise and assess transferable 'core' skills, 2nd language skills • Transfer information to Record of Achievement	• Skills Audit • Relevance of general and 'core' skills to qualifications and NVQ	• Matching specific knowledge and skills to the standards or learning outcomes specified in the qualifications • Developing an action or assessment plan
• Drawing out evidence information using appropriate interview procedures/task-based assignment • Raise awareness in candidates of culturally based teaching and learning methods • Gathering of evidence by methods suitable to students' cultural education and background	• Formative Assessment • Portfolio of evidence	• Assembling evidence from a range of sources, recording and organising evidence • Negotiating assessment of evidence from prior achievements and contemporary assessment • Presenting evidence for accreditation

APL Induction Module

Chapter 3

A holistic APL profile

INTRODUCTION

A closer examination within this chapter will reveal the processes and methodology of assessing bilingual learner's language competences and common learning outcomes which would link into the GNVQ core skills. The six core skills used by most colleges approximate as closely as possible to the National Curriculum Council (NCC) publication 'Core Skills' (1990) and are a set of transferable skills considered central to academic, vocational and personal development with an emphasis on processes/abilities as follows:

- communication;
- problem-solving;
- personal skills (working independently and working with others);
- numeracy;
- information technology; and
- a modern language.

A strictly narrow interpretation of APL would only allow for the candidate's vocational experience, prior skills and knowledge to be matched against units and elements within accredited options. However, gathering evidence of the candidate's aptitude and levels of competence in the areas of the broad common learning outcomes as well, which may actually go beyond the core skills by putting an emphasis on skills, value and knowledge, will lead towards a holistic APL profile of the mature bilingual candidate.

The common learning outcomes as developed by the Confederation of British Industry (CBI), 'Towards a Skills Revolution', stress the work values and skills required by employees and are as follows:

- values and integrity;
- effective communication;
- applications of numeracy;
- applications of technology;

- positive attitudes;
- understanding of work and the world;
- personal and interpersonal skills; and
- problem-solving.

The majority of mature bilingual learners have undoubtedly been in employment in different cultural settings and would have developed processes/abilities, skills, knowledge and experience in these 'learning' areas. Although the direct relevance and appropriateness of some of the cultural work values transferred into a British context is arguable, never-theless, building in a holistic appraisal of a candidate's hidden attributes alongside the work experience, gives him/her an awareness of their importance. This highlights the increasingly crucial role of 'core skills' in the assessment of vocational learning as an essential part of learning for candidates who have not had previous contact with the British edu-cational system, nor any work experience in British society. Attitudes to work differ, for instance, in many developing world countries and former communist Eastern European countries; the key to getting a high-level job is to get a high-level qualification.

A Ghanaian refugee has made the pertinent comment:

You are paid for having a degree back home, not for the work you do.

A Chilean woman who has been in the UK for 15 years observed:

We refugees from the Third World, in our culture, feel that if you get a Master's Degree you will get a good job. Here it is different in that academic life is separate from working life and higher qualifications do not necessarily help people to get jobs in Britain.

(Examples taken from Tony Marshall 1992)

By contrast, what is comparatively more important in Britain is *work experience* and a positive *record of achievement* in work.

The advantages in developing a *holistic profile* for bilingual candidates are numerous. The profile would be a report that would provide separate assessments for the different attributes of the candidate. It would be a means of recording information rather than an aggregation within a single grade, score or statement. A profile would have the potential to provide information of greater variety and subtlety than single statements or grades. It would be much easier to present a quantity of information in a profile. The information may be presented in the form of a grid with a series of statements, related to each skill area, which are informed by the linguistic profile key. This approach to communications-skills assessment is more positive in relation to bilingual learners, and it agrees with the general philosophy associated with profiles; that is to say, the centrality of the learner, the importance of the formative role of profiling and the range of qualities and skills to be assessed, especially in relation to the self-evaluation of common learning outcomes.

It is vital that the information documented in the profile pertaining to the candidate's attributes and areas of difficulty or improvement be recorded in such a clear and concise manner as to be 'user-friendly'. That is to say, there needs to be clear recognition that the profile will form part of the portfolio which will be viewed not only by the APL team, but by course tutors within the college and eventually by staff in other training and educational establishments, employers and other selectors.

What is suggested then is that within the framework of the staged interview with the guidance advocate and/or APL adviser, there should be two types of assessment to form part of a *reflection* on candidates' experience and accomplishments:

1 self-assessment by the bilingual candidate in areas of common learning outcomes and work experience; and
2 formative assessment by the GA/APL adviser of the candidate's language and 'core skills'.

Candidate *self-assessment* within the context of the APL system is vital, if ultimately, the aim of the process is the development of reflective and analytical abilities. If the desired outcome of demonstrating the core skill of problem-solving is an autonomous, pro-active individual, it follows logically that the individual should be self-reflective about performance. A student needs to take responsibility for his or her own learning and to monitor self progress.

This chapter will suggest a variety of approaches for the implementation of candidates' self-assessment, centring on self-evaluation of generalised common learning outcomes, and preferred learning patterns, using group interviews, inventories and checklists.

Formative assessment by the GA/APL adviser of the candidate's language and 'core skills' involves:

(a)   collation of relevant evidence
(b)   making a judgement as to whether the evidence meets the standards required and is sufficient to attribute competence or achievement.

The assessment of a 'core' skill other than communication need not be divorced from the assessment of language and does not need to be based simply on the evidence of one demonstration in one activity. Evidence can then be collected over a number of demonstrations from different activities over a period of time for more reliable assessments, if carried out within the context of 'learning units' as part of an APL Induction Module. This offers the candidate the opportunity to enhance the 'enabling skills' and to make him/her aware that skills are transferable.

PORTFOLIO PREPARATION WITH GUIDANCE ADVOCATE

Initially, the Guidance Advocate would need to compile a generalised portfolio of the bilingual candidate. A format which has been designed and used with bilingual candidates successfully (cf Appendix 3.1) is based on the notion of a curriculum vitae. From earlier experience in a college of FE, using a traditional CV, which simply asked candidates to outline qualifications and work experience, elicited a fairly negative response, in so far as candidates would not record overseas qualifications or work experience gained in their own country. Once again, this demonstrates the low self-perception that many bilingual learners have in relation to their past accomplishments outside Britain. In order to encourage bilingual candidates to record all their accomplishments, it is necessary to highlight this on the form. The boxes on the form that categorise learning and past experience into different vocational and academic skills areas are not exhaustive, by any means. They are intended as prompts or triggers for candidates to embark on the process of reflecting on their past accomplishments and to begin to record this.

Preparing a personal portfolio is a particularly useful exercise which:

• raises the confidence and motivation of bilingual learners by focusing on their concrete achievements and by building an awareness of marketable experience, skills and qualities;
• provides a relevant tool for use in guidance by enabling the candidate in collaboration with the GA and APL adviser, to identify skills and interests that could usefully be built upon or used for reorientating the candidate to new directions thus engaging him/her in 'life-long learning'.

The portfolio creates a heightened awareness of his/her skills and acts as a stimulus to encourage the candidate to keep demonstrable evidence of these skills as part of an on-going process.

SELF-EVALUATION AND ASSESSMENT OF 'CORE SKILLS' AND LANGUAGE

This stage will occur after the learner has filled in the CV giving a general outline of work experience and qualifications as part of the initial interview with the GA worker. At entry stage, asking bilingual learners initially to complete a self-evaluation form in the areas of common learning outcomes gives an overall picture of candidates' strengths and areas of improvements. It is vital that learners are familiar with the concepts and language of common learning outcomes. Providing translations for learners is useful as it enables them to understand and to discuss these concepts with their peers and with the guidance advocate worker prior to filling in self-evaluation forms. This element of interactive discussion and reflection is crucial to the learners' understanding of basic concepts which hitherto may not have formed part of their conscious learning process.

Providing candidates with a key to evaluating themselves in a more focused way, typically initiates a self-evaluation process which all students need to become familiar with, in competence-based learning, and therefore provides a model of good practice. The self-evaluation form should be part of the process which involves the learner in outlining his/her generalised portfolio. The role of the GA is essential in guiding the learner to assess his/her competence in the common learning outcomes area. The bilingual learner needs to reach the stage where he/she can make the link between the work experience gained, and the types of evidence that he or she would need to offer, to gain elements of units, as part of the APL process. Consequently, it is essential that an interim process be added, to enable the learner to deconstruct his/her experience in a meaningful way. Stage 1 can be split into two parts as follows:

- Stage 1 (A): Candidate self-evaluation of common learning outcomes and work experience; and
- Stage 1 (B): Candidate evaluation and assessment of language and communication skills.

Following on from Stage 1 is Stage 2 – Work Experience and Evidence Identification (formative stage of assessment). Typically, at Stage 2 the candidate can proceed to the APL adviser with a concise and thorough record of his/her skills and abilities, language knowledge and work experience. Then with the help of the APL adviser, it is possible to demonstrate specific evidence acquired through practical experience as matched against the elements and units desired for the qualification.

Deconstructing the APL process into these two separate but interdependent parts of Stage 1 (Stage 1(A) and Stage 1 (B)) is necessary for bilingual learners on account of specific language needs but would be equally advantageous for monolingual candidates. Let us then focus on Stages 1 (A) and 1 (B).

Stage 1(A) – candidate self-evaluation of general skills in terms of common learning outcomes and work experience

(a) Learners complete exercise on 'Using Communication Skills 1' (Appendix 3.3), which will give them a template of their skills and abilities at a glance in the area of the GNVQ core communication skills. Developing computer software for use with learners who are computer-literate would provide a print-out record for the learner to keep as part of an on-going, self-evaluation record-keeping exercise. A similar grid can be developed for self-assessment of the other 'core' skills, i.e. numeracy, information technology, personal skills and problem-solving;

(b) Learners complete self-evaluation exercise in the area of common learning outcomes (Appendix 3.2);

(c) Learners complete skills breakdown exercise which involves them in identifying their work experience in terms of duties, skills and knowledge – as the example in the case study demonstrates (Appendix 3.4);

(d) The job content skills would eventually be deconstructed into three separate areas: working with data, working with people, and working with things (Appendix 3.5). The case study of Saira Sandhu demonstrates how this is organised.

Working with groups of homogeneous learners

Stage 1 (A) can be effectively carried out as a group session with the GA facilitating groups of candidates towards recognition of their skills and abilities. This session works most successfully when candidates share homogeneous backgrounds, i.e. the same language, culture, similar educational and work experiences. Candidates who feel underconfident about their accomplishments and/or language are still able to draw on their experience and skills and to list them through the supportive and interactive nature of the group work. A standard 'interview' using both client-centred and open-ended questions may not be as effective precisely on account of the pressurised reflective and analytical nature of the communication processes involved on a one-to-one basis. There can be an internalised feeling among bilingual candidates that language is a means of power and a way of determining people's status. A combination of the candidate's poor self perception in terms of language, lack of fluency or accuracy in English and possible unconscious bias on the part of the APL adviser may result in the candidate being unable to focus on the relevant evidence of his/her skills, abilities and prior experience.

Two pertinent comments from refugees illustrate this graphically:

People do not meet as equals. For example, in an interview situation the poor language speaker is seen as lower and stupid. (A Latin American refugee.)

If two people from the same culture or class meet you know what the other is thinking. You then communicate well, get on well. .... If one is from a different country/culture you don't know what the other is thinking, what you see is different, your expectations are different.

You can find it hard to relate to each other, you may be off cue, and in a job situation this is disastrous. (An Iraqi refugee.)

(Examples from Tony Marshall 1992)

Although these comments are made specifically in relation to job interviews, nevertheless the comments are equally valid for pre-entry assessment situations where candidates are applying for entry to vocational courses in colleges of FE. Therefore, enabling candidates to gain self-confidence will result in greater fluency of self-expression.

Familiarity with technical jargon

The second main advantage of approaching the profile in this way is to familiarise candidates from the outset with the 'technical jargon' of competence-based learning. An 'interview' process implies that all candidates are able to evaluate their experience and articulate it using 'appropriate' language and couching it in 'intelligible' English. In order to achieve this goal, bilingual learners need to be equipped with the tools, i.e. the jargon of skills, knowledge and evaluation. Much of this language is totally unfamiliar to bilingual learners or is only familiar in other more specific contexts. Language such as the following occurs repeatedly in competence-based learning when outlining elements/ units:

Skills; devise; role; identify; promote; effect; affect; interpersonal skills; communicate; value; enable; contribute; evaluate; performance; assess; peer group; underpinning knowledge; initiative; managing own learning; supervise.

Both bilingual learners and native speakers will benefit from a compiled a list of 'core' language and terminology, based on the 'core skills' and the jargon of the APL process, available in translation and in accessible English. Enabling *all* learners to have access to a wide range of language in English empowers them to articulate their experiences in a more meaningful way. Candidates need access to an inventory of transferable skills to enable them to distinguish between those work duties and skills that lead to *common learning outcomes* ('core skills') and those that lead to *specific vocational outcomes*.

Skills breakdown

In the skills breakdown case study (Appendix 3.4) the candidate Nusrat Ahmed eventually becomes aware that the experience she gained as an accounts assistant is potentially categorised as in Table 3.1.

As can be seen from the breakdown of 'Common learning outcomes' in

Table 3.1 Breakdown of skills and learning outcomes

Vocational underpinning knowledge + skills	Common learning outcomes
• collating information	• knowledge of information technology
• book-keeping	• working as part of a team and on own initiative
• filing	• writing skills in Gujarati and English
• typing	• verbal communication skills in Gujarati and English
• knowledge of word processing/ spreadsheet/database	• time management and prioritisation of tasks
• answering telephone enquiries/ writing letters to clients/reception skills	• problem-solving in predictable and unpredictable situations

Table 3.1, the general areas covered can be found in the BTEC GNVQ Core Skills Personal Skills, Improving Own Learning and Performance and in the GNVQ Core Skills Communication.

Increasing the candidate's awareness of her abilities at this stage increases her chances of being much more active and successful in the learning process. At a later stage of her 'student journey', having achieved the AAT (Assistant Accountant Trainee) NVQ Level 2, the student returned for further advice and guidance on the possibility of undertaking a Nursery Nurses Examining Board (NNEB) course, NVQ Level 2, because she wanted to open up her own creche. She had had prior experience in working on a voluntary basis in a creche in a local Asian community group when her children were much younger. Having achieved a relevant qualification in business administration she now felt that she did not want to pursue book-keeping or accountancy as a career but wished to combine her business skills with her interest in working with children to open up a creche primarily for Asian children in her locality. She was referred to the APL adviser who was able to begin the process of identifying and locating sources of evidence. In her case, the childcare experience had taken place too long ago for it to be relevant. Nevertheless, she had decided to return on a voluntary basis in another local nursery so that she could demonstrate some of the evidence needed for assessment/accreditation of prior learning towards the NVQ Childcare and Education (work in a community run pre-school group) Level 2, which was felt to be a more appropriate course for her than the NNEB.

The main point worth stressing here is that at an initial stage, Stage 1, the discussions and self-evaluation/transferable skills exercises which the student undertook with the GA pointed the way towards her potential in an unrelated area, other than the very obvious one in which she had had substantial work experience. This enabled the student to have a wider variety of career options and vocational areas of study than if she had pursued the very obvious ones relating to her recent work experience.

A continuous evaluative approach of this kind involves the students carrying out periodic self-evaluations with tutors in the areas of common learning outcomes. In this way, the course tutor can assist the student in evaluating his/her ipasative progress (individual's progress as monitored against level at point of entry) and can monitor the learner support element of the course accordingly. A recommendation would be for the student to carry out self-evaluation at three junctions - entry point, formative/halfway through the course and summative or exit point of the course.

Stage 1 (B): evaluation and assessment of language, communications skills and 'core' skills as part of an APL process

At entry stage, assessing a learner's language is a result of a need to collate the following information:

1 to find out which languages a learner uses; levels of fluency and contexts; to assess the levels of competence he/she has attained in the four language skills;
2 to locate the skills areas in which he/she will require the greatest input for personal development purposes;
3 to compile information on which routes of proposed study the learner would probably take and to assess the suitability and adequacy of his/her language in relation to this;
4 to evaluate the best and most cost-effective learner support methods to achieve development in those areas of a learner's profile which are in need of support (the APL services staff should have at their disposal a nationally recommended minimum threshold level of English language competence necessary for learners to achieve targeted outcomes in the specific vocational areas). These threshold levels need to be designed with vocational staff working in conjunction with language and communications skills specialists and with input from the External Validating Body (EVB).
5 to evaluate the most appropriate course for the development of English and communication skills leading to a recognised accreditation;
6 to evaluate the most effective form of record keeping for the learner. Currently, limited use is made of computerised 'expert systems' for initial and diagnostic assessment, although clearly, the potential is considerable, especially for self-assessment and reducing costs. The quality and effectiveness of such programmes need to be evaluated, and their availability publicised and extended. Moreover, instructing

and guiding students towards computer-literacy is a major issue for APL services staff.

7 to assess the learner's competence in the 'core' skills, with reference to the GNVQ Levels.

BENEFITS OF A HOLISTIC PROFILE FOR LEARNERS

A key for establishing a linguistic profile is necessary for cross referencing a learner's abilities with the minimum threshold level of English language competence (cf Appendix 3.6). The key that has been developed and is used in the case studies presented, breaks skills usage down into four areas as follows:

1 speaking and discourse skills;
2 active listening skills and comprehension;
3 active reading skills and response to comprehension; and
4 literacy writing and style.

A fifth area needs to be included. It assesses a bilingual learner's skills in the area of 'study skills'. This would encompass the following:

(a) to identify the learner's abilities in the area of comprehending successfully the assessment task/assignment/exercise questions in the area of English study and vocational skills; generally to identify to what extent the learner can comprehend the assessment task as outlined;

(b) to identify whether a learner can focus on the skills needed to carry out the assessment task and understands fully/partially/not at all what is required of him/her;

(c) to identify whether a learner is able to set himself/herself, through a process of analysis and reflection, an action plan to carry out the assessment task;

(d) to identify whether a learner is capable of locating and retrieving appropriate information from various sources for use in the assessment task and to identify whether the learner is able to manipulate the information as required, in the most effective way;

(e) to identify whether the learner is able to use a variety of appropriate learning methods and is able to use effectively various sources of learning support and to identify the learning strategies brought to the assessment task by the learner;

(f) to identify finally whether the learner is able to perform the assessment task as required fully/partially/not at all.

INTEGRATED TASK ASSIGNMENT AS A MEANS OF ASSESSING LANGUAGE

The most effective way in assessing all five areas of language skills at entry stage is to present the candidate with an *integrated task assignment*. An example of a vocational assignment used for assessing aptitude and evidence of prior knowledge and experience for entry to the City and Guilds 324.1 Childcare course, is available in Chapter 5. The integrated task assignment could be based on content lifted from the specialised vocational area and/or generalised content taken from current events/ media. It would seem appropriate to ask the candidate to carry out assessment in both areas of knowledge, in order to assess general awareness, and more specifically, familiarity with everyday vocabulary and more technical jargon. It needs to be stressed that the aim of the assessment is not to exclude candidates, but to identify their learning support needs and to match the candidate's attributes with the most appropriate course. The objective of the integrated task assignment is to focus on all five areas of a learner's skills in order to determine:

- whether a learner is able to comprehend what is required of him/her;
- whether he/she is able to digest the information given, analyse and reflect; and
- whether he/she is able to produce the outcome of the learning process which can be a word processed or written narrative, a verbal presentation, role-play or interview, or discussion/debate or any combination of these 'product' formats.

The skills required to carry out the task may, or may not be all the skills required by the learner on the desired academic or vocational course. In the first instance, the purpose of the assessment task is a diagnostic one, to provide an analysis of the learner's strengths and areas of difficulty. Second it would be possible to build up a general profile of the learner's different capabilities, to enable the following to take place:

1 the APL team are able to make effective decisions concerning the most cost-effective level and type of learning support required by the candidate, plus possible intensive provision in English language learning;
2 the APL team are able to ascertain the areas of potential difficulties for the candidate in terms of the four skills, language concepts, vocabulary and grammar, discourse skills and prosody;
3 the APL team are able to make reliable and valid decisions concerning the suitability of the candidate for her chosen course/courses;
4 the APL team are able to ascertain the strengths and weaknesses of the candidate in the area of the 'core' skills.

However, prioritising areas for development and support should take into account and balance the immediate skills needed for successful learning on the vocational course with the long-term goals of the candidate, such as developing confidence in speaking for employment purposes or developing the skills of formal letter writing for use in working in a self-employed business.

Example of an integrated task assessment

Open University programmes provide a good selection of materials that can be used in this way. Video materials that specifically present areas of good practice in vocational work, or material developed for teaching the underpinning knowledge of specific vocational areas, lend themselves very well to being adapted for assignments. However, it is very important that bilingual candidates be familiarised as far as possible with the terminology, keywords and phrases and technical jargon which they would not necessarily be expected to know before entry on the course. In this way, they can concentrate on the skills and aptitude involved in developing the task, and not be distracted by unfamiliarity with the jargon.

Language programmes such as the BBC's 'Inside English' (1992) are a good example of a starting point for diagnostically assessing candidate's core skills, (communication skills) and language. The aims and objectives of the series of language development programmes have been described as such:

> a series for all those wishing to improve their functional English for work and study. . . . It will also be of use to students developing language skills in vocational education and training courses. It addresses the theme of access and progression by focusing on some of the key language skills set in a variety of contemporary vocational and study contexts and offers a framework of core authentic language functions and skills. The programme reflects a communicative approach and is based on complex functions of language such as description, explanation, comparison and contrast, formulating argument, persuading and negotiating. These functions form part of the implicit language demands of many first level vocational courses such as BTEC First Diploma or academic courses such as GCSE.
>
> (Europe Singh, Education Officer, BBC Education Unit)

Three of the programmes provide very appropriate material for the candidates to demonstrate communication skills and 'core' skills. As the language and contexts used throughout are authentic, it is feasible to develop a method of assessment as follows:

1 Show a clip of the chosen material from the series to the candidates:

   (a) making a case – gathering and presenting evidence and coherently debating and arguing a case which involves the skills of 'stating an opinion – making arguments for and against (consequences) – supporting the case with evidence and examples'

   (b) using technical language – following instructions that involve technical language which require both good receptive skills and the ability to learn new vocabulary in context and discourse markers which help find a way through a set of instructions

   (c) handling clients – handling complaints and dealing with customers involving verbal and non-verbal communication – questioning, listening skills, ability to show empathy and to employ a body language that can be welcoming and sympathetic.

2 The candidates are presented with a tapescript and terminology of the clip and given time to familiarise themselves with it, using whichever learning strategies they have, i.e. bilingual dictionaries, work in mother tongue, in peer groups and so on.

3 Candidates are presented with the assignment and the clips are replayed. The ideal situation would be for candidates to work with TV monitors in small groups so that they may replay the tape as often as they need. Moreover, the adviser may observe any of the interactive skills and learning strategies listed in the checklist and evaluate candidate performance accordingly.

4 The assignment may take the following form:

   • *Clip 1* The candidates listen to the case for and against the Cardiff Bay Barrage as delivered by a small selection of individuals, council employees, residents and college students. They are then given written information which outlines the case briefly with the pros and cons. They may discuss the arguments in small groups or pairs. Finally, they would need to:

     (a) transfer the written information to a grid format;
     (b) develop a piece of narrative/report which outlines one side of the case; and
     (c) present verbally to the group (which would be taped) the point of view in the narrative.

   • *Clip 2* The candidates listen to an instructor delivering fairly technical instructions around advanced driving and photography and are given some similar back-up instructions in writing taken from a manual or log on the same subject. Candidates are asked to:

     (a) transfer the instructions to a 'sequence' sheet which displays understanding of order and sequence;
     (b) develop a sequenced set of instructions from instructions which are jumbled up on an unrelated subject;
     (c) develop a set of instructions on an unrelated subject which they are familiar with; and
     (d) present verbally the set of instructions to the group (which would be taped) either on audio or videotape.

   • *Clip 3* The candidates watch a customer complaining to an employee of a large company and are asked to focus on the aspects of verbal and non-verbal language. They need to:

     (a) complete a grid/checklist which identifies aspects of body language/non-verbal behaviour demonstrating dissatisfaction, anger and so on, from the point of view of the customer and empathy from the point of view of the employee

> (b)   carry out a role-play in pairs, to demonstrate a similar complaint situation (taped)
> (c)   write a formal letter of complaint to the company to outline the complaint.
>
> In all three contexts, the evidence (i.e. products of learning) will be kept for discourse analyses and diagnostic assessment by the course tutor and learning support tutor. These can be used to formulate further learning support strategies during the course. At all the stages of assessment using video material, the exercises and tasks are specifically designed so that there is a focus on integrating all four language skills and on assessing the 'core' skills in terms of the common learning outcomes, such as:
>
> • problem-solving skills, working in groups;
> • communication core skills;
> • taking part in discussions;
> • preparing written materials;
> • using images to illustrate points made in writing and discussions; and
> • reading and responding to written materials and images.

THE LEARNER PORTFOLIO AND ASSESSMENT PROCEDURES

In the learner portfolio, there needs to be standardised information on the aims and objectives of the assessment procedures carried out with the candidate. This information should show that the diagnostic assessment carried out with the candidate has employed a set of processes, which have been designed to identify the nature, cause and extent of any specific weaknesses or strengths in the candidate's performance. The selective assessment procedures should use a combination of criterion-referenced assessment procedures, which give information on whether the learner's performance would meet specified standards, and norm-referenced assessment procedures, describing the learner's achievements in relation to others in a defined group. If the external validating body – EVB – is setting the criterion-referenced standard, then it needs to be made very clear to the candidate that he/she does not meet the stipulated entry requirements or criteria of the course. However, what usually happens is that vocational course tutors focus on what they perceive as being the criterion for 'success' on a particular course. This criterion is usually informed by linguistic and cultural factors. The assessment procedure is then developed around this criterion and very obviously militates against those bilingual candidates who have not acquired the same skills and abilities as others in their peer group.

A good example of this is the entry stage assessment procedure for the NNEB course for Nursery Nurses. In one college of FE, candidates are required collectively to view a video of children being cared for in different ways and in different cultures. The emphasis of the assessment is on the *active reflective* and *analytical thought processes* of the candidate who is required to take notes during the video and to make evaluative judgements about child psychology in the format of a written narrative. In the duration of the two-year course, the student will be expected to become conversant with child psychology as part of his/her acquisition of underpinning knowledge. If this is a stated aim of the course, then testing potential candidates and excluding them on the basis that they have no concept of psychology at the pre-entry stage would seem culturally biased to many candidates, not least to bilingual candidates. What happens in practice is that candidates with substantial work experience in creches and nurseries can be excluded on the basis that they do not ostensibly appear to have underpinning knowledge at pre-entry stage, even though the intention of the EVB is to give credit to candidates with relevant work experience. In this case, if the intention of the assessment is to locate whether a candidate has aptitude in the field of child psychology, it would seem more reliable and valid in terms of assessment to carry out a *diagnostic* assessment and not a *selective* assessment.

By expecting bilingual candidates to analyse and reflect on child psychology, at pre-entry stage, without recourse to clear reference points to their own experiential learning, places them at a definite disadvantage and is not acceptable to the ethos of the APL process. The following examples of exercises to assess aptitude and to diagnose areas of improvement would be in greater harmony with the philosophy of APEL by assessing prior learning and experience.

Example 1

Candidates could be shown a video and have access to a terminology of 'core' expressions and words used in child developmental psychology. Staff could initiate a discussion with candidates in English and facilitate candidates' discussion in shared language peer groups, followed by a multiple choice paper to assess comprehension of the material in the video. The questions could then be used to enable candidates to infer, to analyse and to deduce information from the material presented.

Example 2

By this stage, the candidates would be familiar with the vocabulary and concepts both orally and in recognising the written work – through the tutor input, discussion and multiple-choice paper. The candidates could then be asked to submit a written account on the same basis as before. The written narrative would be subjected to a diagnostic discourse analysis for recording potential areas of improvement. Areas to be checked include order and sequencing of thought, use of time markers and use of discourse markers such as however, then, etc.

Example 3

The candidate is asked to view a video clip again and to make notes on a specific area and in response to some specifically directed task, for instance; 'Outline activities staged by children in video. Focus on appropriateness of activity to age of child.' The quality and depth of the note-taking would shed light on the degree to which the candidate has acquired one crucial element of the study skills: summary and note-taking linked to listening comprehension.

Example 4

At this stage, candidates can demonstrate the 'products of learning' and provide evidence of their work experience in an analytical way, thus demonstrating underpinning knowledge gained experientially. The second stage of the exercise above involves candidates reflecting and analysing information through the perspective of their work experience.

The assessment procedure as it stands originally aims to *test* and not *assess* candidates' prior knowledge and study skills, in a criterion-referenced way. That is to say, certain standards are set which relate to the on-course or summative standards of the accreditation. Candidates are expected to meet those standards at the pre-entry stage, with minimal or no support. This form of assessment would deliberately exclude certain groups of candidates.

The alternative assessment exercises outlined above rely on the principle that if at the core of assessment lies a need to analyse and assess a candidate's aptitude, then aptitude to understand, acquire and use knowledge in the widest sense should be assessed. In order to gauge a candidate's aptitude and capability, it is necessary to focus on the processes of comprehension, acquisition and utilisation of knowledge. Some candidates will be in a 'privileged' position, in so far as they will have had exposure to formal education and language within the context of British culture, which will mean that they will be entering the assessment process with enhanced chances of success. It does not mean, however, that these candidates are better suited to performing in the workplace, or even to producing better learning outcomes at the end of the course. What is important to recognise is the duplication of the learner-supported teaching input for all candidates at the pre-entry stage of assessment, during the APL process. The candidates who will eventually be in need of learner support during the course will be most likely to 'perform' in the same way at pre-entry stage as they are likely to perform during the course and at the summative stage of assessment.

Undoubtedly, a bilingual learner in need of substantial support at the pre-entry stage in terms of his/her English language and acquisition of knowledge may not have access to this substantial level of support and needs to be counselled to a more appropriate course. On the other hand, most candidates need a decreasing level of support or alternative models of support as the learning progresses and candidates undoubtedly develop greater confidence and fluency with a more developed sense of analytical and reflective thinking.

USEFULNESS OF DIAGNOSTIC ASSESSMENT

Diagnostic testing in a learner-supported environment generates information on the holistic state of the candidate, which can be used to manage the learner's future learning programme. Diagnostic assessment may also lead to more gradual adjustments of the learner's programme – in terms of determining the pace of learning, models and levels of learner support and intended outcomes.

Diagnostic assessment is also useful in identifying programmes of study for those bilingual learners who want a customised training programme which addresses the gaps in the areas of skills, experience and knowledge. In other words, where a programme is developed for a candidate on a modular basis, and allows access to a combination of units such as business administration, marketing, health and safety and certain elements of underpinning knowledge, or in a vocational area, where the candidate is already employed or self-employed. The language skills and 'core' skills demonstrated by the candidate might go beyond those identified as needed on a vocational course. As such, the full potential of a candidate risks not being identified.

Analysis of 'core skills' incorporated in the area of diagnostic assessment would play a major role by illuminating skills which candidates with work experience had not previously recognised, for example, the planning and problem-solving skills required in otherwise 'practical' activities. These skills would form part of the 'common learning outcomes' which are assessed through candidate self-evaluation and through tutor evaluation using the integrated task assignment approach.

USE OF SELF-PACED COMPUTER PACKAGES

Self-paced computer packages have a number of applications:
(a) for candidates who are familiar with, and are comfortable with information technology skills, this would be an ideal way of facilitating the assessment process;
(b) for candidates who are not familiar with information technology, access to word processors will provide diagnostic assessment of a

candidate's aptitude in relation to the use of information technology. This can encompass evaluation of one area of the Common Learning Outcomes, i.e. information technology;

(c) word processors are generally recognised as being very helpful to bilingual learners who are trying to improve their literacy using CAL (Computer Assisted Learning).

Many types of commercial software currently available on the market have been especially designed with bilingual learners' needs in mind, therefore, with an emphasis on enhancing the development of language alongside a vocational specialism. 'Go to Work on Your English', developed by Robert Leach (NEC, 1993), is a particularly good example of this. Using and adapting these softwares enables candidates to be assessed at pre-entry stage for levels of competence for evidence of prior learning in vocational areas. During assessment, the element of learner support can take the form of a demonstration to candidates on how to use the computer. They would then be left to practise and experiment, either individually, or in small groups, with the back-up of written instructions. The GA and/or APL adviser is focusing on a candidate's aptitude and 'core skills', i.e. problem-solving/working in groups/use of language.

As part of specific assessment procedures for entry to a business administration or engineering course such as NVQ Level 1/2, City & Guilds 4242 Information Technology, RSA CLAIT, or any other vocational course which requires specific computing skills such as ability to use spreadsheets and databases, the assessment procedures could include graded integrated task-based assignments. At the very simplest level, this could involve the candidate being given a set of tasks which would assess his/her aptitude, in terms of computer literacy as well as in the area of communication skills:

1 logging into the computer;
2 accessing a 'menu';
3 retrieving a file;
4 storing information on a database;
5 using a spreadsheet;
6 describing/explaining the process in writing and on audio tape; and
7 using the word processor to write a report, memo, letter, short story and so on, subsequent to a role-play or simulation during which the candidate has gained the necessary information.

The software could be made available in different languages as well as English, so that English and lack of confidence does not present a demotivating barrier to the candidate and affect his/her performance adversely. The demonstrations of all the tasks by the GA would be in English. The guiding principle should be that candidates are not under 'test' conditions but in a 'normal classroom' learning situation. The role of the adviser would be as a facilitator to guide and advise the candidates to perform to the best of their abilities and to fulfil their potential. Nevertheless, the adviser's function would also be to observe and monitor diagnostic assessment of the candidates, and to note learning patterns as outlined.

HOW TO CONSTRUCT A LEARNER PROFILE THROUGH DIAGNOSTIC ASSESSMENT

Historically, learning support is provided according to the individual needs identified during initial assessment, and subsequently reassessed and monitored during tutorials with the course tutor. However, in order that a suitable model or models of learner support be identified to serve the potential student's needs, it is important that during the initial assessment process, the candidate's performance is monitored to assess how he/she approaches the integrated task-based assignment. It may well be that through observation, the course tutor can make some judgements concerning the individual learning styles of the candidates. For instance, some candidates would work better through interactive discussion with peers and with the tutor, whereas others prefer to work through their ideas in writing on their own, asking for support and clarification when they need it from the tutor. A third option would be to enable candidates who feel more comfortable with this style of learning to use self-paced computer packages and/or video. Once again, the role of the APL team, in this case, the GA and APL adviser, would be to identify and then help candidates to analyse the styles of learning they find most effective, so that the learning support options offered to the candidate may reflect their preferred styles.

Initially, candidates need to be asked to reflect on the teaching and learning styles which they have experienced and to analyse the ones they have found effective and those which were not. The grid in the Appendix entitled 'Teaching and Learning Methods' (Appendix 3.7) focuses on some of the most broadly defined categories which can act as triggers to enable candidates to think through their own experiences which could eventually lead into discussions on experiential learning.

The following checklist provides a suggested format for the adviser to establish the learning patterns of the candidate, which would eventually contribute towards creating a profile for the candidate's learning support needs in the following areas:

1 vocational specialism
2 common learning outcomes
3 communications skills.

CHECKLIST FOR USE BY APL ADVISER/GUIDANCE ADVOCATE

A tutor demonstrates and/or explains the task/assignment while the adviser observes the candidate to assess whether the candidate can show evidence of the following skills and aptitudes:

• active listening strategies;
• comprehension of text – written and aural;
• summary and note-taking;
• interactive behaviour with peers and assessor;
• asking for clarification/discussion with assessor and peers;
• use of mother tongue;
• asking for guidance and help from peers;
• giving guidance and help to peers;
• ability to locate and retrieve information from appropriate sources, i.e. written instructions, manual, blackboard, log book, dictionaries and so on;
• ability to problem-solve, to show initiative, to self-motivate;
• oral and writing skills;
• confidence in use of vocational specialism language;
• confidence in use of mother tongue;
• confidence in use of English;
• ability to articulate problem and ask for appropriate help from assessor or peer group.

In terms of assessment, it is suggested the candidate's abilities are classified in the above areas on a scale of 1 to 4 as described below:

Levels of learner support

1 the candidate shows a lack of ability/understanding/confidence and would need specialised intensive input in order to build up positive strategies in his/her learning style in order to learn and communicate effectively – and to attain learning outcomes.
2 The candidate has limited ability/understanding/confidence and would need some intensive input in terms of communication and core skills, in order to develop further his/her learning strategies to attain learning outcomes.
3 The candidate has credible ability/understanding/confidence and needs support, guidance and advice on developing and improving his/her learning strategies to attain learning outcomes.
4 The candidate has substantial ability/understanding/confidence and needs accordingly limited support, guidance and advice on how best to maximise his/her potential and to develop a variety of learning strategies.

Broadly speaking, the area of the four language skills (*communication skills*) is analysed according to the key Linguistic Profile (cf Appendix 3.7). The overall factors to be taken into consideration would be:

1 The active listening skills as evidenced through comprehension of the instructions and the assessor demonstration, through appropriate feedback, through appropriate clarification questions, ability to understand text with high/low redundancy;
2 The reading comprehension skills – ability to read and understand high/low redundancy text, ability to locate and retrieve relevant information and to use information appropriately from a variety of contexts; ability to 'gist' read – skimming and scanning;
3 The speaking and discourse skills - ability to communicate effectively, to make herself/himself understood, to articulate problems, ability to use mother tongue in appropriate context, ability to work and communicate in pairs, small groups, ability for verbal presentation in front of peers;
4 Written skills – ability to summarise and make notes, ability to write a piece of narrative, ability to change writing styles, formal and informal, according to context e.g. reports, letters, memos, narratives and so on.

Once more, the candidate's abilities are classified on a scale of 1 to 4 so that 1 is the lowest point and 4 is the highest.

CONCLUSION

The APL process has great potential for bilingual learners as the ethos is an enabling and empowering one. However, it needs to be recognised that as the process stands presently, the holistic needs of bilingual learners – especially the support needs – would not be addressed through the role of the APL adviser alone. As stated previously, if the assessment and placement aspects for the bilingual learner are not given due importance as the linchpin for the whole of the learning process, then students will underachieve or not achieve targeted outcomes. The particular skills that are brought to the APEL process by the GA worker enables all bilingual learners to be screened effectively. The role creates a safety net which ensures that the learner support needs of bilingual learners can be addressed.

A note about the appendices

In the interest of confidentiality, real names of students have not been used in the sample documents reproduced as Appendices.

APPENDIX 3.1

BILINGUAL LEARNER
SUPPORT SECTION

CURRICULUM VITAE

(1) *NAME*:   (2) *MARITAL STATUS*

(3) *ADDRESS & TELEPHONE NUMBER*	(4) *DATE OF BIRTH*	(5) *NATIONALITY*

(6) *HOW LONG HAVE YOU BEEN IN THIS COUNTRY?*

(7) *EDUCATION IN YOUR OWN COUNTRY AND IN BRITAIN*

NAME OF SCHOOL/INSTITUTE	QUALIFICATIONS – Subjects studied Title of course	DATES

(8) *EQUIVALENCIES OF OVERSEAS QUALIFICATIONS*

OVERSEAS QUALIFICATION	COUNTRY	DATE	NAWRIC BRITISH EQUIVALENT	STAFF SIGNATURE

(9) *OTHER QUALIFICATIONS* (*includes driving licence etc*)

(10) *WORK EXPERIENCE IN YOUR OWN COUNTRY AND IN BRITAIN (PAID AND VOLUNTARY)*

EMPLOYER	JOB TITLE	JOB DESCRIPTION – list of duties, skills etc. What did you do?	DATES

(11) *SKILLS/KNOWLEDGE/EXPERIENCE (includes your interests and hobbies)*

Can you write down what you have learnt in any of the following areas in your country and Britain?:

Fashion/Beauty/Hairdressing	Catering and Food

Child Care/Youth Work	Maths/Budgets/Numeracy

Computing/Information Technology	Business//Administration//Cataloguing/Typing/ Filing/Word Processing/Office Skills/ Reprographic/Clerical Work/Working in a Library

Science/Biology/Chemistry/ Agricultural Work	Engineering/Electronics/Civil Engineering/Mechanical Engineering

Construction/Plumbing/Tiling/Wiring/ Bricklaying/Roofing	Art and Design/Designing Posters/Theatre Design/ Working with Musical Instruments/Photography

Communication Skills – Learning Languages/Writing Stories/Poems/ Giving Lectures/Talks, Finding Out Information/Giving Information	Any other areas?

(12) *LANGUAGE PROFILE: OUTLINE THE LANGUAGES YOU KNOW AND USE*

Language	Spoken	Written	Reading	Listening

(F) = Fluent
(C) = Conversational/Confident
(B) = Basic
	Level 4 Advanced
	Level 3 Intermediate/Upper
	            Intermediate
	Level 1/2 Beginner/Post
	            Beginner

If you need help with reading and writing please write (L/D) (Literacy Difficulties) in the boxes. If you want to improve your study skills write (S/S) in the boxes.

(13) *WHAT WOULD YOU LIKE TO SEE YOURSELF DOING IN 1 YEAR'S TIME?*

(14) *WHAT WOULD YOU LIKE TO SEE YOURSELF DOING IN 3 YEARS' TIME?*

(15) *PLEASE TICK WHAT YOU CONSIDER IS YOUR ETHNIC ORIGIN* (This information will be used for planning and monitoring purposes only)

Arab	1		Indian	7	
Bangladeshi	2		Pakistani	8	
Black African	3		White European	9	
Black Caribbean	4		White other	10	
Black other	5		Other	11	
Chinese	6		Information refused/ not known	12	

(16) *DO YOU REQUIRE?*

(a)   creche   Yes/No

          numbers and ages of children

(b)   help for disability   Yes/No

          If so what is your disability?

(c)   classes at the following times: please tick

Day 9–12	Afternoon 12–4	Twilight 4–6	Evening 6–9

Student signature _____ date _____

Staff signature _____ date _____

Course/s studied   Year 1 _____

                       Year 2 _____

                       Year 3 _____

> FOR STAFF USE ONLY

> REVIEW SHEET AND PROGRESSION

Course Tutor/s _____

Accreditation entered for _____

Course desired _____ Year

                                        1)

                                        2)

                                        3)

Course/s enrolled on provisionally _____

_____

_____

Action taken/pending _____

_____

_____

APPENDIX 3.2

PRE-ENTRY SELF-EVALUATION SHEET
To be filled in by the student

Difficulty in areas of common learning outcomes

What help would you like from the tutor?

Put 1, 2 or 3 in the ☐
and please specify areas/situations/contexts

Key: ☐1   = I have difficulty

☐2   = I can do it with some help

☐3   = I can do it with little or no help

1) I can communicate effectively in the following languages, I can read, speak, write, understand information and study in these languages:
----

2) I can compile and use numerical information; I can calculate using information from graphs, tables and by budgeting ☐

3) I can use information technology (computers) to calculate information, to store information, to write letters, stories and reports ☐

4) I can understand the organisational systems and structures in the workplace. I know how to use the organisational systems and structures in the workplace effectively. I am familiar with, and know how to use these structures in terms of my relation to my supervisor/manager, working with colleagues as part of a team, working with clients:

(A) in Britain ☐

(B) in other countries ☐

5) I can develop effective social and interpersonal skills in the following languages and cultures:
----

6) I can work independently, and on my own initiative and in teams ☐

7) I can solve problems and deal with the unexpected ☐

8) I can cope with change and everyday pressures ☐

9) I can express my needs and wants to family, friends, colleagues, fellow students, educational staff, supervisors/managers in the work situation in the following languages:

_____ ☐

_____ ☐

_____ ☐

_____ ☐

Mark down on 1 – 4 how you rate yourself

1 I would like to improve
2 I usually/sometimes need help
3 I am generally OK
4 I am confident

1 – 10 GNVQ Core Skill
- Taking part in discussions with a range of people on routine matters.
- Reading and responding to written materials and images.

	1	2	3	4
1 When I explain processes to people they usually understand me in English				
2 When I explain processes to people they usually understand me in my first language				
3 I can understand people when they are explaining things to me or asking me to do something in my first language				
4 I can understand people when they are explaining things to me or asking me to do something in English				
5 I can complain to someone I know in English. I can negotiate what I'd like with this person				
6 I can complain to someone I know using my first language. I can negotiate what I'd like with this person usually without misunderstanding				
7 I can complain to someone I don't know, an official, shopkeeper, restaurant manager, and get what I want in English. I can negotiate what I'd like with this person without misunderstanding				
8 I can complain to someone I don't know, an official, shopkeeper, restaurant manager and get what I want in my first language. I can negotiate what I'd like with this person without misunderstanding				
9 In any interview situation, in English, such as housing, immigration, welfare benefits, I can answer questions fairly quickly and appropriately. I can talk about my qualifications and work experience in a job interview. I can talk about my abilities and skills and show clear understanding of the interviewer's questions				
10 In any interview situation in my first language such as for housing, immigration, welfare benefits, I can answer questions fairly quickly and appropriately. I can explain about my qualifications and experience in a job interview. I can talk about my abilities and skills and show clear understanding of the interviewer's questions				

11 – 13 GNVQ Core Skills
- Reading and responding to written materials and images
- Prepare written material on routine matters

	1	2	3	4
11 I can use the telephone, the library and find out information when I need it				

APPENDIX 3.3 cont.

1   I would like to improve
2   I usually/sometimes need help
3   I am generally OK
4   I am confident

	1	2	3	4
12 I can read and understand most official forms and letters and can write an appropriate response in English				
13 I can read and understand most official forms and letters and can write an appropriate response in my first language				
14 In a work situation, I can write letters, memos, reports which can be understood in my first language				
15 In a work situation, I can write letters, memos, reports which can be understood in English				

16 – 22
GNVQ Core Skills

- Taking part in a discussion with a range of people on routine matters
- Reading and responding to written materials and images on routine matters
- Preparing written materials on routine matters
- Using images to illustrate points made in writing and discussions

	1	2	3	4
16 In a classroom learning situation, I can join in a discussion in English				
17 In a classroom learning situation, I can act out a situation with a partner				
18 In a classroom learning situation, I can work on a project or an assignment and get together the necessary information				
19 In a classroom learning situation, I can listen to the tutor and make notes				
20 In a classroom learning situation, I can make notes from a text book and write an essay using the information and I know from where I can get the relevant information, i.e. text books, dictionaries, reference books, etc				
21 In a classroom learning situation, I can talk on a subject in front of the class and the tutor fairly confidently				
22 In a classroom learning situation, I can select information and images to illustrate points made in writing and in discussions, such as sketches, diagrams, still photographs and charts using images to illustrate points made in writing and discussions				

APPENDIX 3.4

WORK EXPERIENCE SKILLS BREAKDOWN

Case Study – Name: Nusrat Ahmed

JOB	DUTIES	SKILLS + KNOWLEDGE	TYPES OF EVIDENCE	SOURCE OF EVIDENCE	NVQ ELEMENTS/UNITS
'Carer' –Housewife	– voluntary work in local creche – looked after family, brought up children – organising social/ religious functions – helping voluntary organisation to organise social events – organising family budget	– organising play activities – underpinning knowledge and skills of childcare – organisation and prioritising of time, people & resources – cooking, sewing, budgeting – working in a team and on own initiative – communication skills in Punjabi and English			
Family grocery business (assistant)	– till opener – serving people – stock control: checking stock re-ordering stacking shelves pricing	– working in a team and on own initiative – time management – communication skills in Urdu/Punjabi/English – managing resources – budgeting – stock taking			
Accounts assistant in a family business	– book keeping – filing – typing – VDU/word processing – answering phone enquiries – writing letters to clients in response to enquiries	– book-keeping – filing skills – communication skills in Urdu and English – typing skills – word processing on computer – working as part of a team and on own initiative – time management – prioritisation of tasks – writing skills in English and Urdu			

STUDENT'S PERSONAL PROFILE   SKILLS AUDIT   **NAME:** Saira Sandhu

JOB CONTENT SKILLS & KNOWLEDGE	DATA: WORKING WITH INFORMATION	COMMUNICATION SKILLS & PERSON MANAGEMENT: WORKING WITH PEOPLE	CO-ORDINATION & DEXTERITY SKILLS: WORKING WITH THINGS
Primary School Teacher: Delhi (India) 1976–86 Explaining information to children orally; responding to questions; asking questions; testing comprehension orally/written; writing information on boards and books	Transfer of information from written to oral. Writing clearly to be understood by others. Eliciting information. Communicating information to others; seeking feedback	Giving appropriate feedback; listening actively; using appropriate register and discourse skills: using appropriate language; speaking in Hindi and English	Working with different mediums, i.e. chalk, pens, coloured paper, card
Classroom management; exhibiting children's work; organising pair work and group work for teaching assessment/play	Communicating instructions clearly. Ability to memorise. Numerical ability	Giving appropriate feedback; listening actively	Organising classroom furniture, stocktake of materials, manipulating items rapidly and efficiently; artistic and creative skills; being logical; being able to design and create; sharing resources with children
Taking register; writing reports; writing and marking tests	Recording official information for statistics. Making written assessments	Numerical skills; writing in appropriate style and register	
Working with children; dealing with problems in classroom/playground; exhibiting children's work		Motivating; dealing with conflict/crisis; advocacy skills; counselling skills; being persuasive	Using resources to reflect children's cultural background and interests
Working with staff in a team	Communicating information to others; giving appropriate feedback	Offering support; sharing credit/maintaining relationships; being co-operative; being understanding; taking initiative; demonstrating leadership qualities	
Working to manager	Responding to instructions; giving appropriate feedback	Listening; developing rapport; helping; being of service	Carrying out instructions
Volunteer in school in Newham for disabled children 1990–92; working to classroom teacher	Responding to instructions	Giving appropriate feedback; demonstrating comprehension	Carrying out instructions; dealing with child's physical disability; handling wheelchair; lifting children
Organising and helping children to work individually, in pairs and in groups; helping children to work creatively and logically; helping children to read and work with numbers	Numerical skills; literacy skills, reviewing, evaluating, testing and screening work	Communicating instructions clearly; ability to memorise	Being able to design and create; being logical; motivating; working with materials, card, ink, paint; manipulating items

APPENDIX 3.6: KEY FOR LINGUISTIC PROFILE

SKILL	Level 1 – Basic	Level 2 – Conversational	Level 3 – Fluent	Level 4 – Native-speaker standard
Speaking and Discourse skills	Can express simple utterances, needs and wants. Limited vocabulary, very little awareness of tenses and grammar	**Conversational** Can speak about own life situation and ask questions about routine matters. Has difficulty sustaining simple conversations/dialogues. Frequently responds inappropriately on account of misinterpretation and incomprehension	**Fluent** Sometimes responds inappropriately on account of misinterpretation and incomprehension. Can participate and initiate complicated exchanges such as in complaints/negotiations etc. Can use idiom in a limited way. Has greater understanding of prosody than usage (i.e. intonation, rhythm, stress)	**Native-speaker standard** Has developed a range of critical, reflective and problem-solving skills and competences. Can maintain fluent, culturally appropriate discourse with good prosody plus pronunciation and few errors in a range of situations
Active Listening skills and comprehension	Can understand and respond to basic questions about self. Cannot develop conversations or give responses to more complicated questions. Cannot respond to idiomatic language	Has difficulty with idiom. Can understand and respond to requests from others. Can understand basic travel announcements and messages, e.g. TV/radio/public situations. Cannot follow idiomatic sustained conversation/dialogue with more than one person	Can understand and respond to longer conversation pieces of discourse, in group and one-to-one. Can understand news TV/radio/short plays, complicated instructions, certain forms of jargonese/idiom	Can understand different dialects and registers. Can respond appropriately. Understands nuances and ironic humour, sarcasm and wit
Active Reading skills and response to comprehension	Can read and understand short pieces of simple writing signs/notices and simple readers (small articles from magazines/small ads)	Can read level 2/3 readers/instructions/short stories/forms on a day-to-day basis. Can use indexes, directories and dictionaries	Can read complex forms. Can get gist; read articles in magazines/newspapers. Can scan advertisements/job ads. Can use indexes, directories confidently	Can identify different layouts and writing styles – formal and informal. Can read novels, specialist journals, etc.
Literacy Writing and Style	Can write short notes and fill in simple forms if language of form is within range familiar to individual	Can write short formal and informal letters and cards. Can fill in forms for passports etc.	Can fill in forms for job/study application, CV. Can write longer formal/informal letters of complaint, etc. Can write short articles with limited fluency and accuracy	Can write short articles/reports with extended fluency and accuracy. Can use different styles and registers appropriately. Is accustomed to using idiom, complicated syntax appropriately.

APPENDIX 3.6 *cont.*

This profile provides a *snapshot* of the four broad levels of language competence from Basic through to Native-speaker standard. Within each level exists a whole range of language aptitude and expertise in each *skill* area. The quantum leap occurs between Levels Two and Three and is arguably the most difficult grey area of language competence to assess. This is because individuals may well straddle the two levels. They will on occasion show evidence of progression to Level Three and will sometimes revert to a level of fluency, accuracy and comprehension in keeping with Level Two. This may, of course, happen between any of the levels as language acquisition is not always a linear process but is a state of flux and transition. Progress is dependent on frequency of exposure and usage in authentic meaningful contexts and levels of motivation.

'Risk-taking' in language competence as in 'concentric comfort learning', the ability to develop self-confidence and self-assertion in order to explore vocabulary, idiom, use of prosody, discourse skills, varies from level to level and within each level and skill area. It would be true to say that the rate of risk-taking would reflect an individual's ability to progress through the levels, as at any given point in time an individual's language development would be classified as L + 1 = language level. That is to say, present language level plus element of 'pushing on' and risk-taking equals a new language level.

APPENDIX 3.7

LEARNING AND TEACHING METHODS

Which teaching/learning situations do you remember from school, college or any other learning situation? Which methods do you like or dislike? Why? Talk about what you achieved e.g. an essay, a talk, a test, etc as a result of these methods.

Key
1 = I didn't learn much using this method and didn't enjoy it
2 = I found this way of learning satisfactory, but not that enjoyable
3 = I learnt a great deal using this method and enjoyed it
4 = I learnt a great deal using this method but didn't enjoy it

Chalk and Talk from teacher ☐ Working mainly on my own with some help from the teacher in the classroom ☐ Listening to teacher/lecture ☐

Pair work ☐ Working on an assignment or task in the classroom or at home ☐ Making written notes from listening to teacher/tape or outside speaker ☐
Group work
Drills/repetition

Role play simulation ☐ Working on a project or assignment with other students in a group ☐ Copying information from the blackboard or text book ☐

Discussion and Debate ☐ Working with a video camera or tape recorder and making notes ☐
Individual/group Presentation

Watching a video tape or listening to a cassette ☐

Written tests ☐ Solving problems on my own or in a group as part of a task ☐
Exercises (e.g. grammar)
Oral tests
Listening tests

Outings ☐ Using reference books and finding out information ☐
Outside speakers
Games

APPENDIX 3.8

```
---------------------------------------------------------------
ROCKET              Student Record : Satish Kumar              21/06/93
---------------------------------------------------------------
```

BTEC Nat. Diploma in Engineering

Date of Birth	: 20/02/69	Telephone	:
Left F T Educ.	: / /		
Start Date	: 14/09/91	Week	: 92
Expect Finish	: 26/09/93		
Actual Finish	: / /	Ethnic code	: 3
Address	: 183 Byron Ave	Sex	: Male
	Manor Park	Disabled?	: No
	E12	NVQ level	: 0
Postcode	:	ID Code 1	: 9300012
Extra Field	1 :	ID Code 2	:
	2 :	Trng Crdt	:
	3 :	Nat. Ins.	:

SUMMARY OF PROGRESS

Competence Unit	Achieved	Average level of competence
		0———+———+———+———+———4
Managing and Developing Self	3 / 4	
Working & Relating to Others	2 / 3	
Communicate	3 / 4	
Managing Tasks & Solving Problems	3 / 3	
Apply Numeracy	1 / 1	
Applying Technology	1 / 1	
Applying Design and Creativity	2 / 2	

PROGRESS REPORT
Managing and Developing Self

1

2
Satish has negotiated action plans and completed these in the specified times (see log for evidence). Action Planning is an important aspect of an activity-based program. Satish has much evidence of completing action plans on time.

3

Satish has completed a substantial report with others on careers in engineering. He has identified opportunities in engineering and is using this to his advantage.

4

Satish has completed a number of integrated assignments which incorporate activity-based programmes thus satisfying the full range. He has used his skills to his and others' advantage in differing situations. Evidence includes 555 Timer, Power Supply, and many others.

Working & Relating to Others

5

6

Satish has worked satisfactorily as a team member and has received as well as given advice to others. Evidence of team work can be seen in projects such as Function gen., Capacitor ass., Statistics ass., PLC ass. and others.

7

Evidence as above. Satish has worked effectively in a team situation and recognised his responsibilities within that team. He has taken on team leadership role in function gen. ass. and worked within role play situations in an activity-based programme.

Communicate

8

Information has been interpreted from found and given sources and used in an appropriate way. Evidence can be seen in a variety of assignments such as Stats ass., Wordprocessing ass. and many more.

9

There is a great deal of evidence to show that Satish has completed the range. Information from found and given sources have been produced to publication standards.

10

Information in the form of memos, letters, reports has been produced to the required standards. Evidence of this can be found in the Stats ass., power supply ass.

11

Managing Tasks & Solving Problems

12

Satish has completed the range when doing an activity-based programme of assignments and has sufficient evidence to show that he has managed to solve problems from given and found sources. Evidence is found in his portfolio of work.

13

as above

14

as above

Apply Numeracy

15

Satish has completed the range and has produced several projects which reflect the different techniques needed in applying numeracy. This includes the Stats. ass. funct., Gen ass., 555 Timer ass. Satish has recognised his weakness and has improved his numeracy to obtain good results in his phase tests.

Applying Technology

16

Satish has produced a wide variety of evidence to show that he is capable of completing the range. Evidence includes Computer app. and control, 555 timer, data comm. and many more. He has completed a questionnaire on safety and procedures.

Applying Design and Creativity

17

Satish has used his skills effectively in design and creativity when producing a series of projects as well as developing ideas. These have been evaluated and tested to complete the range. Evidence includes conveyor belt ass., traffic light ass., computer app. ass., data comm ass. and 555 timer ass. Con. Tester.

18

Satish has used his ability to design and create into differing situations and apply thought processes in evaluating how his ideas can be used in other situations. This has been achieved in an activity-based programme of assignments allowing this to be developed. Evidence as above.

Newham Community College

APPENDIX 3.8: ALBSU ASSESSING READING AND MATHS (extract)

A Screening Test

**READING AND MATHS
ASSESSMENT**

Name: _____

Date of Birth: _____

Company/College/Organisation: _____

_____

_____

Department/Sector/School: _____

_____

_____

Date: _____

DO NOT TURN OVER THE PAGE UNTIL YOU ARE ASKED TO DO SO

For Assesor use only

Marks: Reading: Section A   ☐

                              Section B   ☐

            Numeracy: Section A   ☐

                              Section B   ☐

ALBSU
The Basic Skills Unit

READING ASSESSMENT

Safe as houses?

We think of our home as a safe place to be, and are more worried when someone goes out of the house than when they stay at home. In fact (1) ———— people die from accidents in (2) ———— home every year than are (3) ———— on roads or at work.

(4) ————-are the causes of these (5) ———— in the home? Many people may (6) —— of fire as the greatest (7) ————, but in fact more people (8) ———— from falling than from any (9) ———— cause. Tragic accidents, some fatal, (10) —— caused by children and adults (11) ————, walking, or falling through glass (12) —— and windows. Poisoning can also (13) ———— illness or death. This may (14) ———— from medicines or from household substances (15) ———— as cleaning materials. Food (16) ———— is also a common danger.

Statistics (17) ———— that most accidents happen on Mondays (18) —— at weekends. People are at work (19) ———— now and have more leisure (20) ————. They therefore spend more time (21) —— home. This has led to (22) ———— increase in the number of (23) ———— in the home. The two (24) ———— vulnerable groups of people (25) —— young children (especially pre-school (26) ————) and the elderly. These groups (27) ———— more time in the home (28) ————, for example, older children who (29) ———— at school, or adults (30) —— are out at work during the (31) ————. The elderly are weaker and (32) ———— slower reactions. Young children are (33) ———— aware of the dangers in (34) —— home, and are dependent on (35) ———— carers being aware of dangerous (36) ————.

Total

Total: 36 marks

This is the end of the Reading Assessment. Go on to the next page when you are told to.

READING ASSESSMENT   10 minutes

PRACTISE

Every year there are over 55,000 fires (1) —— the home which kill and injure many

(2) ————. Most of these (3) ——— could have been avoided.

SECTION A

Fire Drill (at work)

Fires are a danger. Wherever you are working, make sure you know the fire drill. If you (1)

—— working in a new place, make (2) ———— you know where the nearest alarms (3)

——. Ask about this on your (4) ———— day at work. If a fire starts, (5) ——— should

never try to put it (6) ———— yourself.

This is what you (7) ———— do:

If you have time close all (8) ———— and windows. Leave the room (9) ———— the near-

est exit and close the doors behind (10) ———. Find the fire alarm button and raise (11)

—— alarm. Go to the nearest assembly (12) ———. Read the fire safety notices (13)

—— that you know what to (14) ———— if there is a fire. Remember that (15) ————

can cause death.

Total

Total: 15 marks

Go on to the next page when you are ready

Chapter 4

Learning styles

INTRODUCTION

This is an area that is crucial to potential failure or success for all students, but especially for bilingual students. It is not traditionally an area associated with discussions on APL but generally with curriculum development. However, as with the area of communications and other core skills, a prior assessment of the candidate's learning styles is a critical part of the learner profile.

The recent HMI report 'Bilingual Adults in Education and Training' September 1990 – April 1991 (HMI 1992) emphasised the need for certified vocational and academic programmes designed to improve the learner's chances of getting a job, promotion or progressing through further education and into higher education. Teaching and learning styles need to be examined more closely in relation to this and as part of an APL Induction learning module integral to vocational and academic courses. Bilingual learners, by and large, are accustomed to a more 'passive' and prescriptive style of learning. Part of the reason for low attainment and drop-out is on account of a failure to adapt to new learning styles on the part of the student, coupled with the attitudes of staff who are wedded to the notion of learners as deficit models and do not wish to discuss their past experience in learning. Vocational and language tutors see students as ciphers who will respond to learning styles imposed on them. The HMI report has provided evidence of this scenario taking place in colleges of FE and adult education institutes. It offers examples of good, inspired and innovative work which resulted from teachers identifying and responding to individual need and building on students' considerable experience. They are thus able to expand their knowledge and skills. The report also focuses on the least successful provision, where there is an inappropriate choice of teaching styles and learning activities with a low level of student involvement.

Teaching in some classes fails to recognise individual student needs and differences, and consequently does not capitalise on individual experience and expertise.

(HMI 1992)

Particularly good examples of practice in colleges and educational institutions responding to learners' needs, and allowing the student to develop positive learning strategies at the outset are outlined in the report. On one 'taster' course, students kept daily learning diaries and attended regular seminars at which their learning was reviewed. Their personal portfolios enabled them to assess, analyse and record their learning prior to entry and during the course. Another example cited involved a minimum of teacher involvement with emphasis on problem-solving activities and project work on a law access course, where students were working on case studies in the library researching a particular field such as family or consumer law. Interestingly enough, many had made their choice through reading reports of legal cases in the press and had been inspired to read law books. The Inspectors observed them working with 'autonomy, confidence and purpose'.

EXAMPLES OF BILINGUAL LEARNERS' PREFERRED LEARNING STYLES

Example 1

In a London college recently, a Nigerian student was told to leave a City & Guilds 730.7 Adult Teacher Training course, a few weeks into the first term, because he was asked to carry out a micro-teaching lesson and did not fulfil the 'competences' according to the course tutor. His style was apparently authoritarian and didactic and did not allow for feedback from his students. He was not given the opportunity to facilitate a discussion as part of the lesson because the tutor made the assumption that he was unable to do so.

The student was no doubt delivering a classroom style to which he was accustomed in his own culture but obviously needed further training and insights, i.e. role-play, discussion and introspective reflection on other styles used more commonly in Britain. An effective APL process would have sifted out the student's skills, abilities and strengths in other areas in conjunction with the student, and at the same time, focused on the areas for improvements with an appropriate action plan for learner support prior to the student joining the course. This might well have averted the need for failure and drop-out, as the student would have been aware from the outset that he needed to become more introspective and flexible in his approach to teaching styles, if he was going to succeed on the course.

Example 2

In an outer London college, a Punjabi student enrolled on an NNEB Nursery Nurses course, where no diagnostic assessment of any kind took place at pre-entry level. Consequently, the student, who was the only bilingual learner in a group of twelve students, was compelled to develop learner strategies to deal with the demands of the course which were unlike anything she had experienced in India, where she had obtained a Bachelor of Arts degree in political science, history, English and Punjabi. She had undergone a one-to-one interview where she had talked about her experiences in childminding for a friend's children and presented a testimonial to the interviewer. With virtually no, or very little, help from the learning support team she realised that through watching Open University videos at home, reading books on child psychology and carrying out play experiments with her own children and those in her work placement, she could arrive at an understanding of the underpinning knowledge in child care, psychological development of children and play. She needed structured help in writing out assignments. The only help she received from the learning support team was in the area of grammar and spelling. What she needed, however, was to know how to structure essay plans with the appropriate discourse skills. Her experience of essay writing, sixteen years previously in India, had involved writing biographical accounts in which there had not been much element of analysis and reflection. She was faced with working largely on her own and finally developed a style of writing which was very successful. Overall, she was able to pass the examinations and produce a series of excellent assignments through great motivation, perseverance, basic aptitude and confidence in her own ability.

Once again, an effective APL system would have addressed these issues during the profiling assessment process and enabled the student to build upon the strategies she had, whilst compiling information on her preferred ways of learning so that she could have received the appropriate support, advice and guidance from the course tutor and/or learning support teams. She had obviously developed her own strategies in experiential learning and preferred to work with her own children and those in her care in a pro-active way, so that she could arrive at a clearer understanding of the underpinning knowledge. This needed to be acknowledged and actively supported by the staff.

Another strategy which she would have liked to develop but was unable to do so, was discussion in mother tongue with peers. The staff could have actively encouraged use of bilingual diary or log, translation, glossaries, bilingual dictionaries and encouraged the student to work with a student who shared her mother tongue in another group on an Open Learning basis, so that both could pool similar educational and cultural experiences and share resources. The overall conclusions which emerge as a result of these two examples, are as follows:

1 If learning and teaching styles are 'culturally' biased, then there should be a frank and overt discussion of these at the APL pre-entry stage, and as part of an APL Learning Induction Module.
2 If at this stage, it becomes evident that a student has inflexible and entrenched styles of learning inherited from his/her own culture and educational system, then he/she needs to experience an amalgam of teaching and learning styles which borrow from various educational experiences and would give to him/her a sampling of new and unfamiliar modes of learning, in a supportive environment.

WHAT IS EXPERIENTIAL LEARNING?

The principal processes in the assessment of prior learning and achievement have been described by Norman Evans (1989). They can be represented by the abbreviation SISE where:

S is Systematic reflection on past experience
I is Identification of significant and relevant learning and experience
S is Synthesis of evidence into a portfolio or similar compilation
E is Evaluation by the assessor through assessment, or recommending credit or exemption.

This may be amended to SLISE in the case of bilingual candidates to include the following:

L is Language for articulating reflection on past experience.

A form of experiential learning was demonstrated by the Punjabi student on the NNEB course. However, she arrived at this style of learning through necessity and experimentation and not because it was promulgated as being integral to course delivery. The principles of experiential teaching may best be described as follows:

1 Learners are encouraged to be involved in an active exploration of experience. The experience gained is used to test out ideas and assumptions in a pro-active way rather than to obtain and accept practice passively. The practice needs to be enhanced and consolidated through reflection.
2 Learners must be encouraged to develop a process of reflection and analysis so that they are able to reflect on their experience in a critical way, rather than take that experience for granted and assume that the experience on its own is sufficient.
3 Learners must be encouraged to take full responsibility for their learning and must be committed to the process of exploring and learning, to reflecting on the experience, reassessing and adjusting the strategies accordingly.

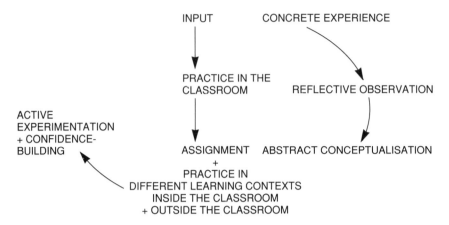

Figure 4.1 Adapted from 'A model of the experiential process of learning'
Source: Kolb 1984

4 The learner needs to establish some independence from the tutor so that he/she is able to exercise reflection and analysis, and not be under the illusion that the information transmitted by the tutor is the ultimate product of learning.

Authentic external situations/contexts allow the student more opportunities for reflective observation and abstract conceptualisation concerning the experience of applying communicative grammar in different situations. By allowing the student opportunities to discuss his/her learning experiences in the classroom, the tutor will gradually encourage reflection and analysis in a safe and supportive environment and one that encourages learners to value their own experiences.

In essence, experiential learning involves a cyclical sequence of learning activities with different teaching methods which can be selected to provide a structure to each stage of the cycle. The following example can illustrate what happens to the learning product when students approach a task by focusing on simply one aspect of the experiential learning process and have developed an inflexible learning style.

Learning 'language' experientially

In terms of language learning, the above descriptors of experiential learning might be illustrated in the following example:

A student needs to learn the mechanics of formal language structure, i.e. grammar. A student has opportunities in the classroom, through role-play to 'test out' learnt theories on specific grammatical points. He/she is then in a position to readjust the strategies of communication according to feedback received from peers and tutors after the role-play, as to whether the grammar was correctly used to convey meaning. The acid test of a student's use of communicative grammar is whether it works for the student in authentic 'real life' situations. The tutor may ask the student to complete an integrated assignment, which involves the student in assuming independence and responsibility for his/her learning, but in a different learning environment outside the classroom. He/she could be asked as an individual or in a group to undertake a questionnaire, to interview someone, to carry out a survey, collate specific information or to research a piece of information, depending on the language skills and learning outcomes being taught, reinforced or assessed.

By ensuring that the student feeds back both the *experience* and the *evidence* to the tutor, which is then recorded, the student will have had the opportunity to be actively involved in the learning process. She will also have been given the opportunity to reflect and analyse the experience in a critical way, as there would be a 'learning time gap' between the three stages of the process. By making the assignment relevant to the student outside the classroom, the tutor inbuilds a different set of variables in the structure within which learning can take place and can be reliably monitored for validity.

Approaches to a language task

In an English-language-learning classroom situation in a college of FE, students were asked to listen to a news broadcast at home on TV or radio, to select one item and to write a detailed précis of that item:

- *Student A* concentrated on the content of the news item, was eager to note down the details and paid no attention to accuracy, fluency of thought or sequencing.
- *Student B* was more concerned with accuracy than with content, was not prepared to take risks by putting down unfamiliar expressions or words, and preferred to limit the article to the bare minimum of meaning and content.
- *Student C* was concerned with the content and with quantity rather than quality. She had noted down a quantity of 'English phrases' but did not necessarily demonstrate comprehension of the phrases as the sequencing was incorrect and evinced jumbled thought processes.
- *Student D* took the initiative to read the news item from a daily paper and then to watch the news item on TV. The end result, however, is a plagiarised narrative expressed out of sequence.

These four approaches to one task signify four learning styles that have become fossilised at a specific stage of the experiential learning process.

In the first three cases, the students missed out the reflection and analysis process. In the last case, the student reflected on the task and using her initiative, read the news item prior to watching it on TV but did not familiarise herself with the vocabulary, expressions and so on to enable her to write a narrative in an accurate way in her own words. Although she was fairly familiar with the item and could talk about it in general terms, she was unable to write about it in detail in her own words having not internalised the new vocabulary.

Student A and Student C displayed similar learning styles in so far as both were so concerned with 'getting on with the task'. This meant putting down on paper as much evidence of English that they could demonstrate – but they were unconcerned with accuracy. They did not seem to grasp the connection between accuracy and fluency for conveying communicative meaning. In other words, they did not demonstrate comprehension of the task itself and rather seemed to approach it in a trial and error sort of way. Student B was so concerned with accuracy that, once again, he did not realise that the aim of the task was to communicate as much accurate information as possible in order to convey the full content of the news item.

It was possible for the tutor to generate a discussion on learning styles by sharing the different copies of the work with all the students. Collectively, and with the tutor facilitating, the students worked towards a process or learning style which would obtain the best results. In the case of this task, the students felt that they would need to read the news item in class first in order to familiarise themselves with expressions and vocabulary. In doing this, they used dictionaries, bilingual and mono-lingual, and talked through meanings with peers and the tutor. They then looked at a video of the news item and discussed the notes taken while watching the video, in pairs and small groups. Finally, they wrote out the detailed précis incorporating any new vocabulary into their own style of writing. They also presented the news items orally to their peer groups, which acted as consolidation and enabled further active experimentation to take place in a different context.

Once the students had established sufficient confidence in carrying out this preferred learning style in class, they were able to do the same at home as part of a weekly assignment. It was not an easy process for students to adapt their learning styles to incorporate all stages of the cyclical process. The home assignments demonstrated that some had reverted to their old learning styles. The tutor then prompted the student with a reminder of the stages of learning and the student redrafted the piece of work. Students were constantly reminded that the *process of learning* was crucial to successful outcomes and that the student should take care to implement each stage in sequence. In the case of language learning, the tutor emphasised the following:

- the importance of reflection and internalising new structures and vocabulary;
- analysis of the task at hand and knowing what is required of the learner;
- the importance of correctly accessing sources of support, e.g. dictionaries, reference books, back-up materials, talking to peers and to the tutor; and
- asking for clarification, more information and feedback.

The students were continuously involved in reflection of the learning process and of evaluating and validating their accomplishments. They were also involved in specifying their learning objectives and devising strategies that would enable them to identify their learning goals and the sequence of learning activities involved in achieving them. Self-assessment and peer group assessment are invaluable ways of helping bilingual students identify evidence of accomplishments, acceptable to the task objective.

Developing a process of assessing and teaching learning styles is invaluable as part of an APL Induction Learning module, as it leads to an assessment of a candidate's prior learning style and can be a useful starting point for inducting the candidate into the various stages of the experiential learning cycle.

Barriers in experiential learning

P. Honey and A. Mumford (1986), developing ideas from D. A. Kolb's experiential learning styles, have suggested that people develop learning styles that emphasise some learning abilities over others. Although different disciplines tend to emphasise one type of learning style, nevertheless, different activities within the discipline would require different learning styles. If it follows that individual learning styles are developed as a result of conformity to different cultural and education pressures, then most people have developed one or two predominant styles which they feel comfortable with, and with which they have achieved a fair degree of success. Honey and Mumford have argued that we all have preferred and habitual ways of learning (see Figure 4.2) and that few people are effective in all stages of the cycle. At each stage of the cycle, different demands are placed on the learners.

This model presupposes that learners are operating in a language where they feel comfortable. The stark reality is for bilingual learners that very often they are operating in a language medium in which they feel under-confident. Consequently, this self-perception usually creates a stumbling block which will prevent them from moving to stages 3 and 4 in the learning process. This is especially so if the tutor expects that the student has

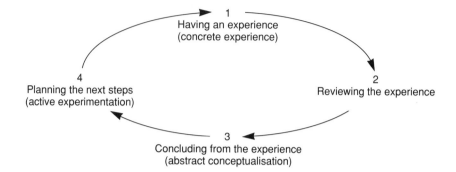

Figure 4.2   The process of experiential learning
Source: P. Honey and A. Mumford, *Using Your Learning Styles*, Maidenhead, 1983.

developed learner autonomy sufficiently to work on a study, assignment or project by themselves, but in reality the student does not feel so confident. It may or may not be the case that the actual language competence of the student is inadequate to the task in some way. But the point that needs to be reinforced, is that it is the students' self-perception and low self-esteem in their language competence which often create the problem. Experience in FE colleges with bilingual learners has demonstrated unequivocally that students whose grasp of English is both accurate and fluent to just below native-speaker standard (level 3/4) in English, continually question their language competence and consequently their ability to carry out verbal presentations, assignments and so on.

Evidence from the FEU project, 'Cultural Bias in Assessment' (1983), maintains that students with problems in literacy did not seem to understand the true meaning of assignment writing, i.e. for gaining information or for working independently or for finding out new ways of doing things; rather, they focused on assignments as examinations and were daunted by the 'written page'. Following on from this evidence, I would contend that the model put forward by Honey and Mumford can be adapted for bilingual learners and learners with basic skills difficulties, i.e. literacy and numeracy (see Figure 4.3).

On account of the real or self-imposed stumbling block, i.e. difficulties with language, the 'experience' then becomes the focus for the learner who is unable to develop other learning strategies at stages 3 and 4 of Honey and Mumford's model.

Demonstration of different learning styles

This can be illustrated by the case of two Zairean, French-speaking students on an NVQ Level 1 Office Skills course in an FE college. They

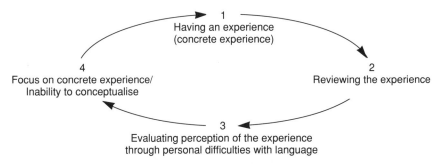

1
Having an experience
(concrete experience)

4
Focus on concrete experience/
Inability to conceptualise

2
Reviewing the experience

3
Evaluating perception of the experience
through personal difficulties with language

Figure 4.3 The process of experiential learning for bilingual learners. Adapted from Figure 4.2

both had substantial experience as bilingual secretaries, receptionists and administration workers plus two certificates in business management from Zaire. Prior to entry on the course, they had not undergone an APL process nor an assessment of their language competence and consequently their experience was not taken into account to gain exemption from units. They were discouraged from fully exploring other styles of learning by their own and the tutor's perception of their language competence.

Their whole learning experience was perceived in terms of the limitations imposed by their language competence which actually prevented them from exploring their full potential. In a work placement situation their main concern was whether they would be able to 'cope with the tasks' (basic tasks such as filing, word-processing of letters, photocopying), which they had already performed successfully in the simulated training office in the college and in their work situation in Zaire. They were capable of working at supervisory level and spoke of undertaking tasks such as helping to set up projects in an engineering firm, undertaking visits for marketing purposes for a sugar production company, the verbal presentation of the processes and production of various food products, e.g. Coca-Cola, to visitors and delegates in the sugar production company, and the induction of trainees to the firm. All of these in terms of occupational competence feature at NVQ Level II and above.

During the work placement situation, they demonstrated very competently that they were able to 'update records in a computerised Database' (NVQ Business Administration Level 2). As part of the underpinning knowledge and skills in this element, they needed to demonstrate competence in 'reading and interpreting manufacturer's and/or organisation's instructions'. When a relevant situation arose where they did need to in fact demonstrate understanding of instructions, they were able to do so because the content of the instructions were similar to ones they were used to following in French. They could make the transfer of knowledge from one learning situation to another and overcome the hurdle of understanding specialist jargon because they were already familiar with the *context* from their prior work experience. Another requirement of the underpinning knowledge is the 'planning and organising work within deadlines' which they were able to do very competently on account of their prior work experience.

Within the 'cycle of learning', they were able to progress from the 'abstract conceptualisation' stage to the 'active experimentation' and revert to the 'activist' style of learning, to which they were accustomed. This they managed to do in the workplace and not in the classroom, because in the classroom they were inhibited by the tutor's and their own perceptions of their 'limited language ability'. In the workplace, their confidence in their occupational competence overrode any misgivings which they may have had concerning language and allowed them to progress to Stages 3 and 4 of the learning cycle.

Interestingly enough, as the NVQ criteria are fairly ambiguous as to whether the database should involve a simple file on the BBC or Nimbus, or could be a custom-designed system in a large bank or insurance company, the scope for the two learners to demonstrate their potential was both viable and achievable. The ability in the workplace context to read and interpret manufacturer's instructions, does not necessarily mean an ability to set up and work with a new database package from scratch. The underlying assumption is, in fact, that the candidate needs to find a single command in the manual and to interpret that. The two learners in question were able to do that successfully. The implications for an APL process which encompassed work-based learning are far-reaching. It would be necessary to set up systems which allow the learner sufficient flexibility to return to the tutor/assessor and to claim elements of a unit and/or units from the next NVQ level, if the learner has been able to demonstrate his/her experience in the context of the workplace. The mechanism whereby learners are encouraged to claim more competences in the workplace other than the ones for which they are currently studying, particularly benefits learners working in a bilingual workplace environment. In actual fact, the two Zairean learners in this case study were placed in a bilingual workplace where they felt confident of their own language competence in French and this had an overall enabling effect on the development of their English. Therefore, to some degree, they were arguably in a strong position to bridge the gap between their occupational competence and their language competence.

The point to be made here is that, in general, learners can only expand on learning styles that feature in the 'experiential learning cycle' developed by Honey and Mumford if they are confident of their language and literacy. An open agenda of regularly assessing progress on language competence will demonstrate to the learner that the levels of language competence are progressing in tandem with his/her levels of occupational vocational competence.

Honey and Mumford have distinguished four different learning styles, which can be identified as being broadly equivalent to the four learning stages:

- *Activists* learn best from constant exposure to new experiences and like to involve themselves in short, 'here and now' activities. They learn least from activities that require them to take a passive role.
- *Reflectors* learn best from activities where they can ponder over experiences and assimilate information, reaching decisions in their own time. They learn least from activities where they are forced into situations which require action without planning.
- *Theorists* learn best from activities where they can integrate observations into sound theories and can explore the interrelationships between ideas. They learn least from situations that they do not have the opportunity to explore in any depth.
- *Pragmatists* learn best from activities where they can see the practical value of the subject matter and where they can test ideas and techniques to see if they apply in practice. They learn least from situations where learning is unrelated to an immediate, recognisable need or benefit (Jennifer Kidd NIACE 1988).

The two Zairean students' natural styles of learning in the language class veered towards activist and theorist. They enjoyed role-play, discussion and debate and were vocally very articulate. They invariably expanded on any new input from the teacher by asking questions about the applicability of certain language structures in different contexts, and actively experimented by using new language in different contexts.

In a language-learning situation they were able to explore all four stages of the experiential learning cycle but informed the language teacher that they were unable to do the same in the vocational subject. In other words, the vocational subject teacher held them back from conceptualising and experimenting with the learning experience in new and different contexts. They were not given opportunities in the class to talk about or to build upon their Zairean work experience, skills and knowledge.

It can be seen from this example that the APL process, once initiated at pre-entry stage, should be and can be sustained in the classroom with tutors building on individual's prior experience and knowledge. This is especially important with bilingual learners as a positive self-image has an enabling effect on their communication and other core skills.

ASSESSMENT OF PRIOR LEARNING STYLES

What needs to be assessed is the extent to which learners have made the transition from a passive teacher-centred learning style to an active, participative and independent learning style, and are able to adapt their learning styles according to circumstance and context. Candidates are generally inhibited from developing autonomous learning strategies. Exploring learning styles with students breaks through barriers of poor self-perception and enables students to think positively about their past and present learning experiences.

The project set up by the Department of Employment Group 'Quality in Teaching and Learning' (1992) provides evidence of the link between learning styles and successful outcomes in the classroom. The project's target group were British-born ethnic minority students engaging on a BTEC First Programme. The focus of the study was classroom interaction and its importance in accounting for student success. Strictly speaking, the relevance of this study to the present volume is limited, in so far as the target groups are vastly dissimilar in age and the amount of contact with the British educational system. Nevertheless, some valid general points do emerge, and need to be heeded. The project's findings concerning successful students can be summed up, that 'learning skills' and positive social relationships are just as essential to successful assignments and to outcomes, and yet they remain largely invisible:

> The crucial process of 'tuning in' to these skills and relationships is neither specified nor taught ... the classroom learning skills referred to are the kind of management and problem-solving skills expressed through talk which are the routine repertoire of all good teachers. They include reformulating the task in your own words, defining, giving examples and so on.
>
> (Department of Employment Group 1992)

The study goes on to suggest that teacher attitudes affect motivation positively and can also create the kind of teacher-student talk that provides day-to-day opportunities for learning. If learners are expected to operate in an environment that is vastly different from what they have been accustomed to and one that imposes different expectations of learning styles centred on a specific model of classroom interaction, then learners need to be aware of this at the initial stage of the learning process. Mature bilingual learners entering the APL process have very often achieved a high degree of academic or vocational success in their own countries with very specific teaching and learning styles and need to be presented with very convincing arguments as to why they might need to adapt to a different set of learning strategies.

The FEU project (1993) examines an interesting case study of a Malaysian student who was hoping to become an electrical engineer and was advised to start on the BTEC First Diploma. Whilst he recognised the importance of certain common skills, especially communication (since he saw this as being the key to success in terms of being as good as anyone in the class) he was puzzled by other common skills, such as problem-solving ('the English way of learning, so I have no choice but to do it'). However, discussion on a one-to-one basis in a tutorial enabled him to demonstrate effective problem-solving skills (for example, in the way in which he enlisted help from others in the group); it also enabled him to explore constructively his strengths and weaknesses in terms of communication in English and encouraged him not only to request language support, but also to specify those areas in which that support was needed.

RECOGNITION OF A RANGE OF LEARNING STYLES

Valid evidence from the FEU project supports the contention that a discussion of students' perceptions of learning at an initial stage of the learning process is a key factor in motivation and successful outcomes in learning. Some of the monolingual and bilingual students educated in the UK perceived assignments in terms of projects to be researched, in order to find out information. However, this was in marked contrast to the three bilingual students with limited or interrupted education in the UK, who perceived assignments in the terms of questions to be answered, without any focus on the research element. Interestingly enough, this perception was also shared by a monolingual student (with weak literacy skills) who was struck primarily by the 'printed papers' which made him think of assignments as 'like an exam'. On a more general level, the findings suggest that those students (bilingual or monolingual) who experienced literacy difficulties, tended to equate assignments with exams.

Learners' perceptions of learning projects, i.e. assignments, examinations and so on, are a realistic indicator of their personal individual learning styles. This inevitably has an effect on the 'tuning-in' process in the classroom between the learner, his or her peers and the teacher. For instance, the FEU project findings focused on the fact that some 'stronger students' saw the purpose of the assignments in terms of the role of the teacher who would be in a position to 'see how good we are', 'helps the teacher test your English, understand your weaknesses and give you extra practice'. Some monolingual students perceived the purpose of assignments in terms of fostering greater independence so that 'it makes you think differently and helps you to think for yourself'. Other bilingual students expressed the benefits in terms of obtaining information. Some placed greater emphasis on gradings because 'it shows me that I am ahead of most of the class' and/or 'my parents understand Distinction, Merit, even if they don't understand exactly what I am doing on the course'. As the findings suggest, these approaches were in marked contrast to the perceptions of the weaker bilingual and monolingual students who all saw the purpose in terms of a test or exam, related to grades or their report, and they were not able to recognise any benefits for themselves beyond this.

Obviously, if a learner is made aware of the importance of developing a range of learning styles which link in with the 'products' of learning and is given access to benefits for himself/herself, he/she would be much more motivated and gain ownership of the learning process. The result will be a shift in emphasis on the continuum of learner from reactive to active and participative.

Further evidence from the findings quite clearly demonstrates that 'while the content of assignments may appear closely linked to the world of work or vocational studies, it cannot be assumed that this will be recognised by all students unless made explicit, for example through group discussion. Under these circumstances, the core skill of problem-solving for example, is likely to be totally ignored. This is more likely to be the case with students accustomed to a more formal and examination based educational system' (FEU 1993).

This evidence can be linked up with the attitudes of teachers teaching on BTEC or any other assignment-based courses in FE colleges where there is heavy expectation that students will achieve successful learning through interaction, which depends greatly on good relationships with their peers and with the teacher, and that the role of a teacher is more like that of a facilitator. This in turn, depends on how socially confident mature bilingual learners feel in a classroom environment alongside monolingual learners, together with their personal confidence in their language competence.

Independent learning, and to a greater extent Open Learning, is greatly valued by tutors. Learners are expected to research projects, studies, assignments for various assessment purposes. The underlying assumption in an FE environment is that learners irrespective of their educational and cultural background, have the required study skills, e.g. library research skills, and know in which context to use them. Moreover, they are able to undertake a study or piece of research in a practical context, e.g. in the real world outside the class and recognise its relevance to the general underpinning knowledge which is imparted to the learners by the teacher in class. There are, however, differences in the types of transmission models and definitions of knowledge in culturally different educational systems. A learner who has not operated in an assignment-based learning system previously and whose whole life experience and prior knowledge has moulded his learning styles and expectations differently, will be disadvantaged in an educational system which does not prepare him adequately for the transition.

The 'hidden agenda' in managing learning and developing learning strategies may be summed up in one way in the table entitled 'Learning Skills in Classroom Interaction' (Department of Employment 1992), which identifies two aspects or groups of skills:

- the organising of the procedural aspects of learning, e.g. 'what are we doing?' or 'who is involved in this learning?' and
- the negotiating of the cognitive aspects of the learning itself, e.g. 'clarifying a problem', 'defining a concept' or 'generalising'.

As the study concludes, there is a paradox inherent in the findings, that although learning skills such as these are required to negotiate the taught curriculum, they are not specified by examining boards as part of the curriculum content or curriculum outcomes. They may be acquired in the classroom, but, initially at least, are more likely to be the product of previous education experience and social background.

The classroom 'interaction' learning skills are equally as essential as the *'access and transfer' learning skills*. By the latter, I mean those skills needed by the learner to widen classroom-based learning and to encompass the outside world. Not only would this include research, study and project work, but also work-based training and learning. This is the ability of the learner to demonstrate the symbiotic nature of the relationship between input of knowledge in the classroom and its practical application in the 'real' world. The learner is thus able to transfer learning strategies from the theoretical to the practical and to access into the learning product or outcome by developing more independent and problem solving strategies for learning. Those skills include:

- target-setting;
- clarifying tasks;
- identifying sources of information;
- understanding information;
- understanding the task
- organising the task;
- analysing information gained from knowledge both learnt and based on practical experience;
- reformulating ideas;
- transferring information;
- reflecting on result/reformulating ideas;
- summarising; and
- evaluating the task.

DEVELOPING FLEXIBILITY IN LEARNING STRATEGIES

Certain conclusions which emerge from the 'Quality in Teaching and Learning' document (Department of Employment 1992) demonstrate that students with developed classroom learning skills 'performed' well in the classroom where there was more focus on the analytical, on tightly structured tasks and the display of knowledge. Conversely, students who had well-developed social and interpersonal skills performed well in the classroom where there was a focus on student experience and informal social relationships. It follows logically that 'students rated as successful in one classroom might not have been able to "tune in" to other types of classroom.'

A crucial part of the APL process implicitly demands that the learner be equipped with those learning skills which enable him/her to recognise valid experience and to demonstrate competence through performance evidence either within the workplace or through simulations in the context of the college. Those same Access and Transfer learning skills are used in this context. The following example illustrates the process. Two Asian female students who were on a City & Guilds 325 Community Care course in a FE college, were asked to undertake a study of a local community centre. However, it was not made clear to them that a gurdwara (Sikh temple) would qualify as a local community centre as language classes in English and Punjabi were held there as well as classes in Punjabi culture – folk dance and music. They had not undergone an APL process and the tutor at the initial stage of interview had not questioned them on the whole breadth of their voluntary activities, i.e. teaching Punjabi and catering for religious functions at the gurdwara, preferring to concentrate instead on their childminding experience and paid employment in a local creche.

The students did not see their experience in the gurdwara as relevant to the assignment, as the tutor had not shown any interest in it previously. Subsequently, they were unable to access and transfer this information as being relevant when given the 'theoretical' definition of a community centre. They eventually undertook their studies in local community centres where they felt they had great difficulty in accessing the information they required because they felt they were not asking the right questions. Gradually, the tutor received full details from them of their involvement in their gurdwara and encouraged them to undertake a study of the centre, where they asked questions in Punjabi, but finally wrote the study in English.

The following conclusions may be drawn from this example. First, in terms of the 'tuning in' process in the classroom, the women, although fairly articulate in English, felt their experience was not as valid as others in the group; moreover, their perception of a gurdwara was first and foremost a place of worship rather than a social community centre.

Second, the tutor had made the erroneous assumption that everyone's understanding of a community centre would be the same and not need explanation. The absence of an APL process in this case which would have facilitated the gathering of a portfolio on learner's competences, prior knowledge and experience in all contexts, clearly prevented tutor and students from working together in a constructive way.

Third, and most importantly, this example would consolidate the argument for developing an APL process which focuses on learning skills and strategies and enables learners to gain the necessary skills through an induction module. In the case of these particular students, they needed to develop a range of more assertive and independent learning styles in the classroom, which would enable them to take responsibility for their own learning and not to rely on the tutor as the source of all information.

CONCLUSION

Two of the major areas of underachievement for learners, and bilingual learners in particular, are their inabilities to:

(a) develop flexibility in learning styles; and
(b) to focus on their personal experience as being valid and relevant to learning outcomes.

Part of the curriculum entitlement should be opportunities for learners to undergo a process that assesses their prior learning styles. They are given the opportunity to attend an APL Induction module of 'learning to learn', prior to joining a course of study, so that their learning skills could be developed sufficiently to enable more successful outcomes. The process of APL is primarily an overarching process, concerned with clarifying aspirations and identifying potential in all areas of a learner's 'profile'. Harnessing a learner's potential involves unlocking the learner's ability to refine the 'access and transfer' learning skills. The end result would be the learner's ability to recognise his/her practical experience and place it in a formal framework, in other words, he/she would be able to refine his/her experience into heuristics, i.e. the rules of thumb describing know-how – the underpinning knowledge. Only through achieving this will he/she be able to bridge the next stage, which is to combine the transfer of theoretical or formally acquired knowledge with the practical experience in a formal assessment situation.

APPENDIX 4.1: THE HOPSON-ANDERSON HIERARCHICAL MODEL OF STUDY SKILLS

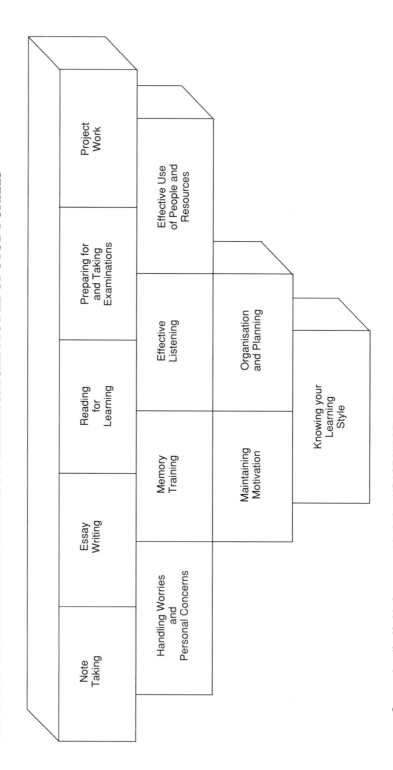

Source: Jennifer Kydd, Assessment in Action, UDACE/NIACE, 1988.

Chapter 5

Case study

The aim of this chapter is to focus on recent illustrative examples from FE colleges which serve to highlight the need for a specific APEL framework for bilingual learners, as discussed in the previous chapters.

A case study of six Asian women – who were refused entry to the City and Guilds (Caring) course (also known as CGLI 324.1) and NNEB (Nursery Nurses) courses and subsequently undertook to follow an Open Learning Foundation or preparatory programme leading to the City and Guilds 324.1 in a London FE college – illustrates the barriers and successes inherent within the entitlement curriculum framework, in relation to its stated claim of extending access to all. The aim is to illustrate the benefits of the recommended APL framework outlined in the previous chapters for all types of bilingual learners from settled 'immigrants' to more recently arrived refugees and arrivals from the EC.

CASE STUDY OF OPEN LEARNING FOUNDATION PROGRAMME LEADING TO CITY AND GUILDS 324.1

Aims and general background

The City and Guilds 324.1 is designed for those who work in care posts, to recognise and respond effectively to the variety of family settings within which children (0–7 years) live.

All six students on the course were female and Asian – Pakistani, Bangladeshi or Indian. Four of the students had commenced the course in September after being interviewed by the course tutor and being informed that their English would not be good enough to undertake the course successfully. The course tutor and the bilingual learner support tutor then designed a package of learning which could take place in an Open Learning workshop with the bilingual learner support tutor facilitating the learning process on the basis of three hours a week maximum. The students were informed that they could come to the workshop at other times to work and to use the facilities offered. They preferred to take up the option of visiting the workshop only at those specified times when the bilingual learner support tutor was present. All four students were also attending a CGLI 361 (Communications English) course for four hours a week and an advanced class to improve their oral and communication skills entitled 'Speak with Confidence'.

One of the other students had been attending a GCSE course but had found the work too demanding and had felt underconfident of her ability in literacy and study skills. She had subsequently left the GCSE course in January and joined the group of learners in the workshop after talking to them informally about the CGLI 324.1 course. The final student who joined the group was referred to the bilingual learner support tutor in March/April after being refused a place on the NNEB Nursery Nurses course on the grounds that her English was inadequate in order to successfully complete the course.

The students' names have been changed for publication. Their potted biographies were:

Sitha was 40 years old and had two children. She had received education to the age of 18 in Bangladesh and had lived in Britain for nine years. She was working in a paid capacity as a creche assistant in a voluntary community organisation on two afternoons a week. She wanted to build upon her work experience and to obtain formal qualifications which would enable her to gain paid employment on a more substantial basis as a nursery nurse.

Radha was 39 years old and had had three children. Two children suffered from muscular dystrophy. One child, at the age of 9, had died the previous year. Since the death of that child she had decided to work on voluntary basis for two days a week in a local special needs school where her eldest son, suffering from muscular dystrophy, was a pupil. She was a single parent, in so far as her husband lived in India and did not want to live in England. She had lived in England for eight years. Her aim was to obtain a formal qualification which would enable her to gain full-time paid employment, preferably in order to work with special needs children. Halfway through the year in March, she secured a temporary position as a dinnertime supervisor there.

Anjana was 45 years old and had three children and initially seemed to join the course because she wanted to improve her English further and stay with the other three students with whom she had spent one year previously, studying for a RSA Profiles Objectives Certificate in ESOL. She was quite clear from the outset that her husband's work as a publisher had brought the family to England and that her main aim was to educate her children to university level and to return to Pakistan.

Two of her children were already at university. She did not appear to have any personal ambitions in the way of employment aspirations in England although she had worked as a teacher in Pakistan for five years teaching children between the ages of 5 and 10 years. She appeared the least motivated student in the group initially.

Nimini was 25 years old and had no children. She too did not appear especially motivated to undertake this course but wanted to gain some skills in childcare so that she might eventually look for some employment but was not under financial necessity to do so. She wanted to gain greater self-confidence in her English language and communication skills and enjoyed the social interaction and support of the group. She had lived in Britain for four years.

Devi was 38 years old. Initially she did not want to take up employment but although she had started the course in a very ad hoc manner on account of a chance conversation with the other students, nevertheless, she became very motivated as the course progressed and eventually began to talk of gaining employment once she had completed the certificate. She had visited her daughter's school and had worked there voluntarily on occasion, helping young children to read.

Shaheen was 32 years old. She had lived in Britain for fifteen years and had worked for a period of eight years as a dinnertime supervisor. She had undertaken a computing course for a year and had stopped the course as she was to be married. She could not understand why she had not been 'allowed to undertake the NNEB Nursery Nurses Course' and why her English was not considered adequate. After careful observation by the bilingual learner support tutor, it became evident that the problem was not English as much as the learner's inadequate ability to concentrate on input in the classroom and to cognise information in a relevant way. In other words, the 'problem' was with the learning styles and strategies of the student and not the language. Her spoken and written English was fairly fluent. Her aim was to gain a credible certificate such as NNEB Nursery Nurses or CGLI 324.1 in order to gain paid employment.

Aims of the pilot

At the time of the pilot the City and Guilds course was not classified as an NVQ qualification, therefore the students were unable to claim exemptions for units by providing evidence. The central aim then of this course was to enable the students to accumulate a portfolio of evidence in specific areas of childcare which would result from work experience either in a voluntary or paid capacity in schools, nurseries or creches, and tutor input to facilitate underpinning knowledge. The students would then be able to present the credible evidence to an NVQ assessor for exemptions to units. Second, the course would provide an emphasis on students developing confidence in their English and communication skills. Third, the course had integrated a strong focus on developing experiential learning strategies in the context of the student's prior learning styles.

All the students managed to gain voluntary or paid work experience once they began the course. Apart from Anjana, none of the other students had *formal* teaching experience or qualifications in caring of any kind. The case study took place over one academic year – 36 weeks consisting of one three-hour session a week in the workshop plus work experience in the College creche and private creches in the local community. The constraints faced by the two tutors were as follows:

- City and Guilds specifies a syllabus in some detail but offered no recognition of prior learning for exemption to units.
- The students came from a range of backgrounds with personal and emotional problems which overspilled into the contact sessions with the bilingual learning support tutor. As they were a small group, initially they were keen to use this group as a way of developing emotional and practical support links and to use the tutor as a counsellor for their 'problems'.
- The students were unaccustomed to working in an Open Learning format and had not developed the independent and autonomous learning strategies they needed to be successful on the course. They were very dependent on the bilingual learning support tutor and felt 'lost' if the tutor needed to attend to other students in the workshop. Even if the tutor had set them a task, i.e. a discussion on how to work on an assignment or a discussion/brainstorm of ideas on a specific area, the students would use the tutor's absence to discuss personal or social issues unrelated to the 'task'. They were used to working in a pedagogically teacher-centred way and found it very difficult to reorientate their strategies to accommodate a more andragogical and experiential style of learning.
- Frequent interruptions experienced by the bilingual learning support tutor from other users of the workshop made facilitating contact with the students very difficult.
- Students' self-esteem and self-confidence in relation to their English language competence and communication skills were very low and proved to be major obstacles to enabling the students to recognise the positive aspects of their experience and learning progress.

- The students all arrived on the course with varying degrees of motivation, which altered as the course progressed through the year.
- The students had virtually no contact with the vocational course tutor and perceived her role as an obstacle to entry on the course CGLI 324.1 the following year. They felt they needed to provide the evidence at the end of the Open Learning course to prove to the course tutor that their English was good enough to be allowed entry on the course.
- The APL process was explained to the students but they still continued to undervalue their experience skills and prior knowledge. However, the current experience they were gaining in their work 'placements' seemed to hold greater credibility and currency value as the year progressed and they could perceive links between their work experience and the underpinning knowledge they gained on the course.
- The vocational course tutor perceived the students as a group of 'needy' learners who would have to develop more independent ways of learning if they were going to succeed on the course.

Conventional didactic knowledge-centred methods were not useful in the above context; the variations in knowledge, skills and interests were too great, the motivation problems too acute and the intended outcomes of practical demonstrable evidence needed to be addressed. The vocational course tutor provided an outline of a selected list of areas with corresponding assignments (cf Appendix 5.1). This was taken as a starting point and the bilingual learner support tutor grafted onto the blueprint other areas of development which corresponded to the experiences and interests of the students, so as to build upon their potential, plus areas of development for language. The students were all following the CGLI Communications English 361 course at the same time, which also served to consolidate their language learning.

Broadly speaking, the programme addressed six main areas:

1 input of underpinning knowledge for specific areas,
2 English language development and exposition of nomenclature of vocational area;
3 development of English and communication skills;
4 exposition of the language of instruction within the framework of different learning styles leading to different outcomes/products of learning, e.g. assignment, task, etc.;
5 the development and accumulation of different types of evidence to be part of a portfolio; and
6 introduction to experiential learning styles.

In the first few sessions, the bilingual learning support tutor took on the role of a 'guidance advocate' within the framework of an APL process. The students were required to focus on their qualifications and work experiences in the different areas as laid out in the 'CV', and then the bilingual support tutor facilitated deconstruction of their experience into broad skills areas:

- skills working with people;
- skills working with information; and
- skills working with things.

The broad skills were cross-mapped with the list of occupational competences listed in the City and Guilds Guidelines Booklet (Appendix B) Design and Marking Schedule for Integrated Assignments (324–1–01). The students were able to contextualise the work experience that they had gained or were gaining in the context of the occupational competences which they clearly needed to achieve on the course in order to demonstrate underpinning knowledge and competence in the workplace.

The students were asked to keep a learning log of their work experiences – known to the students as a diary (cf example Appendix 5.4). They were told that the aims were to:

1 improve confidence, fluency and accuracy in their written English;
2 enable them to observe, reflect and analyse teaching in the classroom in general and their teaching or caring activities in particular;
3 enable them to observe the progress that they would make in the areas of communication skills and teaching/caring; and
4 enable them to perceive their work experience in terms of occupational competence, so that eventually they could build up evidence which would form part of their portfolios.

Notes for the log were written in their first languages – Hindi, Urdu, Bengali, but the log was in English. At the start of each week's session, the students shared and discussed the outcomes of the activities observed. Students were set observation and reflection tasks to undertake in the college creche with the care assistants. They were also asked to observe and reflect on the teaching of the bilingual learning support tutor in the context of a 'conventional English language classroom' and to evaluate in general the following points in both contexts:

1 What were the aims of the activity in the creche/classroom?
2 How did the teacher/carer prepare the students/children for the activity?
3 How did the teacher/carer carry out the activity?
4 How did it meet the needs of the students/children?
5 What was successful and why?
6 What was not successful and why?
7 What would you have done differently and why?

The actual skills of questioning themselves and others, evaluating, reflecting and analysing were radically new to the students and, therefore, disorientating. The 'language' of evaluation was unfamiliar and the purpose of the exercise needed to be explained repeatedly. Students were told that unless they were able to observe and analyse others in the classroom, they would not be able to improve on their own teaching/caring. Their past experiences of learning, both in Britain and abroad, had consisted very much of essay writing either in narrative or biographical form. Some study skills formed a crucial feature of their learning strategies and the bilingual support tutor was able to build positively on this. However, being told 'how' to do the task and what sorts of 'answers' to expect formed an integral part of their expectations of the teacher's role.

Once the students had surmounted the initial hurdles of their own insecurities in language and had become familiarised with the new ways of working, they began to learn a good deal from these exercises.

Creating a supportive framework within which students could observe and reflect on the activities of other professional carers in the college creche was crucial to successful outcomes. They visited each other in their places of work and were encouraged to be constructively critical of each other's caring activities. They found it difficult to differentiate between a professional criticism and a personal criticism. Being able to give and take constructive criticism was one learning experience they gained from the activities. By staging the activities, in a gradual way they were able to make the transition from observing others to becoming more reflective and analytical about their own caring activities.

Developing task-based skills

One of the final assignments they needed to undertake was an integrated *Practical Care Tasks Skill Assignment*. They needed to plan an activity for children in their care, to stage the activity and to complete a checklist to indicate whether they had achieved the occupational competences. As with all occupational competence-based courses, the language and literacy needs are implicit and not overt within the assessment of the practical care tasks skills. In order to prepare the students adequately for the task, they were asked in the first instance to observe a carer in the workplace and to assess his/her occupational competence in the course of carrying out an activity such as painting, making a collage, etc. and to observe in particular the language used by the care assistant with the children. Students were asked to carry out the observations in pairs with one student observing the carer's occupational competence and the other student observing the carer's language being used in relation to each of the competences, as follows (occupational competences taken from the CGLI 324.1 Syllabus):

- observed safety and hygiene in carrying out the task;
- left child feeling satisfied;

- developed two-way verbal communication and non-verbal communication with the child;
- dealt patiently with the situation;
- showed empathy towards the child;
- used humour, where appropriate, to develop positive responses and attitudes; and
- left child feeling positive and in charge of the decisions.

Developing reflective skills

A list of activities was developed and cross mapped with the occupational competences within a framework of appropriate language. A particular difficulty with this group centred on *reflective discussion* as discussions digressed into a largely irrelevant swapping of anecdotes. The bilingual learner support tutor focused the students' attention directly on what a reflective discussion could be like by 'modelling reflection', i.e. providing a clear model or example and shaping the learner's behaviour towards the model. In the case of this particular group, the bilingual learning support tutor asked two female Asian students following an NNEB Nursery Nurse course to discuss their experience of observation in the form of a reflective interchange of ideas. The Open Learning students were asked simply to listen and not to comment. As all students were unfamiliar with this way of working, the tendency initially was for the CGLI 324.1 students to interject and to ask questions and for the NNEB students to try and involve the others by asking their opinions. The ground rules were made very explicit and the bilingual learner support tutor demonstrated the 'modelling' process by improvising a reflective monologue on observation of her own teaching in a lesson. She included the following features:

- (descriptions of events) How was this different from other teaching experiences? What was good, successful, unsuccessful? (Judgements)
- Why was it good/bad/successful etc? (Analysis)

Once all students realised the aim of the process and how it would be helpful to them to be able to identify and evaluate good and bad caring practice, the modelling exercise continued and students noted down specific language structures and expressions used by the tutor in the course of the monologue on analysis and evaluation. They verbally presented their observation of care activities in the workplace, to a class of students with whom they attended the 'Speak with Confidence' advanced oral skills class and received feedback.

The peer group of students were asked to be judges and to award points on the basis of:

- clarity of meaning;
- sense of audience;

- fluency and accuracy of language; and
- interest value of content; humour, use of idiom, etc.

The students felt more confident as a result of these learning activities and were able to progress to the next stage – the identification of a *Care Task Skills* activity which they had to carry out in the workplace. They needed to choose and design an activity individually, and to self-assess their occupational competence during the course of the activity. As the students shared languages with some of the children in their care, they were able to demonstrate verbal communication in two or more languages, although this did not achieve extra credit with the CGLI criteria, neither was the verbal presentation part of the City and Guilds 324.1 criteria. A valid APL process needs to acknowledge these two important outcomes for the relevant evidence in terms of the 'core skills'.

This simulation motivated the CGLI students to work towards greater cohesion and clarity of delivery in terms of their language input. In terms of back-up for the CGLI students, their peer group in the language classes consisted of a reliable and consistent source of support, who were able to provide constructive criticism in a safe and friendly environment.

Another way of encouraging the students to review and reflect upon experience involved the use of role-play, video and audio recordings. The students were given a 'difficult' situation in a workplace to act out in the advanced oral skills class. This involved some element of conflict, frustration and/or anger which the students found difficult to deal with, without the necessary interpersonal skills in English. Situations were taken from 'real life' problems such as coping with aggressive/demanding parents in the nursery, coping with aggressive members of staff, justifying to another member of the team the course of action which had been taken to deal with a disruptive or hysterical child or one who was having tantrums.

Role-play facilitated the flow of language and students could experiment and risk take with different types of language in a safe and supportive environment. Video and audio recordings provided a very powerful tool to aid reflection on experience. Peer appraisal as part of a structured debrief was also a valuable source of feedback for the student. As the students were generally very underconfident of their language, the tutor felt it was very important to encourage all peers to focus on positive and negative aspects of a student's 'performance'.

Although comments and appraisal from the bilingual learner support tutor and peers proved valuable for these students, ultimately it was the individual student's self-assessment which mattered. The conclusion of the process of reflection was initially of direct experience and finally of what personal conclusions could be drawn having analysed that experience. The process of self-assessment started to take place successfully just over halfway through the academic year in February/March. It was a wholly unfamiliar process for these students and took them a long time to understand and appreciate the value of the experience.

Once the process of self-assessment was initiated, the students were able to develop action plans which incorporated the conclusions into planning for the next experience.

Working in a group on assignments

The group of students were a mutually supportive group and actively sought assistance from each other. One of the dominant learning styles they shared in common was a lack of competitiveness combined with an overwhelming sense of loyalty to the group (and a recognition that within the group was a communal need for support and help). Although this was a source of strength within the group in terms of identifying language needs, ironically, the group had great difficulty in adjusting to working together on vocational group assignments. The aims of the bilingual learning support tutor were to:

• facilitate the individuals within the group to appreciate the varied work experience of their peers and to utilise it during group assignments;
• reorientate and direct the group's communal energies towards undertaking a group assignment;
• create awareness within the group of the differences in learning styles in all six individuals and to set up ways of working which would effectively complement each other;
• encourage reflectiveness and self-assessment; and
• mobilise enthusiasm from individuals within the group to undertake work towards the group assignment outside contact sessions in the workshop.

The individuals within the group were conscientious and well motivated. If a task was set, the students would spend time doing it at home, and hand it in for marking. The students relied heavily on the tutor for all decisions about how well they were doing, when they should move on, types of assignments set and so on. Although the students themselves came with a wealth of experience, they did not initiate talking about that experience at the outset.

The students were asked to complete an assignment on *Outdoor Play Provision*; it became evident that three of the students did not perceive this group assignment as something 'serious' as it involved a visit to the local playground with the tutor. In order to assess the quality of the equipment in the playground the students needed to examine the equipment, to draw a layout of the playground and to reflect and analyse the whole experience with conclusions as to how the playground facilities could be improved. Their reaction was that ordinarily they would have expected to have undertaken an exercise of this type by studying photos in a book, reading a text and working on this at home. After the visit, they realised by actually examining playground equipment in closer detail and thinking about the potential dangers, in the context of their work experience, they had probably learnt a lot more from this 'unorthodox method'!

The next stage was for the group to visit another local park with better facilities for comparison and contrast. Although the students were in the habit of meeting one another socially, they did not seem able to organise a joint visit or even individual visits to the park without the tutor. Similarly, when asked to undertake a group assignment on teaching the hazards of fire and road safety to young children, they initially had great difficulty in formulating a joint action plan to co-ordinate the identification and retrieval of resources, i.e. leaflets etc, from local libraries, CAB and so on.

Development of 'core' skills

Students had been informed that part of the assessment centred around core skills, i.e. working in a team, independent learning and problem-solving. It was essential then, for the tutor to facilitate the students' clearer understanding of the group assignments and the need to develop the 'core' skills when carrying out the assignments. Consequently, she had to address three main issues which she identified as 'gaps' in the learning strategies of the students:

1 the development of 'active listening skills';
2 the development of learning strategies that would involve experimentation, risk-taking, taking the initiative, action planning; and
3 the development of core skills, i.e. working together as a group/team.

It is well researched that unless the student recognises some 'pay-off' in the process of problem-solving and working with others, attempts at problem-solving are unlikely to be sustained or non-productive. Five preconditions are normally stipulated for the solution of a problem:

1 the existence of a gap between what is and what should be;
2 an awareness that a gap exists;
3 the motivation to decrease the gap;
4 an ability to measure the size of the gap; and
5 the abilities and resources required to close the gap.

In the case of these students, they were simply not aware of the importance of evolving learner strategies, to develop the 'core' skills in tandem with carrying out the assignments. The motivation in their case stemmed from their desire to demonstrate to the course tutor and the Bilingual Support tutor their ability to undertake the City and Guilds 324.1 course. However, their prior 'learning styles' originating in India, Pakistan and Bangladesh had not prepared them for this way of studying and consequently, they felt that what they were doing constituted an 'unorthodox method'.

In order to introduce to the students the four stages of developing *problem-solving* as a 'core' skill, the tutor embedded the assignment on *Outdoor Play Provision* into a framework which focused on the following:

1 communication skills/problem recognition, identification and definition;
2 analysis and delegation of roles within group;
3 implementation and use of communication skills in the four discrete language skills areas; and
4 review and evaluation of peers' and groups' learning outcome.

The four-stage model of problem-solving was adapted by the author from the framework used with substantial success as an 'integrating concept' at an American college, Alverno. Here then is an attempt to incorporate and assess 'core' skills throughout the entire curriculum, in higher education. (The original examples appear in NCVQ 1990.)

Assignment: Outdoor Play Provision

Communication skills/problem recognition, identification and definition

1 Identify problems in design of outdoor provision.
2 Contribute to a group problem-solving activity where the exact nature of the problem can be determined, i.e. comparing and contrasting outdoor provision through site visits to two parks.
3 Write a short report on the identification of the problem.
4 Interview a person to ascertain discrepancies in provision, cost of setting it right – to ascertain the nature of the problem.

Analysis and delegation of roles within the group

1 Describe (orally) alternative strategies for dealing with the problem of assigning roles to members of group for research and collation of information, organisation of playground visits and so on.
2 Contribute to the analysis and generation of solutions in a group.
3 Review a proposed solution to a problem.
4 Write a short report providing an analysis and potential solutions to the given problem of poor outdoor play provision.

Implementation and use of communication skills

1 Assuming a given perspective in role-play, complain to an official of the Leisure Services on the nature of the problem in outdoor play provision.

2 Write an article for a local newspaper or local council on how you would deal with the problem of poor outdoor provision and proposing necessary changes.
3 Give a short presentation to your peer group on how you would implement the changes.
4 Write a letter of complaint to Leisure Services complaining of poor outdoor play provision.
5 Organise a group activity such as designing and constructing the ideal outdoor play provision using model toys, equipment, paint, card, building blocks, Lego, etc.

Review and Evaluation

1 Evaluate the presentation of a fellow colleague and provide constructive feedback in terms of content, discourse skills and communication.
2 Review and evaluate a written report or letter in terms of content, written discourse skills and communication.
3 Contribute to the group review, reviewing the efficiency of the group in achieving its objectives and learning outcomes through the evidence:
   • compilation of a report
   • letter to a Council official
   • design and construction of 'ideal' outdoor play provision
   • roleplay of complaint
   • letter to newspaper or local councillor.

The various stages were presented to the students in more 'accessible' and appropriate English than outlined above.

Developing Learning Styles

At this stage, in December–January, the tutor introduced the concept of 'learning styles' and 'learning strategies' to the students. She asked them to undertake an assignment in the workshop and to fill in a learning styles inventory checklist (cf Chapter 4) which gave her a general idea as to each individual's preferred way of working. From the answers collated, the tutor deduced that by and large, all six students needed to develop an 'integrated learning styles approach' to learning – that is to say, a range of strategies to enable them to view the situation from different angles, to recognise problems, to investigate, to sense opportunities. If students were given a task, the tendency was to proceed with the task without any prior reflection or analysis of what was required in the task. They had developed a trial-and-error style which meant that they set themselves objectives in terms of 'learning products', i.e. a written piece of work produced at home as soon as possible, and handed in for marking. They were more interested in action and results than in evaluating the task and selecting from alternative ways of working on the task.

At this point, it became crucial for the tutor to develop teaching strategies which would address the above issues. The tutor had to overcome resistance from the students in this exercise, who saw all their 'learning problems' as emanating from inadequate English. The tutor addressed the issues in the following ways:

Exercise

1   The students were asked to outline recent domestic or personal situations/ problems which they had needed to solve. They were asked to deconstruct the situation into various stages and asked how they had arrived at a solution, if at all. The students described the alternative solutions and talked about comparing and contrasting advantages and disadvantages. At each stage of the process, it was made clear to the students where they had used *analytical, reflective, evaluative* abilities. It was pointed out they had defined the problem, had established criteria for action, had viewed the situation from different angles, had listened to other's opinions, had set objectives, made decisions and focused efforts to achieve results. Students and tutor used a checklist which enabled the students to see the range of abilities and learning strategies they used in a problem-solving situation. They needed to grasp also the fact that they were operating with these skills and abilities in everyday life with adequate English.

2   They were then asked to focus their attentions on an assignment which did not necessarily involve group work and to carry it out in the workshop. The assignment involved a focus on 'Play Materials' – in particular an examination of books with racist or sexist bias, in terms of developing good practice in equal opportunities. Part of the assignment involved designing a book for children. In order to carry out the assignment they were asked individually to produce an action plan which outlined stage by stage how they would undertake the assignment. Having done this, they came together as a group and brainstormed the ideas into a list. Beside each stage, the tutor prompted the students to identify the learning strategies they were using as in the previous exercise, e.g. 'go to library to find children's books' – investigates, open to experience; 'ask other members of group their opinions' – compares alternatives.

3   The students were then asked to evaluate their experience of the exercises – and to reflect on the following questions individually:

A   Description   What were you asked to do?
                          What did you do?
                          What did you think/feel at that point?

B   Evaluation   What was good/bad about doing that?
                          Were the exercises easy/difficult for you?
                          Which exercise did you find easier/more difficult to do?
                          Why?

C   Analysis   Was it like any experience you have had before?
                          How was it different from the learning/studying you usually do?
                          If you found it difficult/easy, why do you think that was so?

D   Conclusion   What else could you have done if you were faced with that situation again?

Finally, they were asked to get back into a group and to discuss their answers. Some of the comments which were put forward were as follows:

> It was difficult for me.

> Usually, I write my answers – now I had to think about other things not just the answer.

> I realised that when I study its the same as in my life, when there is problem I must solve.

> I know I do many things in my life for solving problems – the same I can do in my study.

> I get information, talk to people, make a plan, change my mind, try out new things – this I can do in my study.

> It was interesting and useful, I find out things about myself and my college work.

> It's very difficult for me changing the way I study. I like to work on my own at home.

> I like the way I used to study but I now want to learn different ways. It is different in this country to the way I learnt to study in my country.

The tutor made the link between the approaches the students used towards problem-solving in their personal lives and the approaches towards learning. For further reinforcement and once again, as part of a modelling process, the tutor talked to the students about how she 'planned a lesson' – she talked through the various stages and once again, highlighted the experiential learning points, the various ways of 'planning a lesson' which illustrated different approaches to learning.

Other areas which the tutor outlined were:

1 Students could learn more from tackling problems themselves than from subject 'input' from the tutor, i.e. experimenting in the work placement, trying out new ways of working and recording what works and what does not and why.
2 Students could learn more by becoming more autonomous, less dependent and more interdependent with other members of the group.
3 Students should develop a more active approach to their learning and move away from an initial focus on particular experience to a focus on general principles. They need to be able to conclude certain generalisations and concepts as a result of specific local experiences.
4 Students need to be able to reflect on their own and their group's learning process and to be constructively critical of one another.

5 Students needed to be involved in setting their own goals and to be involved in negotiation for planning and evaluating the course.

Developing monitoring skills

In terms of their work placement experience, the students needed to develop 'active listening skills', good communication skills and an ability to reflect on theirs and others' teaching/caring practice. The tutor put forward a model of continual monitoring as a cyclical process involving the four stages of planning, action, observation and reflection for their own teaching/caring activities. The model is illustrated as Figure 5.1.

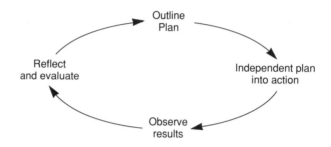

Figure 5.1 A four-stage model of continual monitoring

Once again, the model was illustrated graphically in the college creche with the tutor and the students observing a care assistant and commenting on the activities, behaviour and learning processes of the children. The students needed then to reflect individually on the experience and to analyse how it could have been improved upon – what was successful and what was not. The students were also asked to observe the tutor teaching the advanced oral skills class and to reflect, analyse and evaluate the experience with feedback to the tutor.

The idea was to use the cyclical model which the students would be incorporating into their own work placement experience and to demonstrate to the students how the same model could be used for observation of others. The variation is shown in Figure 5.2.

The students found both experiences immensely useful but very difficult. The difficult part each time was the 'reflection'. The tendency was for the students to accomplish 1, 2 and then 4, but to miss out 3 as they felt that the reflection part was built into 4. Consequently, the analysis was partial and covered parts of the caring/teaching activities. The same would happen in their work placement as was evident from the diary, or learning log.

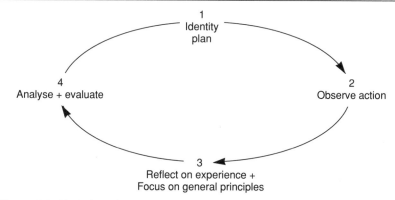

Figure 5.2 Variation of the four-stage model for observation of others

Developing strategies for active listening and reflection skills

Exercise

This was accomplished at the beginning of each session in the workshop. A student was asked to talk about an experience or an activity in which she had been involved in her workplace. The other members of the group needed to listen without interruption,and without giving any obvious feedback. At the end of the 'talk' the students were given one minute timed silence for reflection; all students were asked to reflect in their minds the salient points of the narration. At the end of the minute and not before, they were asked to write down the salient points and then to recount the points to the student who needed to agree or disagree as to veracity. As a group, the next stage was for the student to talk through an evaluation and to say where the activity or experience could have been improved. Other students could then add their own suggestions and advice at this stage after the student had analysed her own experience.

This exercise was a crucial one for these students because they were unable or unwilling to hold a structured discussion, so that every member of the group would be able to speak. Second, there was a tendency for members of the group to speak across, speak over, interrupt another member of the group or to make value judgements about someone else's experience. Members of the group would 'switch off' instead of listening when other members spoke, because their experience was not perceived as being as relevant as the teacher 'input'. This exercise helped students focus on 'active listening skills'.

Finally, this exercise deliberately imposed a structured teacher-led model which students could respond to more easily. At this stage, the students were not comfortable with initiating independent or group learning strategies. If the tutor left the group in the midst of this activity, it would break down, i.e. the students would revert back to anecdote swapping and general chit-chat. They were happy to undertake the exercise as long as the tutor was present to maintain the 'discipline'. By the end of the year, the students were able to undertake the exercise independently much more easily – without the tutor's continual presence. They were encouraged to try the exercise outside the workshop contact time as part of a peer support group activity.

Conclusions

The students were assessed summatively at the end of the course on the basis of the evidence they had accumulated in their learner profile for both language and occupational competence. They were also required to undergo a pre-entry aptitude assessment along with other candidates desiring entry on the City and Guilds 324.1 (cf Appendix 5.6).

The tutor, at all times, sought to build upon the strengths of the group in order to encourage more autonomous and active ways of working. The strengths of the group were as follows:

1 There was an emphasis on mutual trust, respect and helpfulness.
2 The members of the group were able to share ideas and feelings in the group.
3 They met as a peer group outside the college and were mutually supportive of one another.

All the students were very committed, hard working and conscientious. They took great pride in their work and praised each other's work. They spent a fair deal of time examining each other's work with comments as to whether 'this was the right answer', or 'did the teacher want the work written like this or like that'. It was the responsibility of the tutor to guide the students towards the realisation that a 'right answer' as such did not exist but to encourage the students, nevertheless, to be constructively critical and to carry on being mutually supportive of one another. As the year progressed, they succeeded in developing a certain degree of learner autonomy with regard to learning styles.

Focus on experiential learning theory

In terms of experiential learning theory, the effectiveness of this method was in part due to working with the group on account of:

• students identifying their own learning needs by reviewing their work experience and assignments as individuals and as members of a group;
• the definition of problems in terms of situations and experiences rather than in a more abstract way;

- the use of group methods which involved students actively;
- the use of group methods which provided students with substitute experiences of the problems being addressed;
- the use of group methods which took students around the experiential learning cycle, from problem definitions through experiences, reflection and analysis to action plans;
- the development of the awareness of learning strategies by using individual's personal and prior learning experience and linking into their learning experiences as a group; and
- moving towards a general awareness of the progress the students had made individually and as a group in their language and communication skills development, once again, through the use of group methods – with substitute experiences and through the experiential learning cycle.

Focus on language development and communication skills

The tutor identified the following areas as crucial for development:

1 Access skills:
   - for sources of clarification;
   - for the identification and use of sources of information, advice and redress; and
   - for the understanding of information, ideas and feelings expressed in oral, written, tabular and graphic forms.
2 Transfer skills:
   - for the transfer and expression of information, ideas and feelings from one mode, person or function to another, expressed in oral, written, tabular and graphic forms; and
   - for the selection and organisation of information, ideas and feelings for a particular purpose.
3 Discourse skills:
   - for the culturally appropriate sequencing and layout of ideas, feelings and information, expressed in oral, written, tabular and graphic forms.
4 Interpersonal skills:
   - for the development of 'culturally' appropriate personal, interpersonal and political skills;
   - for the generalisation of information, skills and concepts acquired in one context for use in another; and
   - for the development of 'active listening' strategies and appropriate 'culturally determined' communication skills.

As far as possible, the tutor's teaching strategy involved integrating the language and communications skills into the overall learning process of the vocational subject. The following methods were used as there was considerable overlap in the two areas:

- role-play/simulation for confidence and fluency;
- collation of information and transfer to different contexts, i.e. tabular, oral, written and graphic;
- video/audio recordings of students leading to discourse analysis for monitoring and screening of appropriacy of context, grammatical correctness, accuracy and fluency, and for the development of active listening skills;
- focus on developing autonomous learner strategies through peer group support, assignment-based learning, student responsibility for record keeping, development of learning resources by students, problem-solving activities, tasks for developing learner initiative and working in groups.

The students were encouraged to keep a portfolio of their learning both in the area of language inside and outside the classroom and in the area of the assignments for the CGLI 324.1. They were encouraged to keep a learning log, which was also used as a record of their achievements. The record-keeping was designed to encourage the students to reflect on and evaluate their strengths and weaknesses in their learning and in the products of the learning, i.e. the tasks and assignments. Informally, peer group appraisal took place but was not recorded on the individual student's record sheets. However, formalising the process of giving and receiving constructive criticism as part of a learner's personal assertive behaviour would be a recommendation. This could add to the holistic profile of the learner.

It was stressed to all the students from the outset that the most important learning opportunities would take place, not on the course, but in their work placements, and that the course was designed to help them to make the best use of this opportunity by:

- supporting risk-taking and experimentation, including creating a supportive climate for learning;
- offering new ways of learning and new methods to try out in their work placements;
- helping them to share experiences and make sense of them as individuals and as a group;
- encouraging them to develop a portfolio of evidence which could be used to demonstrate occupational competence in certain areas of childcare;
- encouraging them to use learning logs to record their reflections on their work-based activities and experiences and on their language and communication skills development.

CONCLUSION

The specific aim of this pilot scheme was to prepare the students to undertake a caring course, be it CGLI 324.1 or NNEB Nursery Nurses. What emerged from the pilot was the students' ability to harness their overall potential and their prior and current experience in 'caring' at work and in their roles as 'carers' in the home.

The pilot was a testimony to the way learners can – given the right learning environment, adequate support and a structured framework for the recognition of their abilities and experience – demonstrate their potential in a specific vocational area. Moreover, the barriers normally faced by bilingual candidates concerning entry to courses of study in colleges of FE are in three main areas:

- language;
- non-recognition by college staff of prior experience, knowledge and overseas qualifications as relevant; and
- inability of candidates to adapt flexible learning styles as appropriate, especially for systematic reflection on past experience.

These were demonstrably addressed in the course of the pilot study.

APPENDIX 5.1

Case Study (Materials used with Students)

C & G 324.1/ Foundation O/L   **Name:**

                                                   Date:

PLAY & PLAY MATERIALS   **Competences: 1, 2, 4, 10, 12, 13**

"The Individual and the Group"

Books: Task 8 Integrated Assignment

'Promoting Equal Opportunities for Young Children'

*   *Choose a book for a child aged 0–7 years*

*   Write a little description about the story

*   What is the age group? Do you think it can be used with a different age group in a different way?

*   Look at the illustrations. Are there any stereotypes? Would the children like the illustrations? What do you think?

*   Would children enjoy the story?

*   What do you think the language is like? Easy, difficult, just right. Do you have any ideas for improvements?

*   Any other comments?

*   *Design and make a book for a child aged 9–10 months and one for a child aged 2–3 years (the book mav be bi-lingual)*

*   Use it with a child and evaluate the child's response

APPENDIX 5.2

Choosing a Toy

(2) I chose this toy because it is _____

I found this toy _____

In my opinion this toy is _____

In terms of major Motor Skills this toy will help develop

In terms of fine Motor Skills this toy will help develop

The child also benefits from using this toy by/through development of his/her emotional and social character.

He/she will play with this toy through discovery play / physical imaginative/ creative play / pretend play / manipulative play

This toy will help a child to play with other children / will give a child a stimulating environment to play in / will allow children to work out their stress / aggression / will keep a child occupied for a long time / will help a child develop concentration/co-ordination.

(3) Yes, this toy is good value because it will last a long time, it is durable, affordable, washable and can be used with other siblings in different ways.

(A) Choosing a Toy Play + Play Materials

(1) Choose a suitable toy for a child aged 2 years. Stick the picture here

(2) Why did you choose this toy? What skills, abilities and emotional development and physical development will this toy develop?

(3) Is this toy value for money? Why?

(B) Choosing a Toy + Play Materials

(1) Choose a toy which is *not* suitable for a child under 3 years/under 2 years/under 2½ years. Stick the picture here

(2) Why did you choose this toy? In what ways is this toy unsuitable? Does it present any dangers to a child under 3 years?

(3) Could this toy be used with a child under 3 years with adult supervision? In what ways?

APPENDIX 5.3

Name

Date:

PLAY & PLAY MATERIALS: Competences:

BOOKS   1, 2, 10, 12, 13, 3, 4

INTEGRATED ASSIGNMENT: TASK 8/ TASK 3

TITLE: The Individual and the Group

PURPOSE: To examine your contribution to meeting the whole needs of the child

"Promoting Equal Opportunities for Young Children"

• Identify equipment and material with which you can develop equal opportunities through play:

    (a)   Evaluate the book you have designed with the checklist and note down a child's response

    (b)   Look through some children's books and report on 2 examples of bias in these books

    (c)   Look through some children's books and report on 2 examples which promote equal opportunities

• At work, select an activity that you can organise, carry out and evaluate with 2 or more children. In your written account, include the following:

    (i)   Why did you choose this activity? What is its purpose?
    (ii)   How will you plan it?
    (iii)   What equipment / materials/ castings will you need?
    (iv)   How long will the activity take?
    (v)   Evaluate the activity in terms of its usefulness to
        – the group of children
        – individuals within the group
        – observe differences and similarities in behaviour of boys and girls, eg language, choice of toys.

• If you were going to organise the same activity again, what would you do in the same way and what differently?

APPENDIX 5.4

DIARY: Work Experience	NAME: Radha	DATE: 20.9.92
WHAT I DID	WHAT I OBSERVED	SKILLS I USED
I left my house 9 am. 9 to 12 I left the children in their classroom. Children made a lighthouse. Teacher explained it to me and I told the children how to make it. I helped other children too. I helped three children go to the toilet when the children lined up for their dinner. I helped them to take their dinner to the table. 1 to 4 o'clock. All children made a lighthouse. They enjoyed making it. I supervised the children, while teacher told the story about lighthouse. I helped a child to put on his coat. I helped strap two wheelchairs.	I saw children make a lighthouse. After that children to make it. The teacher told them a story about the lighthouse. The children were feeling tired. Then the teacher said to them 'now you have a rest. You can play any game'. Then the children started playing the game of their choice.	1) I used child care skills and was responsive to individual children. 2) I observed and responded effectively to different situations. 3) I applied safe working practices in terms of health and safety. I made sure children did not throw paint at one another and washed their hands and cleared away afterwards. 4) Anticipated and responded appropriately to children's needs while making the lighthouse and helped them to get ready. 5) I used listening skills with children in responding to their needs. 6) Children felt at ease with me and trusted me.
WHAT I COULD DO DIFFERENTLY DIFFERENT STRATEGIES		
One day one child asked me for a tissue. Then I gave to her. Teacher was near me. Then she asked the child, 'did you say Please?'. She said 'No'. The teacher said to her 'you give tissue back to Radha and you say "Please"'. And she again asked me 'Can I have a tissue Please?' After that the teacher said to me 'children should say please and thank you. If they do not, you remind them.'		
WHAT I COULD DO DIFFERENTLY DIFFERENT STRATEGIES		
Now I can begin to understand the needs of the children. One day a child said to me: 'Could you help me colour this picture?' Then I helped him. The teacher asked me 'did you help?' I said 'yes I did'. Then she said 'He can help himself. You just tell him how to do it. Only one or two children can't do it for themselves, they need help.'		

APPENDIX 5.5: MAPPING OF THE ASSESSMENT OPPORTUNITIES

List of competences with particular reference to occupational competences *The student has shown ability to:*	MANAGING AND DEVELOPING SELF	WORKING WITH AND RELATING TO OTHERS	COMMUNICATING	MANAGING TASKS AND SOLVING PROBLEMS	APPLYING NUMERACY	APPLYING TECHNOLOGY	APPLYING DESIGN AND CREATIVITY
1 Plan, organise and complete the tasks and activities in the assignment as agreed with the tutor/work-based supervisor	a) Manage own roles and responsibilities b) Manage own time in achieving objectives c) Transfer skills gained to new and changing situations and contexts	a) Treat others' values, beliefs and opinions with respect	a) Receive and respond to a variety of information a) Present information in a variety of visual forms b) Communicate in writing c) Participate in oral and non-verbal communication				
2 Find and use relevant information from a range of resources				Use information sources			
3 Observe accurately and sensitively. Respond effectively to different situations.				a) Deal with a combination of routine and non-routine tasks b) Identify and solve routine and non-routine problems			
4 Interpret and evaluate work tasks and client situations in the context of the establishment in which they are employed				a) Deal with a combination of routine and non-routine tasks b) Identify and solve routine and non-routine problems			
5 Work effectively with children understanding their own role and that of their colleagues		a) Treat others' values, beliefs and opinions with respect b) Relate to and interact effectively with individuals and groups c) Work effectively as a member of a team					

APPENDIX 5.5 cont.

List of competences with particular reference to occupational competences *The student has shown ability to:*	MANAGING AND DEVELOPING SELF	WORKING WITH AND RELATING TO OTHERS	COMMUNICATING	MANAGING TASKS AND SOLVING PROBLEMS	APPLYING NUMERACY	APPLYING TECHNOLOGY	APPLYING DESIGN AND CREATIVITY
6 Anticipate and respond appropriately to children's needs in a range of work tasks undertaken	Manage own roles & responsibilities	a) Treat others' values, beliefs and opinions with respect b) Relate to and interact effectively with individuals and groups					
7 Communicate verbally with children, colleagues and others in handling information and in giving positive support			a) Receive and respond to a variety of information b) Participate in oral and non-verbal communication				
8 Interpret and respond appropriately to non-verbal signals from children, colleagues and others			a) Participate in oral and non-verbal communication				
9 Co-operate with others demonstrating empathy, initiative, good humour, self-awareness		a) Work effectively as a member of a team		a) Negotiate and solve problems			
10 Use initiative and imagination to develop ideas and good care practice							a) Apply a range of skills and techniques to develop a variety of ideas in the creation of new/ modified products, services or situations b) Use a range of thought processes
11 Apply safe working practices in terms of Health & Safety				a) Deal with a combination of routine and non-routine tasks b) Identify and solve routine and non-routine problems			
12 Select appropriate equipment and use efficiently in client and other work situations					Apply numerical skills and techniques		

APPENDIX 5.6

Assessment GCLI 324.1 (Caring)

1) SIMULATION / QUESTION ORAL SKILLS

The nursery staff say that my child is not allowed to take drinks or crisps to school or nursery. These are the reasons I have been given. Which ones do you think are right? Roleplay a situation between a member of staff and a parent.

2) EQUAL OPPORTUNITIES: CHILDREN'S BOOKS (Oral exercise)

To put Equal Opportunities into practice, we need to show positive images of people from different cultures and races, who speak different languages, men and women, and people with disabilities and learning needs, for example we would ask all children, not just boys, if they wished to play football. Look at the books and decide which is the best book in terms of Equal Opportunities and explain why. (Applicants work in pairs and feed back to group)

3) PRACTICAL ASPECTS OF CHILDCARE: PLAY (Written exercise)

Look at these activities and toys and consider how could you keep two young children occupied/ happy one aged 2 years and the other aged 4, inside your home on a wet and rainy afternoon? (Applicants may discuss in pairs and then are given time to write down ideas individually in full sentences, not note form)

All the above exercises focus on assessment of candidates' **access** and **transfer** skills, **problem solving** skills, ability to work individually and in groups, and general communication skills

Assessment of Prior Experience in relation to GCLI 324.1 (Caring)

Name:		Candidate demonstrated the ability to:		
1) Reflect on experience	2) Demonstrate initiative	3) Active listening skills	4) Assess the appropriacy and relevance of information and extract from source	5) Transfer information to appropriate context

6) Ability to work in pairs and in teams	7) Record ideas fluently	8) Evaluate experience	9) Use language fluently/accurately and in appropriate context

Candidates are assessed according to 'Linguistic Profile' on a scale of 1 to 4

Chapter 6

APL induction module

'LEARNING TO LEARN' SKILLS FOR BILINGUAL LEARNERS

A detailed focus on teaching and learning methodology within the assessment process and incorporated in the APL induction module will be recommended as an integral part of the APL system, as there will be an examination of how all these processes can work towards the potential success or failure of the bilingual student's learning targets. Consequently, inducting learners into more effective learning strategies includes the following:

- using problem-based learning contexts where problems are 'integrated' rather than broken into discrete artificial elements;
- inductive rather than deductive processes, e.g. examples followed by rules (theory);
- encouraging self-directed learning and self-reflection on learning styles;
- using a wide range of contexts in which strategies skills are acquired and practised.

Inherent within the whole process is an emphasis on the overarching role of the GA and that of the APL adviser who would both need to be sensitive enough to create a learning environment which allows the candidate potential to demonstrate his/her prior experience, knowledge and skills in the most holistic sense.

The notion has been put forward in many forums that a distinction needs to be made between assessing prior learning for entry to a course and assessing for exemption from part of a course. For entry, the possession of a sufficient background and adequate learning skills may be the focus; for exemption to parts of the course, assessment is more likely to focus on the possession of competence in one or more areas.

The content of such an APL module must originate from a need to increase a learner's awareness of different learning styles linked into the types of learning and outcomes of learning which a learner will encounter in any culturally based system of education. Undertaking an assessment of prior learning involves undertaking an assessment of prior learning styles so as to confer ownership of the learning process onto the learner. The 'outcome' of this module would be a value-added one and would enable the learner to proceed with increased confidence into the chosen area of study, thus enhancing his/her chances of future success.

The four aims of the module are:

1 to enable learners to develop a portfolio; to give learners opportunities to gather appropriate evidence for entry to a course and/or exemption from units on a course; to make the link between their work experience and heuristics;
2 to allow learners opportunities to gain performance evidence from current practice such as workplace observation, testimonials, simulations, assignments etc;
3 to induct learners into experiential learning strategies for working in groups and in the workplace; and
4 to develop learners' communications skills and 'core' skills, within the workplace and in the vocational area of study.

It is envisaged that the module would be offered to learners' post-guidance advocate stage and pre-APL adviser stage. Learners need to have had initial guidance and counselling in the areas they wish to develop in terms of their prior learning, experience and achievements as well as an outline of their linguistic profile. They would then be in a position to benefit from a module such as the one proposed here. A 'typical' bilingual learner would use the module as a bridging framework to enhance his/her learning skills, build up a portfolio with evidence, develop self-confidence within peer groups, consolidate his/her communications skills, and develop an awareness of the assessment procedure both in college and in the workplace.

More specifically, learners would be inducted into the following areas:

1 awareness-raising of the types of learning methods and teaching methods experienced by learners, including their likes and dislikes and reasons why; and
2 types of assessment processes which learners will meet in the courses of study and the learning methodologies associated with them.

The three stages of assessment are:

1 initial/diagnostic
2 formative
3 summative

Included in this area would be a practical and experiential exploration of different ways of working with built-in self-evaluation and assessment (e.g. peer group assessment):

1 An exploration of assertive and non-assertive styles of learning within a framework of the experiential learning cycle (cf Learner strategies, Appendix 6.1).
2 Awareness of 'bilingual' methods of study and how learners can use their languages positively by developing and experimenting with learner strategies (Bilingual ways of working, Appendix 6.2).
3 Awareness of 'comfort learning circles' and how learners are able to extend or diminish their individualised 'comfort learning circles' through risk-taking and experimentation.

COMFORT LEARNING CIRCLES

The concept of the *'comfort learning circle'*, which I have developed, focuses exclusively on learning strategies (see Figure 6.1).

A = Learner's language and self-confidence

B = Learner's vocational academic know-how – underpinning knowledge

C = Task/role/skills practical application in the workplace

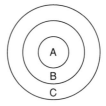

Figure 6.1 Concentric 'comfort learning': the ripple effect

As the learner becomes more confident and is prepared to take more risks, he/she will expand the 'comfort circle' of his/her learning strategies. As he/she receives positive feedback and/or positive outcomes in learning, the 'comfort circle' will gradually get bigger and feel more 'comfortable' and the self-confidence will increase, thus resulting in more risk-taking and outward increase in the circle. However, the flip side is that the circle can retreat if the learner receives negative feedback from peers, tutor, the 'real world' or 'learner outcomes'. This model presupposes a state of constant flux with the learner experimenting, risk-taking and increasing or decreasing in confidence during these stages.

In the context of the bilingual learner, my contention would be that he/she has three comfort learning circles which are interdependent in terms of the interaction of learning. For instance, Comfort Circle A would be for language development and Comfort Circle B for the development of a learner's vocational and academic competence, and Comfort Circle C for the practical application and development of skills in the workplace.

The learning strategies, as demonstrated previously, may or may not, be mutually exclusive to the three areas. The learning strategies that a student may use or be encouraged to use in one area may eventually be transferred and used very effectively in the other areas as part of a 'ripple effect' process. For instance, as confidence increases in Comfort Circle A, it has a ripple effect on B and increases risk-taking in Comfort Circle B, which in turn creates greater access to areas of knowledge and this can only have an enhancing effect on skills gained in the workplace, Comfort Circle C. The areas of competence defined within the circles are not fixed or static but interchangeable. Arguably, developing confidence in language leads to improved performance in the areas of underpinning knowledge and occupational skills. Nevertheless, it may well be that opportunities to demonstrate prior underpinning knowledge or occupational skills in the classroom or workplace have a beneficial knock-on effect on a student's acquisition of language. Ultimately, it is the area in which the student feels that he/she is able to experiment with and to consolidate learner strategies most successfully which would lead to the greatest progress and desired ripple effect in the other two areas.

The model of the 'comfort learning circle' needs to be explained to students through the 'learning skills' induction module via video/audio recordings, diaries, peer group observation and so on, so that they may learn from their own and their peers' practical examples the phases of experiential learning. Students may be asked to focus on learning strategies for problem-solving, action planning, structured discussion and role-play and to evaluate their learning over a course of time.

PEER GROUP LEARNING/OPEN LEARNING

A large part of the success of the case study lay with the students' group solidarity. A recommendation to learners as part of the induction module would be the formation of *peer groups* and/or supplementary instructors which would meet on a regular basis in an Open Learning workshop. The aims of the group would be to:

- offer mutual support and constructive criticism to all members of the group;
- encourage consolidation of autonomous learner strategies and ways of working as part of a group;
- monitor mutual progress of individuals within the group in terms of language and literacy;
- help individuals within the group identify and accomplish learning goals;
- offer practical help, e.g. role-plays, listening to review and reflection of experience;

- form a link with a tutor in the workshop for more directive guidance and advice; and
- offer mutual help, guidance, swapping of tips on learner strategies, record-keeping and so on.

The vast majority of learners would probably feel most comfortable forming peer groups with colleagues studying for similar vocational/ academic areas. However, some learners may gain other benefits by forming peer groups with students who share their languages and culture. Once again, one of the major strengths of this group was the homogeneous nature of the background of the students. Although the tutor shared the language of the students, the greater part of the learning process was carried out in English. The students undertook social discourse with one another in their mother tongue independent of the tutor. This was a major contributory factor in building up the mutual trust, commitment and supportive nature of the group.

The case study was designed on an Open Learning basis but the learners did not have the necessary learner strategies in order to benefit from it initially, and consequently insisted on a teacher-centred learning approach. An initial introduction in a classroom with a larger group of learners, for greater cost-effectiveness would induct learners into new ways of working. They could then progress to an Open Learning situation where they could benefit from Open Learning packages on language and communication skills learning strategies and self assessment. There needs to be a heavy emphasis on the development of the ACCESS and TRANSFER skills as outlined previously and a focus on computer assisted learning packages as well.

Once the learners are in an Open Learning situation, they should benefit from individual tutorials and/or group tutorials, to enable them to undertake the following:

- formulating individual development plans;
- formulating action plans for tasks/assignments/activities in the work-place;
- monitoring their learning;
- evaluating progress/setbacks/areas of improvement;
- assessing evidence for the portfolio from outside the classroom and the work placement;
- compiling the portfolios and evidence; and
- monitoring of peer group activities.

A previous chapter focused on the use of task assignment for assessment of a candidate's *language and core skills*. The following assignment is used as an example for assessing the *learning skills* of a candidate and is adapted from *Case Studies and Projects in Communication* (Neil McKeown 1990).

Assignment F (Document 7) (AEB specimen case study)

You have decided to support your local school which is mounting a local campaign for the improvement of facilities for games and general leisure activities in your area. You have been given ten photographs by the secretary of the school's photographic society and asked to prepare a variety of drafts using the photographs to support your writing.

During the assignment and especially at the initial planning stage of deciding how best to tackle the assignment, students can be given a checklist which outlines various options, ways of working and skills which students may use or need during this stage. The student needs to self-assess and tick the checklist for him/herself.

The ways of working and the learning skills would be equivalent to the four stages of the experiential learning cycle.

Learning skills checklist

1 I started working on the assignment straight away.
2 I checked all the vocabulary and grammar I didn't know.
3 I used a dictionary.
4 I asked my colleagues in the class for help.
5 I asked the teacher for help.
6 I made a list of the words I didn't know in a special vocabulary book.
7 I made a list of the words I didn't know on a piece of paper.
8 I checked with the teacher that I knew what I had to do for the assignment.
9 I checked with my colleagues in the class that I knew what I had to do for the assignment.
10 I waited for the teacher to ask me if I had understood and knew what to do.
11 I spent a lot of time reading through the assignment and making notes in my own language.
12 I spent sometime planning how I was going to do the assignment.
13 I wanted to start straight away and didn't want to waste time planning.
14 I wanted to start straight away after I had checked with the teacher that I knew what I was doing.
15 I didn't know what to do and how to start the work.

This checklist can be presented to the students after they have worked on the assignment for one–and–a half hours. It is presumed that this assignment would take anything up to 4–5 hours. At the end of the assignment, students can be presented with another checklist:

1 I enjoyed working on my own (I prefer working on my own).
2 I enjoyed and found it useful working in pairs or small groups because I could talk through ideas.
3 I found the structure of the assignment confusing because there were too many tasks.
4 I enjoyed doing the assignment because there was a structure to it which told me what to do.
5 I liked working on a variety of tasks and found it stimulating.
6 I felt the tasks were useful for me because they allowed me to develop writing skills such as writing a formal letter and verbal presentation skills, such as speaking to a group of people.
7 I enjoyed doing the presentation to a group of people.
8 I didn't enjoy doing the presentation because I didn't feel confident in my language skills.

9   I enjoyed this assignment because it was about real problems in society.
10 I enjoyed the opportunity to practise my presentation in front of my colleagues
    because it made me feel more confident afterwards.
11 I find the checklists useful because they make me think about what I was learn-
    ing and how I was learning.
12 I do not find the checklist useful because I cannot see what they have to do with
    the assignments.
13 I find the checklists distracted me from the assignments.
14 I find the checklists difficult to understand.
15 I wanted the teacher to talk to me about the work and how I should do it.
16 I wanted the teacher to talk to me about the checklists.

In Britain, criterion-referenced systems of assessment are relatively new and the appropriate learning strategies which enable learners to identify existing competence and to develop new competences need to be actively encouraged and built into a 'learning skills' module.

The area of work which is probably the most neglected in the classroom is the facilitation of learner strategies in the experiential learning cycle between the stages of 'the experience and review, reflection and analyses of the experience'. Developing the learner's abilities and skills in the following areas: active listening, keeping a diary, using video and audio recordings, peer appraisal, self-assessment, reflection checklists and questionnaires and structured discussions, all contribute to enabling learners to reflect on experiences they have had both in the classroom and in the workplace.

Facilitating independent learning and encouraging bilingual learners to take initiatives and to develop risk-taking strategies can be very difficult with individuals who have only experienced situations where they follow 'teacher instructions' in order to achieve 'results'. Bilingual learners need to be able to create independent and collaborative approaches to problem-solving and to be able to function effectively on the 'conceptualisation to the experience' part of the experiential leaning cycle, through formulating action planning and learning contracts.

As has been demonstrated in the case study, the group of learners on the Foundation/Open Learning programme leading to CGLI 324.1 tended to start off with detailed discussion both structured and unstructured in English and in their mother tongue. They were prepared to move onto 'riskier' methods of working together as their own confidence grew and they became more confident and trusting of each other. The predominant strengths which they gained, were most noticeable in the area of problem-solving and structured reflective discussion. At the beginning of the course, their discussion initially centred on their personal self-perceptions of their inadequacies in the area of their English language competence. The discussions became more structured and pertinent to 'problem-solving', including topics such as:

- how to set about doing a group assignment,
- sharing tips on where to get information, resources, etc., shared definitions of vocabulary and tasks,
- exchange of experiences in the work placement,
- a sense of shared purpose and so on as their confidence in their English language increased and they saw the tangible evidence of their successful learning outcomes. The students developed effective action planning skills by the end of the course.

PEDAGOGY AND ANDRAGOGY

The aims of the module, broadly speaking, should be to move from the rigid principles of 'pedagogy' to the principles of 'andragogy'. Many bilingual learners have only been instructed pedagogically. Pedagogy has been characterised by a belief that:

- there is always a 'right answer'
- rote memory is a good way to facilitate learning;
- the need for learning should be dictated by the teacher;
- the teacher should decide the content;
- students lack relevant experience and knowledge;
- the teacher is the source of wisdom; and
- the teacher evaluates the students.

Although these principles of learning may have been valid and successful when mature bilingual learners underwent their learning at schools as young people, the fact remains that, as adults, they are not coming to the classroom devoid of knowledge or tried and tested learning strategies. This philosophy of andragogy is characterised by a belief that:

- the student should accept the content of the programme based on evidence of need, not blind faith;
- students should be active rather than passive;
- all students have experience in the subject and, therefore, bring something with them to the training event;
- the student has individual needs that must be addressed;
- discussion and experimentation are sound ways of fostering learning; and
- the student should evaluate him or herself.

If it is accepted that the underlying principles of an APL process build upon the above principles of andragogy, then it is highly desirable, even essential, to develop a process of learning that mirrors this.

Communality of purpose of the classroom

The principles of pedagogy would lend themselves to the practice of assumption-making which in the case of bilingual learners is clearly unhelpful and non-constructive. For instance, evidence from FE colleges testifies that certain kinds of visual information (in particular the use of rough sketches), far from being a 'universal language', actually pre-suppose specific cultural awareness and may, therefore, place greater numbers of students at a disadvantage. Moreover, many bilingual students make the assumption that *accuracy* is the guiding principle in written English in the tasks, projects and assignments, and that answers need to be written in full and totally grammatically correct sentences in order to achieve a good grade. Very often, this is in marked contrast to the tutor's own emphasis on full information in a comprehensible form. The same may occur at an oral level where students sacrifice fluency for the sake of accuracy and do not engage in interactive discussion for fear of making grammatical errors, thus not engaging in risk-taking.

A similar problem occurs with instructions. The insecurities experienced by bilingual learners in relation to their own levels of competence in English manifest themselves in the comprehension of instructions. Very often, learners will not ask for explanation and clarification of instructions from the tutor, as to precisely what they have to do. First, the assumption is made by the tutor that the instructions are universally transparent; however, these are usually couched in idiomatic language and are therefore obscure, e.g. 'Working in pairs, see how many hazards you can spot'. Second, the learners are not prepared to take risks and explore meanings because they are not equipped with appropriate strategies. Teaching methodology, based on pedagogical principles, often militates against this.

In general, the principles of andragogy assist the learner and the teacher not to indulge in ritual assumption-making and encourage the learner to take risks, experiment and to become pro-active, by taking on ownership of his/her learning, thereby increasing his/her 'comfort learning circles'.

The framework for an APL module

A bridging framework in the specific context of NVQ and more importantly, in the general context of the assessment of prior learning and achievement, needs to equate the experience gained from work/life with the 'know-how', competences or heuristics underpinning this experience.

Even with self-access 'Expert' interactive computer programmes, the experience of tutors in colleges demonstrates that working with a learner as part of the APL process on developing the systematic reflection of past experience and learning and on the identification of significant and relevant learning and experiences, is a particularly lengthy process and one that is not cost-effective if done in isolation from the rest of the learning programme. Given the constraints imposed on the role of the APL adviser with relation to the induction of candidates into experiential learning strategies, it is essential to develop alternative systems which facilitate access to induction; i.e. an induction 'Learning to Learn' APL module.

One system of organising modules is along the lines of recruiting learners from different vocational areas. Another way would be to bolt on a module to separate vocational areas, so that a homogeneous group of learners who share the same vocational area are recruited directly on to the module. Both models have advantages and disadvantages which need to be assessed.

One of the main disadvantages of the learners recruited on to a module from various vocational areas is the organisation and monitoring of the different opportunities for learners to gain their performance evidence (in college and in the workplace). If learners are recruited on to modules which generally speaking, cover vocational areas with broad similarities, then opportunities for monitoring performance evidence within relevant contexts can be more tightly structured and organised. A disadvantage of this may be that recruitment of students on to different courses may vary and fluctuate so as to influence the cost effective viability of running an individual APL module which would be bolted on to the course.

The timing of the module may be organised along the lines of a duration of intensive 2–4–6 weeks depending on the needs of the learner and the module could run at specified times throughout the year for greater flexibility.

The factors influencing design would be as follows:

- cost-effectiveness of both models;
- modularisation of curricular vocational areas;
- availability of expertise on the tutoring staff;
- expertise of guidance advocate;
- expertise of APL adviser;
- availability of open learning facilities;
- availability of language and literacy 'communications skills' adviser;
- cost to the learner; and
- availability of training credits or vouchers for entry to the module.

The performance indicators of such a system would be:

- quality assessment/quality control;
- flexibility;
- cost-effectiveness; and
- value added.

In keeping with FEFC funding guidelines, the module could form part of the 'additional units' which attract extra funding for 'learning support'. Consequently, the module would span the entry and on-programme elements of funding.

Learners would be in a position to benefit from such a module in one of two ways as indicated in Figure 6.2, depending on the assessment made by the GA at point of entry. Appendix 6.3 proposes diagrammatically how the APL induction module would function. Appendix 6.4 illustrates how APL candidates would bring prior experience and skills in the form of demonstrable evidence to the 'APL' classroom as part of the module.

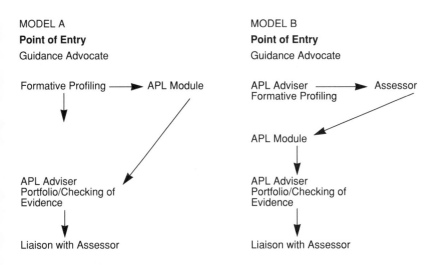

Figure 6.2 Two models of learner benefits using an APL induction model
Source: Jack Nansell, *The Assessment of Prior Learning and Achievement: The Role of Expert Systems*, FEU, 1990.

Jack Nansell (FEU 1990) has illustrated quite clearly the role of the assessment (see Table 6.1).

The example cited by Nansell to illustrate the point is that of an electrician who describes his/her know-how initially in terms of the range of equipment used/installed, and the degree of supervision or autonomy exercised. This is contrasted with the Performance Outcomes stipulated by the awarding bodies' formal assessments which would be likely to require evidence of such skills as ability to estimate voltage drop in particular cables, choose adequate fuses or determine trunking size for a given set of conditions.

Similarly, the students on the 'caring' pilot project did describe their know-how in terms of the different tasks/activities they performed in the

Table 6.1 The role of assessment

Informal context		Formal context		Prior Learning and Achievement
Work	Heuristics	Outcomes	Standards	Applicant seeks to demonstrate achievement: observation, tests, simulation, role-play, discussion, interview, computer-based interrogation, portfolio.
Life Experience (E)	Know-how Competences (D)	Formal assessments (O)	Performance criteria (C)	(A)

Source: Jack Nansell, *The Assessment of Prior Learning and Achievement: The Role of Expert Systems*, FEU, 1990.

workplace with the children, the degree of supervision or autonomy exercised in relation to other carers in the workplace, the types of play they initiated in relation to the needs of the children and the health and safety aspects observed. However, the performance outcomes associated with the City and Guilds formal assessment requires, for example, evidence of the ability to demonstrate in a formal context:

- Need for care: 'to identify the needs of individuals and groups through a study of human growth and development from birth to adulthood';
- Care practice:'types of play and activities and their value in physical, social, emotional and intellectual development, use of language and number concepts'; and
- Provision of care: '"Health and Safety at work"; "legal liabilities"; the consequences of failure to meet the physical, emotional, intellectual and social needs of individuals'.

Therefore, the transition process for the learner to equate experience with occupational competence is a protracted and demanding one and would need to be explored within the module in terms of the *learning strategies* required to undertake the process.

Not all vocational areas have a heavy reliance on the 'role' aspect of the occupational competence. A major requirement of many qualifications is knowledge, understanding, skills and tasks whereas the behavioural and interpersonal skills aspects are not of paramount importance in the successful undertaking of the work. If a comparison for example is made between the role of a 'carer' – creche/nursery assistant and that of an electrical installation technician, it would be clear that a great deal of emphasis is placed on the communication skills and interpersonal skills of the former in terms of occupational competence in the workplace, i.e. relating to children, staff, and parents, notwithstanding the technical 'common sense knowledge' relating to health and safety for children. Conversely, a technician wishing to gain an NVQ Level 2/3 would need to have a far broader knowledge base, skills and technical expertise, some of which would be crucial to areas of health and safety in terms of life and death, and relatively less in terms of interpersonal skills and broad communications skills.

The technician might be required to describe recommendations to a customer on the installation of more light fittings, with respect to the loading of the lighting circuits. A carer might need to explain to parents the importance of not bringing children to the nursery with snacks, sweets, etc. The communication skills inherent in the first example would necessarily involve explaining a technical process in 'accessible' non-jargon language. The second example would involve interpersonal skills such as greater sensitivity, tact and possibly dealing with a parent's anger/complaint. Nevertheless, both types of communication skills need 'finer tuning' in English discourse skills for bilingual learners, so that clarity, fluency and the correct sequencing of ideas minimise cross-cultural misunderstanding.

WORK-BASED ASSESSMENT: SOME ISSUES FOR THE MODULE

Work-based assessment in relation to bilingual learners will become more of a reality with the trend towards the up-skilling of the workforce, which will undoubtedly reveal gaps in the language and communication skills of workers who wish to study for qualifications or parts thereof or keep pace with new technology. Many workers will demonstrate a marked discrepancy between their occupational competence and their ability to demonstrate their underpinning knowledge.

On course work-based assessment generally raises many issues around the areas of:

- cost-effectiveness;
- practicability of carrying out assessment by college staff;
- the extent to which assessment would cover depth and breadth of competence, and would demonstrate a measure of the tasks under-taken by the students, as opposed to the competences they use;
- a move from externally assessed courses to more internal continuous assessment and moderation exemplifying the changeover from norm to criteria referencing for the assessment of competence.

In broader terms, at pre-entry to course assessment stage a number of issues on technical concerns need to be raised, such as the following:

1 It would be desirable to combine assessment of skills and knowledge and approaches to working, which are culturally and gender based, but

related to successful performance of a job. The adviser needs to focus on recording responses to deadlines, critical events, contingencies, etc., as well as recording the more routine aspects of performance which would be influenced by communication skills generally, and in particular language skills.

2 It would be desirable to base the performance criteria of the assessment procedure not only on outcomes, but also on the processes by which outcomes were achieved – for example, responses to clients/customers. Although statements of competence do not necessarily overtly deal with aspects of roles, but with occupational competence, in terms of tasks, it would be advantageous especially with bilingual learners to recognise at pre-entry stage, those interpersonal skills and abilities a bilingual learner may have developed in his/her own culture or language and has the potential to develop in English.

3 In general terms, a recognition at pre-entry stage of a candidate's aptitude in these spheres, documented in his/her portfolio, affects the delivery and development of broadly based competence, such that learners would eventually be seen to be fulfilling a variety of 'roles' as well as successfully completing vocational tasks.

Bias in the workplace assessment

It should be noted that the area of bias in the workplace needs to be addressed in the *module* if assessment of prior learning and experience is genuinely to implement issues of equal opportunities and true access for learners. Examples that emerged from the pilot project indicated that the criteria for the Practical Care Task Skills Assessment in the workplace implied potential cultural bias. The criteria was open to interpretation and as with any professional judgement could be eschewed in the way believed appropriate by the assessor/supervisor.

The following examples indicate possible cultural bias in interpretation:

The student needs to show sensitivity toward the child . . . in the following contexts; and the student needs to describe the context of the task which demonstrates these particular 'qualities':

showed empathy towards the child;

used humour, where appropriate, to develop positive responses and attitudes;

was reassuring, but not patronising;

showed respect for individual's privacy and dignity.

The assumption here is that there is a universal norm in caring for children and that 'empathy', 'humour' and the distinction between 'reassuring' and 'patronising' are universally dictated and not culturally informed. A student in one instance was perceived by the supervisor as 'patronising' a child and not reassuring him. She even perceived the student as unduly 'smothering' a child and not offering him 'respect for an individual's privacy and dignity'. This occurred during a play activity organised by the student who 'cuddled the child excessively', according to the supervisor, after he became distraught.

In this instance, the student's perception of the role of 'carer' may or may not coincide with that 'norm' – if there is one – suggested by examining boards, tutors and/or assessors. In the case of bilingual students a supervisor may judge the *appropriateness* of their social disposition and interpersonal skills in terms of an 'English' standard and may not recognise the cultural bias inherent therein.

Validity and Reliability of work-based assessment

Generally, the point to be made here is not that decentralised local college or work-based assessors cannot assess to an acceptably common standard; they can, but the process itself militates against objectivity because it is complex, incremental and above all judgemental. By being judgemental, it is prone to cultural bias. The actual process of judging whether someone has 'reached criterion' and can be described as able to do something, can be very problematic and open to wide interpretation. The performance observed – directly or in the form of 'artefacts' – is intrinsically variable. Therefore, a student operating in a workplace nursery, exhibiting 'reassuring behaviour' towards the children, by her own definition of the term, would not necessarily be judged by the supervisor in a positive way, if the norm of her behaviour did not approximate to the 'norm' as defined by the supervisor and perhaps as exhibited by the majority of students.

In relation to this, Alison Wolf (1993) puts forward the examples of the SATS (1991) in the new National Curriculum tests. The main point that is relevant here is the finding of major 'differences in the way in which (teachers) interpreted pupils' achievements in terms of the various levels' (Wolf 1993). Even though teachers received explicit instructions on interpretation of assessment criteria, this did not in itself preclude the inevitable probability of the assessment of behaviour, roles, skills and tasks of children not fitting mechanistically to either a written list criteria or an exemplar. What is worrying then in general is the degree of reliability built into criterion-referencing – that is to say, the degree to which different assessments of the same domain do not produce the same results. It follows from this that the implications of this are far reaching for bilingual learners, if assessors and supervisors are working from a standard English norm of behaviour, implicit within the operational 'roles' of the vocational area of work.

In her research, Alison Wolf outlines the practice of 'compensation' practised by assessors, particularly in the workplace. Assessors will judge a candidate's performance or outcome of learning against a performance criterion rather than at element level. This is carried out on a holistic basis with assessors allowing for certain mistakes and accepting less than 100 per cent accuracy on the basis of what they know or think they know about candidates. Therefore, in the case cited by Wolf on workplace research carried out for the MSG, on a standard task descriptor for invoice completion, trainees were judged competent even when they had omitted VAT numbers or had made mistakes when adding or allowing discounts. As Wolf makes the point that 'compensation' will be affected by an assessor's previous knowledge of a candidate and also by his/her preconceptions about what given performance 'really' demonstrates. If this is the reality of assessment, then the judgemental element of assessment as illustrated in the example of the 'care' students, can militate against candidates. In other situations 'overcompensation' can lead to the adoption of below par 'standards' of assessment for performance criteria, which in all cases would affect the issues of reliability.

On the issue of 'overcompensation' the following example illustrates what took place in an FE college with two bilingual learners who were following an NVQ Business Administration Level 1. In carrying out the work experience placement, the students very obviously were not able to demonstrate competence in specific elements relating to photocopying, collating and filing of written materials to the same level of competence as was being exhibited by two other bilingual learners and one monolingual learner. The students had to be asked to redo the tasks three times before they were acceptable. However, they were finally given 'the benefit of the doubt' on the basis that their standard of English did not allow them the flexibility to fully understand the instructions. Nevertheless, the assessor did express concern that she was genuinely puzzled as to the 'source of the problem' as their English was of a reasonable standard and much the same as the other two bilingual learners.

This example illustrates graphically the pitfalls of a system which does not address more careful and detailed specification of outcomes, taking into account 'behaviour' and 'roles'. All five students in question succeeded in obtaining their NVQ Business Administration Level 1 which sheds doubt on the 'reliability' of the criterion referenced assessment. How truly effective would the two bilingual students' real performance be in the workplace once they had secured jobs, in terms of their 'skills' and 'roles'? The students would leave the college with the same difficulties in delivering acceptable standards of work.

In other words, the question that needs to be argued is, how fair and valid is it to the student to lead him/her into believing that the 'standard' he/she has achieved in the workplace experience with a sympathetic assessor will be representative of the tolerance and good will of future employers?

In both the above example and the examples taken from the pilot project, it is important to emphasise that there is a fine dividing line between first, a *justified interpretation* from an assessor on the basis that holistically, a candidate can perform an occupational role in a work context satisfactorily and second, *overcompensation*, where candidates are bestowed assessments of their abilities which do not take into account very real inadequacies which would affect future roles in a work environment. Furthermore, there is a third factor of *unjustified prejudice and bias* which will affect especially assessments of bilingual candidates' behaviours in occupational roles, because these do not measure up to the cultural norm in operation. What is clear is that at this developmental stage of criterion-referenced assessment in NVQs, there is no foolproof way of monitoring individual assessors or centres for how accurately or how unambiguously assessments are applied or for that matter, how much or how little compensation is built into the system and, therefore, there is virtually no control over how much 'slippage' from standards is actually happening.

Avoiding bias in work-based assessment: recommendations for APL module

The issues that need to be identified for the APL induction 'module' in terms of work-based learning are as follows. In order that learners are adequately prepared for the workplace and can make best use of their current workplace experience for assessment purposes, they need to be aware of the separate distinctions between the development of skills, tasks (or activities) and roles in the workplace.

The NCVQ definition of competence relates to performance 'in a range of work-related activities'; it does not specifically include or exclude role competence. However, implicit within the methods of performance assessment will be a series of judgements which would identify the range of competence, which could be biased towards certain candidates. Procedures for checking validity and reliability in all areas of NVQ and in the assessment of prior learning and achievement have yet to be fully developed and monitored.

In this context, it would seem vital to induct learners into the performance of occupational roles which may or may not have a cultural bias. Learners need an awareness of what would be expected of them in a workplace in terms of their interpersonal skills and roles so that they may develop greater confidence and credibility. Once again, the GNVQ framework of 'core skills' could provide just such a vehicle for such an exploration and practice of skills and behaviours.

Learners need to be instructed in the following areas:

1 'norms' of behaviour inherent within occupational roles in the work-place, both explicit and implicit as part of the Awarding Body syllabus and assessment criteria;
2 interpersonal skills – culturally determined – as deployed in the work-place;
3 tutors' and assessors' expectations of the learner's occupational performance in the workplace; culturally specific expectations need to be clarified and compared with learner's prior expectations of the assessment process;
4 criterion-referenced assessment: guidelines on how it operates. Com-parisons with other systems of assessment including systems with which learners are more familiar from other countries, other educational systems; and
5 a range of 'learners' strategies' for use in the workplace to include instruc-tion of 'core skills' such as problem-solving, working independently, working in teams.

IMPLICATIONS FOR STAFF DEVELOPMENT

The CGLI APL adviser 7381/13 award within the framework of the TDLB standards (Training Development Lead Body) specifies the following in relation to a 'mature adult and a non-confident candidate'.

The following list is an extract from 'D36 Identify previously acquired competence: Performance Criteria':

(a) realistic expectations and career aspirations are encouraged
(b) target vocational qualifications identified as appropriate to candidates' current competences and future aspirations
(c) advice to candidate accurately identifies units which might reasonably be claimed on the basis of existing competence
(d) opportunities to use evidence from prior achievement are accurately analysed
(e) assessment plan agreed with candidate provides an effective mix of evidence from prior achievements and current assessment
(f) candidate motivation is encouraged throughout.

In relation to (c), (d) and (e) it is debatable how expedient this process will be, with a 'non-confident' learner – for the purposes of the award. 'Non-confident' may read as a bilingual learner or a non-assertive, diffident learner or a learner with communications skills difficulties. The students in the pilot project could well have been classified as 'non-confident' and 'mature' and certainly gave this initial impression to the course tutor. As evinced from the pilot, 'candidate motivation' and 'confidence building' resulted only after a substantive period of time and with structured input from the bilingual support tutor. They would probably have required protracted sessions which could prove to be too costly and could have acted as a disincentive to them to continue with the process. Conversely, many bilingual learners may have minimal difficulties with communication skills but are still categorised as 'non-confident', even though they would perceive themselves as 'self-confident'. Professional judgements, at the discretion of the APL adviser are made regarding the 'status of the candidate', without substantial guidelines, and may or may not be accurate.

The assessment of prior learning and achievement aims to fulfil a range of needs, from entry to a course to credit for units. The APL adviser is likely to be confronted by bilingual applicants who claim to have competences that are not easily related to a single unit, course or qualification.

It would appear a very daunting task for the APL adviser to undertake a long-term process of encouraging candidates' motivation throughout, given the above areas of difficulty, plus added problems around language and communications skills. This is a more appropriate role for the GA to undertake.

The following list is an extract from 'D363: Help candidate to prepare and present evidence for assessment':

b) guidance provided to candidate during portfolio preparation encourages the development of clear, structured evidence relevant to the units being claimed

d) opportunities are identified for candidate to demonstrate competence where evidence from prior achievements is not available.

For the purposes of gaining the APL adviser award, candidates are asked to demonstrate this performance criteria in relation to at least two applicants; a *special needs learner* and a *mature adult learner*. Once again, it becomes increasingly evident that the APL adviser will be faced with immense difficulties in trying to implement the correct effective guidance and in 'identifying opportunities' for the candidate to demonstrate competence, especially with candidates who do not visibly demonstrate any aptitude in assessing their own experience in terms of heuristic outcomes. Learners who are approaching the APL process with a very traditional notion of 'education' will need a strong emphasis on guidance and induction into experiential and andragogical ways of working. This needs to take place over a sustained period of time and needs to be seen as a separate process to that of the final assessment and accreditation of a candidate's prior experience and achievements.

In other words, the learner – and in particular, the bilingual learner – needs to have access to a separate process which would address his/her needs for guidance, motivation, and identification of competence in a supportive environment along with the learning strategies to enable self-assessment, review and reflection of experience to take place so that the APL process is effectively engaged and genuinely facilitated in a professional and cost effective manner.

RECOMMENDATIONS FOR STAFF DEVELOPMENT

In the training linked to the TDLB APL adviser/assessor awards, the guidelines for practitioners need to be much more clear and substantive so that the potential element of bias in assessment is diminished, leading to more valid and reliable assessment. This needs to be coupled with access for practitioners to staff development training in these specific areas:

- organisational reviews and workshops on assessment skills and techniques; helping practitioners analyse the components of particular skills with practices and feedback;
- development of mechanisms for the valid and reliable interpretation of the range of criteria used in assessment;
- awareness-raising of the potential forms of bias in assessment; allowing participants to gain personal experience of the issues surrounding the assessment process and to promote awareness of skills lacked or those that might be improved; and
- development work by the APL team on written materials for publicity and assessment should include contexts from other cultures so that there is heightened awareness of the validity of overseas qualifications and experience. The probability is that advisers may overlook overseas, ethnic and cultural sources and concentrate on current areas of experience.

CONCLUSION

The rationale for an APL induction module embedded as part of the curriculum entitlement is a strong one. Not least, because definitions of competence and measuring performance outcomes in vocational education are often narrowly based on performance to a standard which does not give overt recognition and credit for vital elements of achievement such as the development of learning skills, persistence, team work, problem-solving or the acquisition of bilingualism. Nevertheless, generalised outcomes of learning usually include the following which need to be acknowledged:

- subject-based outcomes, knowledge and comprehension, the ability to apply knowledge in different situations and the processing skills

acquired through the use and application of knowledge;
- personal outcomes, including language and interpersonal skills like teamwork and negotiation, and interpersonal skills like motivation, initiative and critical self-reflection.

Developing a package of learning in the form of a cost-effective module can potentially address the needs of bilingual learners in bridging the gap between 'experience' and 'heuristics'.

APPENDIX 6.1: LEARNER STRATEGIES (For the learner)

To encourage students to become assertive independent learners in distance learning, in competence-based learning situations, in open learning situations, vocational and academic learning situations

As a learner, you need to be responsible for your own learning. You need to develop the following skills/abilities.

1 'Active' Listening Skills
- How easy or how difficult is it for you to listen and concentrate on what the tutor is saying? ☐
- How easy or how difficult is it for you to listen and concentrate on what the other students are saying? ☐
- Can you usually select what is important when someone is talking to you? ☐

2 Note-taking Skills/Summary Skills
- Do you take down instructions when the teacher is speaking? ☐
  Do you make notes in your own language and then transfer them to English? ☐
- Do you select what is important to you and make a summary without the tutor telling you to? ☐
- Do you wait for the tutor to ask you to write down notes? ☐
- Do you wait for the tutor to draw your attention to an 'important' piece of work? ☐

3 Reference Skills
- Do you look up words in a dictionary? ☐
- Do you use a bilingual dictionary? ☐
- Can you find out information using maps, timetables, diagrams and so on? ☐
- Where would you go to find out information? Who would you ask? ☐

4 Assertive Skills
- Do you ask for information/explanation when you do not understand what a teacher or student is saying? ☐
- Do you find it difficult to interrupt when the tutor is speaking, to ask for an explanation? ☐
- Do you ask a student to give you help/explanation in your own language? ☐
- Do you ask a student to give you help/explanation in English? ☐
- Are you able to give constructive criticism to another student about his/her class work without upsetting him/her? ☐
- Are you able to receive constructive criticism from another student or the tutor without getting upset? ☐

5 Working in groups/pairs
- Can you work in a group? Do you find it easy or difficult to contribute in a group? ☐
- Can you work in a pair? Do you find it easy or difficult to contribute in a pair? ☐
- Do you find it easy/difficult to do a role-play? ☐
- Do you find it easy/difficult to do an individual verbal presentation in front of the class? Why do you find it difficult? ☐

6 Evaluation and Recording of Learning
- Can you evaluate your learning? ☐
- Do you need help from the tutor, from other students? ☐
- Can you record your own learning in the classroom? ☐
- Do you do the work set by the tutor? ☐
- Do you do 'extra' work to improve your language or knowledge of a particular area? If so, what? ☐

APPENDIX 6.2: WAYS OF USING BILINGUALISM IN THE APL PROCESS (For the tutor)

STRATEGIES USED BY TUTOR AND LEARNERS (Tick (√) box where appropriate)	CONTEXTS AND SITUATIONS						
	Publicity on APL process: written information, word of mouth	Counselling + Guidance	'APL' module – learning strategies – gathering of evidence 'opportunities'	Equivalency Building up of overseas portfolio qualifications'	'APL' Adviser – presentation of portfolio	Presentation of performance evidence	Presentation of supplementary evidence
Definite policy on using learner's first language							
T Simplification of materials/explanations Glossary of technical terms							
LR Using L1/L2 dictionaries							
LR Writing down notes in own script							
T Use of bilingual teachers, guidance advocates, APL advisers and APL assessors							
T Making use of bilingual information with homogeneous groups of LR							
T Encouraging interpretation by Learner							
T Using guidance advocate to explain process of APL system in L1 with information publicity on process written in L1							
LR Using L1 reference sources, e.g. library, local community groups, Citizens Advice Bureau, local facilities, e.g. hospital, schools etc.							
T Learning about Learner's culture and using knowledge to draw comparisons							
LR Checking comprehension with other learners of same L1. Group/pair work, discussion/role-play/confidence building/'active' listening exercises							
LR Equivalency of overseas qualifications (College/Community Centre)							

Abbreviations Key: L1 = Learner's first language   L2 = English T = Tutor   LR = Learner

APPENDIX 6.3: APL INDUCTION MODULE FOR BILINGUAL LEARNERS

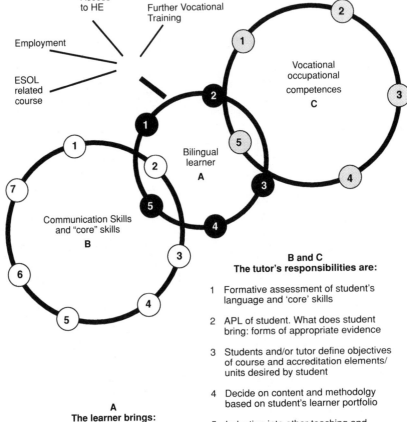

Access to HE

Further Vocational Training

Employment

ESOL related course

Vocational occupational competences
C

Bilingual learner
A

Communication Skills and "core" skills
B

A
The learner brings:

1 Knowledge

2 Skills

3 Experience

4 Qualifications

5 Teaching/learning methodology

B and C
The tutor's responsibilities are:

1 Formative assessment of student's language and 'core' skills

2 APL of student. What does student bring: forms of appropriate evidence

3 Students and/or tutor define objectives of course and accreditation elements/ units desired by student

4 Decide on content and methodolgy based on student's learner portfolio

5 Induction into other teaching and learning methodologies

6 Continuous assessment and evaluation

7 Negotiating assessment and evaluation evidence from prior achievements and contemporary assessment with assessor

8 Presenting evidence for Accreditation and evaluation

APPENDIX 6.4: MICRO-FOCUS ON RECOGNITION OF PRIOR EXPERIENCE, SKILLS AND KNOWLEDGE

Pro-forma of students	Prior experience, skills, knowledge	Skills to develop Topics and areas of interest to students	Evidence of prior learning brought by students to a classroom situation	Accredited course attended for language development in Britain	Common Learning Outcomes The student can demonstrate that he/she can:
Zairean French-speaking male	Bachelor in Science, Mathematics and Physics, Computer programming	• Describe processes • Talk about computer programming • Applications of computer	Results of program print out Describe/explain to class	City & Guilds 7360 Communication Skills WORDPOWER	• Communicate effectively • Use information technology appropriately and effectively • Solve problems
Zairean French-speaking female	Photography, journalism Professional photographer	• Talking about reporting • Describe process of photography • Write article on a current event in the world	Portfolio of work to show class Describe and present work	City & Guilds 7360 Communication Skills WORDPOWER	• Communicate effectively • Use technology effectively • Apply design and creativity • Written communication skills
Pakistani Urdu-speaking female	Working with children Certificate in Education	• Verbal and written instruction giving • Report writing • Giving feedback on performance of child	Can devise: • a plan for organising children's activities (0–7 yr old) • a layout for classroom in accordance with Health and Safety and reflecting multi-cultural ethos	City & Guilds 7360 Communication Skills WORDPOWER	• Communicate effectively and appropriately • Written communication skills • Solve problems • Apply design and creativity • Apply effective personal and interpersonal skills

Chapter 7

The European dimension and APL

INTRODUCTION

The APL process has the potential to be an equitable method for gaining national qualifications, as individuals are assessed on their own skills and abilities, rather than purely on a yardstick of worth placed on their overseas qualifications, which are usually unrecognised and undervalued in Britain. The imminent standardisation of NCVQs across Europe, necessitates a system of APL which can standardise and legitimise overseas qualifications and link them into British/European qualifications.

During the course of this chapter, a general backdrop of current Euro legislation will be outlined, which strengthens the case for formalising an APL framework as part of Curriculum Entitlement for bilingual learners, and as part of inter-agency partnership involving employers, TECs, providers of training and their European counterparts. There will be a focus on assessing language and 'core' skills within the framework of occupational profiles in Britain and Europe with particular relevance to bilingual learners and bilingual employees.

APL AND EUROPEAN DIRECTIVES

In any current discussion on APL since the introduction of the single market January 1993, it appears indefensible to omit the influence of political European initiatives on areas of funding, APL philosophy and APL framework as part of vocational delivery by training providers. An unexpected thrust to the development of an appropriate APL framework for bilingual learners could take place on account of three crucial recent initiatives:

1 The Second EC Directive;
2 The Memorandum on Higher Education in the EC; and
3 The Memorandum on Vocational Training.

The Second EC Directive, to be implemented by 1994, proposes the establishment of a second general system for the recognition of professional education and training (i.e. qualifications gained on the basis of completion of education, training or in certain circumstances, occupational experience) of less than three years (i.e. below degree level). The aim of the directive is to promote the free movement of labour and freedom of establishment for individuals across national boundaries. *'Competent authorities'* will be set up in each member state to receive applications and to take decisions permitting individuals to exercise a regulated trade/profession/occupation (where the content of a qualification differs substantially between one member state and another) to take aptitude tests or for adaptation periods. Aptitude tests will cover the applicant's knowledge of subjects seen as essential to the exercise of the occupation in the member state, but not covered in the previous qualification. Adaptation periods will consist of supervised practice, complemented by training, and subject to assessment.

In keeping with the philosophy of APL, invariably the UK response was concerned that equivalences should be based on competence, rather than on time or on content and on the recognition of prior learning. The directive covers all NVQs at levels 3 and 4, and awards based on professional experience, but the time element of legitimacy (one to three years) remains. The Directive does not propose any measures towards the harmonisation of qualifications, which is the separate work by CEDEFOP (European Centre for the Development of Vocational Training).

The Memorandum on Higher Education in the EC defines HE institutions as including establishments of education and training which offer courses of varying duration and of either a general or specialised nature leading to qualifications of a 'post-secondary level'. This confirms that FE colleges are included and can participate in the EC schemes applicable to higher education. One principle underpinning HE is identified as 'the need to create a "European" education to match the "European" expectations of graduates'.

The memorandum argues for a series of *actions* which would affect FE and consequently the shape of the *admissions* framework which should enable potential students to fully exploit their prior learning. The *actions* are as follows:

- increased access to HE;
- increased resources;
- mobility and credit transfer through modular systems and harmonisation of professional and vocational qualifications;
- partnership with business and industry;
- Open and Distance Learning; and
- continuing education.

In relation to *access*, increased participation rates across Europe for women are recognised and further encouraged, and specific action is recommended to favour mature and non-traditional students, especially those from ethnic minorities. This obviously has implications (yet to be decided) for groups of individuals such as asylum-seekers, settled immigrants, refugees and so on.

The third initiative is the *Memorandum on Vocational Training*. In this area unlike HE, existing policy has seen the recent introduction of major new programmes such as FORCE, PETRA (EC vocational schemes) NOW, HORIZON and EUROFORM (ESF schemes). One of the questions posed for national debate of crucial importance to assessment of prior learning and the recognition of human potential in this area, seeks to link success and lack of success in economic performance with the willingness of member states to undertake 'an aggressive thrust towards structural adaptation and change in terms of opening up access to all groups in the work-force, particularly the disadvantaged and the unemployed'. What is clear here, is the proposal of systems which would seek to harness the potential experience, knowledge and skills in the European work-force as has not been the case before.

Related to this is an interesting section on the growing role of *'intangible capital'* (i.e. workers' competences, flexibility, organisational and communication skills, entrepreneurial spirit). Other areas covered in discussion include:

- training in and for small business;
- a European market for qualifications and training; and
- access to and continuous availability of lifelong training to all social groups.

Three sets of central objectives are then proposed:

1 increased investment in training i.e. in the 'intangible capital' without which the physical capital (of new plant and technology) cannot function, implying better access to initial continuing training for disadvantaged social groups and regions;
2 improving the quality of training – through better links with enterprises and with other member states and across the community, better evaluation of training, improved coherence of training policies with other economic, industrial and human resource policies; and
3 ensuring transparency of the training market – through removing discriminatory barriers of nationality, social origin etc. and by ensuring mutual recognition of national qualifications, with a view to developing harmonisation of qualifications, in order to allow the development of Europe-wide transnational qualifications.

In terms of the last objective the initial EC decision (1985) on comparability, requested CEDEFOP to establish and document the comparability of vocational training qualifications (for skilled occupations only) which led to work on a priority list of nineteen sectors. The full report and a summary of the work are available from the Employment Department's Quality and Standards Branch at Moorfoot.

An example of an initiative in Britain combining bilingual skills and vocational training

The Euroqualifications Project with a UK base at the London Institute addresses issues of mutual recognition and supra-national qualifications, with some input from NCVQ, TEED, CBI and the TUC. The aims are to identify the essential elements in an initial set of qualifications, to develop additional training models for each member state, so that all can reach a common standard for each sector and to equip individuals with the professional skills and mobility to carry out their occupations within the European partnerships.

The twelve occupational fields are:

1 Catering / hotel trade / tourism;
2 Transport;
3 Electricity / electronics / telecommunications;
4 Office automation;
5 Environment / local development;
6 Commerce;
7 Food processing industry;
8 Mechanics;
9 Construction – public works;
10 Car repair / vehicle maintenance;
11 Graphics industry; and
12 Textiles.

The target groups as of 1993 were:

• Young people and the long-term unemployed, prepared to be mobile in the framework of their training.
• People employed in insecure work situations in the countries or regions for which particular conditions are or will be applicable.

In general terms of applicability, the Directive and the Memorandums all laid down proposals and guidelines which aim to harness the human resources potential termed 'intangible capital' through educating and training. Ethnic minorities are a target group specifically selected for this purpose and therefore, by implication existing or potential students who fall into the category of bilingual learners. This objective, coupled with the aim of ensuring 'transparency of the training market' through the removal of barriers of discrimination and ensuring mutual recognition of national qualifications suggests that bilingual learners in Britain and other EC Countries who had gained EC National Status would be entitled to any benefits to be gained from these initiatives.

Many bilingual learners resident in Britain as already noted originate from countries where an EC European language is spoken such as Zaire (French), Angola (Portuguese), South American countries (Spanish and Portuguese), Eastern European countries (French and German).

These groups of people often fall into the category of long-term employed and are very often willing to be mobile in order to build up their expertise and experience. Many have substantial experience of working in other countries, in precisely those occupational sectors under scrutiny by CEDEFOP and the Euroqualifications project. It appears discriminatory and economically non-viable not to target these groups for training under these schemes, thus capitalising on individuals with a fair degree of bilingualism in two or more languages and very probably prior knowledge and experience of operations systems in countries other than Britain. With appropriate training, the experience of these individuals could be put to use in the following ways:

1 Bilingual learners could take part in a 'languages mentor' scheme, working alongside monolingual British native speakers with some vocational competence, thereby enhancing their foreign language competence within the framework of, for example, the Euroqualifications project scheme.
2 Inexperienced young adults with virtually no foreign language competence or vocational competence could 'work shadow' mature bilingual learners in work placements in Britain especially in work environments where two or more languages were required, for example business administration, catering, caring. If bilingual adults with overseas experience had not attained EC national status and were excluded from entitlement of mobility around Europe, then they could usefully be trained and up-skilled in their own area of expertise and language. They would in turn have an enabling and beneficial effect on the training of others by taking part in these 'mentoring' or 'work shadowing' schemes. Young adults could then gain prior experience of both occupational competence and language skills in a work context in Britain *prior* to a work placement in a European country.

If this group of bilingual trainees were able to exercise their rights of mobility in Europe, they would be able to benefit from work placements in a European country where they might be familiar with the language, in a relevant occupational sector, and be able to implement their prior experience, knowledge and skills more usefully.

Two of the five key objectives of the Euroqualification project are:

1 'to train people to carry out their occupation in partnership and/or in occupational mobility situations' (Euroqualifications Information Brochure: DALI). An interpretation of this as outlined above would lend support to the concept of a mentoring or work-shadowing scheme.

2 'To lend a European vocational and linguistic dimension' (Euroqualifications Information Brochure: DALI). Experienced mature bilingual adults, working with young, inexperienced, monolingual adults would be of mutual benefit for both groups to possess a greater depth and variety of experience and thus ensure a greater coherence and convergence of Community vocational training programmes.

An APL module which serves to assess candidates language, 'core' skills and vocational competence could be attached to such a Euroqualifications programme, thus building in the systematic accumulation of accredited units of training within a learner portfolio.

Conversely, candidates from other European countries wishing to gain work experience in Britain benefit from building a bilingual learner portfolio as a result of attending an APL Induction Module. The transferable 'core' skills assessed and accredited within such a module are applicable to work contexts in Europe and Britain.

REFUGEES AND WORK PLACEMENTS/EMPLOYMENT

Certain groups of bilingual adults, for instance refugees, benefit especially from structured work experience and the real possibility of local employment. Without a work element some forms of professional accreditation are not open to refugees as their work experience may not be recognised as sufficient or relevant in this Country. Work placements should allow previous overseas working experience to be given credit within the context of British employment situations.

In the context of the Bourneville Project (1993) work placements had a number of specific objectives, as follows:

• providing the ability for refugees to be supervised in work situations and thus to obtain references and testimonials;
• providing reflection time – i.e. is this the right professional area?
• enabling the possibility of gaining through workplace tasks, modular credits that can be given recognition by accrediting bodies;
• providing opportunities for exposure to the structure and style of work in a British setting;
• creating the opportunity to get inside knowledge of permanent work opportunities.

Findings from the project focused on concern from potential employers who are unsure of the level at which the work should be pitched, especially if there are uncertainties around mismatches between participants' professional skills and their English language skills. This underlines the need for an accurate assessment of trainees' linguistic capabilities aligned to vocational and professional competence. The above objectives add further weight to the argument for providing a structural framework, i.e. an APL induction module which allows refugees and other bilingual learners the opportunities for reflection and development of other necessary skills.

Similar projects which provide suitable work placements to bilingual learners following courses could be funded jointly by TECs and some forms of Euro-funding, e.g. these could focus on refugees' linguistic capability within a work context and individuals could be placed in work situations where full use may be made of their bilingual skills. Opportunities are available especially in the London area, for example export–import firms, guidance and counselling advice workers within colleges, housing and social service providers, citizens advice bureaux and other advocacy agencies. An interesting scheme in Haringey as part of a refugee project secures work placements and employment for refugees in local retail firms such as supermarkets. The refugees are employed not on account of any altruistic gesture on the part of the stores, but because the stores realise they can increase their clientele, i.e. individuals from those refugee groups will shop in the stores because they are made to feel welcome by the refugee/employees who share their cultural backgrounds and languages. Schemes such as this need to be publicised nationally in a directory and actively promoted internationally in the European member states, so that the 'intangible capital' of all European Communities is utilised positively, through the sharing of such a scheme.

Strong evidence from the Refugee Training and Employment Centre illustrates the fact that many refugees are not only educated, but educated to a very high level. A small cohort of the first hundred who came to see the careers counsellor at the Refugee Council for advice provided a snapshot of the educational and employment background of the client group. From published statistics (Marshall 1992), it can be seen that 46 per cent had a degree or were studying for a degree when they had to leave their country. Although not all qualifications match exactly those in Britain, in general, the main point is made that they do equate to a generally similar standard. A point of information which substantiates the argument for capitalising on refugees' linguistic skills and experience is that not all refugees studied in their country of origin. Some went to other countries to study, and often learnt a new language in the process. The examples given include a vet from Sri Lanka who went to Japan to do a Master's degree; several Ethiopians studied in the Soviet Union and some Iranians studied in Italy and in the United States. Presumably, an offshoot of these experiences were the individuals' motivation and capabilities to resettle and integrate into the specific culture and society of the host country and ability to secure some form of voluntary or paid employment. These are the very characteristics which are sought by agencies which set up Euro-projects in order to facilitate transnational work placement exchanges, work shadowing schemes, language and vocational training programmes. Refugees have specific and transferable skills plus a variety of work experiences which taken as a whole are a very valuable asset, particularly in a situation where Britain is faced with severe skill shortages in the labour market. The key to unlocking the potential lies within an APL process which would take into account a framework of national and international qualifications and would allow for:

- short, effective, training courses leading to conversion of qualifications;
- reorientation programmes for those who cannot or do not wish to continue the same type of work;
- up-skilling courses combined with work placements (Adult Compact type programmes) 'top up' training within an 'APL' module to build up a holistic learner portfolio; and
- up-skilling language courses with or without professional and vocations input.

Within the framework needs to be a structure which creates comparability and equivalence of European and International qualifications and a system of *transparency* which enables individuals to assess their occupational profiles according to prescribed standards.

USING BILINGUALISM POSITIVELY IN THE TRAINING WORKPLACE

All this *legal evidence* adds greater weight to the argument that bilingual learners need to be targeted more pro-actively for education and training. Colleges of FE working in partnership with industry, business and local TECs can benefit from Euro-legislation and Euro-funding to facilitate and access these groups onto appropriately designed programmes. Funded programmes need to focus on the prior vocational, academic or professional experience of individual bilingual learners, and to map out clearly an up-skilling or reorientation programme with demonstrable performance outcomes.

The following examples point the way towards an imaginative use of bilingual learners' prior experience and skills as a valuable learning resource to be harnessed pro-actively. In a college where a large intake of students with European languages such as French or Spanish existed, creche workers within the college found themselves in a position where they were unable to communicate with the children of these students in the creche. What the workers found invaluable was the work placement of a French-speaking mature student undertaking a Caring course who had experience of working in a school in Zaire. The creche workers and the other monolingual work placement students carried out, albeit informally, a work shadow experience with the bilingual student. Both the employed creche workers and the work placement students benefited enormously from the experience in terms of developing a limited but useful repertoire of language skills and in developing culturally appropriate strategies for dealing with the children. The Zairian student improved her English in a communicative context as she needed to talk through processes and concepts with her colleagues and gained the experience of working in a British creche which could be added to her already substantial experience of working in an infants school in Zaire.

Similarly, in the area of business administration, Spanish and French speaking students with a business administration background from Colombia and Paris respectively were able to simulate working in a bilingual environment in the college business training office, which was especially helpful for the monolingual students, who were able to gain valuable insights and experience into working in a non-British environment and could develop their language expertise in the foreign languages. They also had access to culturally appropriate discourse skills in those languages; an aspect of language learning which is often ignored in standard language learning classes.

In both cases, students with virtually no language skills, either with or without prior experience in the relevant vocational field, benefited from a kind of 'foundation module' through contact with the bilingual learners. If these concepts of peer group learning coupled with building upon past experience and linguistic skills could be formalised into curriculum delivery, it is possible to generate Euro-funding such as ESF (European Social Fund) for similar pilot schemes to run in colleges. Implicit within any framework which seeks to address the general issue of Euroqualifications must be a respect for prior learning.

Bilingualism, if part of a course of study such as a BTEC course, can be developed particularly through the common 'core' skills outcomes, such as communicating and working with and relating to others. However, it is important for work experience placements to provide opportunities for learners to practise their skills in both languages. Consequently, colleges can set up simulated training environments which are effectively bilingual by capitalising on the language skills of bilingual learners, who are not necessarily on the related course itself. This could benefit not only the students following the course but improve the English language skills of bilingual learners.

For instance, to return to the example of the business training office, there needs to be a simulation of various contexts where students can demonstrate evidence of occupational competence in dealing with clients who are bilingual or who have limited English. Using bilingual learners to interact with the students in authentic and meaningful contexts is a useful way of developing language competence. Bilingual learners can also use these training establishments as opportunities in which to practise their language and core communication skills.

FUNDED SCHEMES INCORPORATING BILINGUALISM IN COLLEGES OF FE

Once bilingual students have undertaken a programme of study which seeks to focus on particular occupational skills and bodies of knowledge, assessment for accreditation needs to take place which would acknowledge and accredit students' skills and abilities as part of their portfolio. Various case studies of Colleges involved in European initiatives with Euro-funding have been collated by the FEU in their excellent document *Working with Europe* (1993). These case studies set out to demonstrate what the 'average college' can achieve in a European context at present and heralds many more initiatives of this nature in the future.

Further implications of activity of this kind are justified on the following lines:

> If colleges put the student at the centre, they cannot avoid a European dimension in the curriculum. Today's students will spend all their working lives in the Single European Market. A curriculum which fails to prepare them for this context will not be preparing them adequately for their future.
>
> (FEU 1993)

The following example is taken from *Working with Europe*.

This initiative involves a private sector agency, France–UK (Luton and Dunstable Engineering Training Group) which works with Colleges and has been involved in the provision of City and Guilds courses with a European dimension. It has formed links with 'Associations' in France: registered Charities which specialise in training programmes designed to 'reinsert' trainees into vocational occupations following unemployment. French students are able to take a nine-month course in secretarial studies with import–export procedures and English as subsidiary subjects and are able to undertake a three week course in English language keyboard skills, office practice and export documentation. The office activities complement what students have already done in France, providing an environment in which students can develop their use of English in a workplace situation. The specialist export documentation work enhances their existing course content as it will not have been covered in France. The group is also able to offer local work placements to some of the French trainees of two to eight weeks duration in the clerical sector.

Commentary on use of funding

All students French and British in this context, can benefit from an APL audit of their experience which would build a portfolio and accredit their work-based learning, on course learning and performance outcomes. Students could develop the core skills of communication and IT/Information skills as well as problem-solving, commercial and enterprise skills if they are involved in setting up a simulated 'company' to run import and export schemes.

TRANSPARENCY OF QUALIFICATIONS

As mentioned previously, the new EC initiative to ensure 'transparency', i.e. making very clear the skills, abilities and qualifications necessary for a job, whilst respecting the principle of subsidiarity would enable individuals to present their vocational qualifications, education and work experience clearly and effectively to potential employers throughout the Community and help employers to have easy access to clear descriptions of qualifications. This would help establish the relevance of applicant's attainments to jobs on offer. Another major benefit to bilingual learners with qualifications from overseas, i.e. outside of Europe, is a mutual recognition of these qualifications and acceptance within the member states, based on 'transparency', i.e. clear descriptions of individual qualifications. If a bilingual adult can have his/her qualification recognised in one member state, it should be possible in the pursuit of equity to gain recognition of the validity of the qualification in other countries.

This process of recognition and comparability needs to slot into a framework of transparency. Individuals could then benefit from an assessment of his/her prior learning so that 'top-up' training can take place in order to align the individuals' experience and qualifications with those of the member state if needs be.

This approach raises the possibility of making available an 'individual learner's portfolio' which would provide a summary of individuals' achievements in a common format agreed between member states, and could be based on the National Record of Achievement (NRA). A Euro-Record of Achievement, which could be used by individuals moving between member states, is a distinct viability and is a necessary adjunct to a Europe with freedom of mobility for individuals to study, train and work. It would offer transparency and would outline performance outcomes, levels of learner competence within a holistic APL learner profile. A model of good practice for a transparent qualifications system, the National Database of Vocational Qualifications could well provide a pro forma for discussion with European partners.

What is needed at this stage is a debate around a clearer definition of the term 'community' which encompasses all individuals resident in the European Community regardless of their country of origin, active in the field of education and training and work. There needs to be a true recognition of, and commitment to, the multi-cultural and pluralistic nature of European society with its recent influx of migrant groups from many countries around the world.

In any audit of the cultural and linguistic backgrounds of a European nation's 'intangible capital', there will be a proportion of the population which is not indigenous to that country, but over a period of time they will eventually be endowed with native citizen status and by exten-sion, EC status. This section of society contributes to its culture and wealth in many ways, and instead of being perceived as a deficit cohort of individuals, they need to be appropriately empowered in order to fulfil their potential in terms of education, training and work.

Within the areas recommended by the British government concerning education, it would be hoped that agencies such as the NCVQ and the British Council would be able to work more closely together with their European partners in order to draw up a transparent database of qualifications, which would be valid in all member states, but includes qualifications from non-EC countries. Defining 'Community' languages, once more initiates an age-old debate which excludes local community languages such as the Asian and African languages, in favour of exclu-sively European languages. Although it is possible to rationalise the reasons as to why this should be the case, nevertheless, in terms of making an impact on the whole of a nation's 'intangible capital', pursuing this path of action would systematically exclude groups of ethnic minorities who do not necessarily benefit from European initiatives in education and training. Narrow definitions of 'community' do not permit colleges of FE to target certain groups.

The ethos of the Memorandum on Vocational Training maintains a commitment to ensuring a 'transparency of the training market by removing discriminatory barriers of nationality, social origin'. This political rhetoric needs to be translated into reality for the majority of bilingual learners resident in Britain and Europe through pro-active targeting of these client groups for access to education, training and work, via a responsive and non-discriminatory APL framework.

OCCUPATIONAL PROFILES AND LANGUAGE COMPETENCE WITHIN A EUROPEAN CONTEXT

The NVQ criteria for assessment and language need to be reviewed so that a greater proportion of bilingual learners from Europe coming to Britain may benefit and also bilingual adults resident and working in the British community may take advantage of training schemes. The following criterion militates against individuals working in a bilingual environment and does not give them due credit and recognition of their linguistic skills:

> *Some* of the assessment for an NVQ may be conducted in a language other than English provided that evidence is available that the candidate is competent in English to the standard required for competent performance throughout the UK.

Until now, this point has been discussed with specific reference to ethnic minorities resident in Britain. It would seem clear that given the backdrop of EC Directives and Memoranda which actively promote and foster multilateral recognition of Euro qualifications, and mobility of training and employment across member states, it is now appropriate to build into assessment criteria, some scope for the recognition of bilingual skills. At the very least, this could include a core of European languages.

The notion of an 'Observatory' which has been studied by CEREQ Paris, (Centre d'Etudes et de recherches sur les qualifications – Research Centre for Occupational and Training Analysis) involves the production of a Euro-database where each qualification is described in a prescribed standardised format. The potential advantages of an 'Observatory' style database would lend itself, first and foremost, to the notion of transparency and would:

- underpin an individual's ability to migrate;
- provide employers with an understanding of the value of qualifications and also information about the way the labour market is developing in terms of the skills needed for the future; and
- provide information which could stimulate the exchange of ideas and expertise in training and assessment – facilitating the transfer of 'training technology and social cohesion'.

APLA / ASSESSMENT OF LANGUAGE AND COMMUNICATIONS SKILLS AND OCCUPATIONAL PROFILES

A Directory of Occupational Profiles currently being developed at CEDEFOP groups occupations according to function which are described on a pro forma, setting out the knowledge, skills and aptitudes required to follow the occupations. The system could be developed so that any occupational qualification could be cross-matched to its profile or pro forma. The different levels of language competence necessary for the job need to be outlined within the profile or pro forma. Defining the levels and establishing a standardised framework would need to take place at national level and then at European level. In Britain with due discussion and consultation, the levels of *language competence* in the occupational profile/pro forma needed to carry out the job effectively could be broadly based on the Languages Lead Body framework, with relevant adaptation. Broad-based profiles for individual occupations could be developed in the following way, for example:

- *A taxi driver*:
    (a) Level 4 listening skills;
    (b) Level 3 speaking skills;
    (c) Level 3 reading skills (map-reading, signs etc.);
    (d) Level 1/2 writing skills.

- *A bilingual secretary*:
    (a) Level 4 listening skills
    (b) Level 4 reading and writing skills
    (c) Level 3 speaking skills.

Whilst the suggested levels above are very much debatable, it is clear that in any job role, language competence is a vital component and with such competence comes the enhancement of other communications skills related to non-verbal communication, i.e. facial expression, body languages, cultural discourse and prosody (intonation, tone, pace and register). It may be appropriate to include assessment of other 'core' skills, such as numeracy, information technology, personal development, problem-solving and so on.

Within a framework or guide which indicates the *Comparability of Vocational Training Qualifications* it would be indefensible not to indicate the aptitude and level of competence in language and communications skills. The example of an *occupational profile* that appears in the official Journal of the European Communities No. C 196/54 25/7/91 of an air-craft mechanic (m/f) maintenance and inspection is a good case in point. (see Appendix 7.1).

By focusing on the 'tasks according to job instructions' it is obvious that a fair degree of underpinning broad-based language communications skills and core skills is *needed to carry out the job successfully but is not explicit within the description* (see Table 7.1).

A further breakdown of the skills inherent in the tasks could be obtained with reference to qualifications.

Table 7.1 Breakdown of communications/language skills and core skills needed in job example

	Core skills	Language skills	Band
Organising his/her workplace	Comm. skills/ working as part of a team/	Listening	4
	working independently	Speaking	4
Aspects 2–5 require a high level of reading skills and the ability to follow through written technical instruction		Reading	4
		Reading	4
Aspects 8 and 10 require a high level of written skills, e.g. report writing and the ability to interpret graphical data and statistics		Writing	4
Aspect 10 may require knowledge of IT	Information Technology		3

By linking up assessment of occupational competence to assessment of core skills and language skills via work-based assessment, assignments, testimonials, certificates and references, it is possible to gain a more accurate profile of an individual's abilities on the job, in terms of the quality standards attained. At this point in time, there is no over-arching template of European *quality* standards applicable to all professions and occupations which ensures parity of the quality within the tasks.

It is well established that different cultures have culturally defined work ethos and prescribed values, which may militate against individuals adjusting to the work ethos and organisational structures of a specific company in another country. By identifying the potential strengths of an individual and areas of training needed to integrate the individual into the organisation, it is possible for employers to:

• gain a more reliable and valid assessment of an individual's potential contribution to an organisation;
• gain knowledge of an individual's linguistic abilities and whether the

lack of fluency and/or accuracy in the host country's language would prevent him/her from carrying out the tasks effectively;

• gain detailed knowledge as to the training needs of the individual and so pre-empt the employee's inability to carry out the tasks successfully owing to a lack of culturally specific training needed for certain aspects of the job. For instance to date, in the field of engineering, Eastern Europeans have not had access to the latest technology in computerisation by and large, and consequently need specialist training in this field to enable them to utilise their engineering skills more effectively, in a Western European work context.

Very clear guidelines on setting up a process of assessment of prior learning experience and qualifications are essential for employers so that they are able to interpret the framework of comparability of Vocational Qualifications in the EC to the best advantage of the employee.

'CORE SKILLS' AND LANGUAGE ASSESSMENT WITHIN FRAMEWORK OF VOCATIONAL QUALIFICATIONS

Two crucial strands need to be added to the framework to make it viable for assessment purposes. First, there needs to be a recognition of the implicit 'core' skills inherent within any job. A combination of the GNVQ 'core' skills together with the fifteen soft 'core' skills drawn up by Eurotecnet could be grafted onto the framework of generic occupational competences, which in itself could be a focal point for discussion with other member states.

In any assessment of occupational competence it is necessary to focus on these skills:

1 the skills required to carry out tasks (task skills);
2 the skills required to manage the relationship between tasks (task management skills); and
3 the skills necessary to manage the work environment, including unexpected occurrences (job/role environment skills).

To the last point can be added the 'cultural' specific dimension of work ethics, organisational systems and so on. The research carried out in this area suggests that important dimensions of occupational competence which encompass the complex reality for most work environments are ignored if there is a traditional focus on task-specific skills. It is evident that the range of skills required in work is diverse and encompasses communication, planning, problem-solving and interpersonal skills, in addition to task-specific skills. It is precisely these management skills which are valuable in terms of adaptability and skills transfer and hold wide applicability in a diverse range of working environments. In terms of cross-cultural exchanges – work placements, work-based learning – it is essential for trainees to understand that developing a parcel of skills (competence) in one work context does not necessarily mean that these are culturally transferable to another context.

Developing language to a sophisticated level of usage, which indicates mastery of the elements of 'finer tuning', can take place usually only when an individual has lived and worked in the relevant country. Individuals working on occupational competence within the context of a foreign language and culture would require the acquisition of a whole battery of skills and talents which can be transferred to culturally different situations. Consequently, a narrow focus on the four discrete language skills excludes the range of communicative core skills which are essential to successful occupational competence. Second, a performance indicator of discrete language skills and more broad-based communication skills need to be grafted onto the framework. Language options on BTEC courses do exist. What is needed, however, is an initiative to produce materials to support the integration of French, Spanish and other languages into engineering and other vocational qualifications at NVQ Levels 2 and 3, so that bilingual learners with the abilities and occupational competence in these areas can gain credit too for their language expertise.

Enabling APL candidates to be assessed and then accredited for their English as just one of the languages available would be a necessary concomitant of an APL process. This would facilitate the inclusion of languages as part of vocational courses and provide these vocational courses for bilingual students who are either resident in Britain or are in the country as a result of a short-term exchange.

However, in reviewing the Languages Lead Body framework for language assessment, it is evident that its applicability is limited in the sense that it does not attempt to cover the wider language and communication processes in such skills as working with others, problem-solving and so on. It is also very much geared to the use of languages within a business/administration framework.

In this way it does not adequately reflect the wide spectrum of English communication skills needed by bilingual learners on vocational courses. At present, there is no leeway within the Languages Lead Body's Framework to assess an individual's ability in two or more languages to different levels. For instance, it would then not be feasible for an individual to have Level 3 in reading and writing in English and Level 2 in reading and writing in French. The reality of the situation for most bilingual adults is that within any one language they may have a Level 3/4 for speaking and listening and Level 2/3 for writing and reading and a matching across two languages or more may reveal greater disparities of levels.

Returning then to the original example of the aircraft mechanic, he/she coming from France may have the sample profile shown in Table 7.2.

Table 7.2   Sample skills profile of aircraft mechanic from France

Language skills	French	English	Core skills	French	English
Speaking	5	3	Communications	4	3
Listening	5	4	Problem-solving	4	3
Reading	5	3	Working with others	4	3
Writing	5	3	Working independently	4	3

Note: Levels of language taken from Languages Lead Body framework for assessment.

It is clear then from the analysis of levels that if this individual wished to be successful in the host country of residence in the daily tasks of 'reading and applying technical documentation', 'referring to manuals', and 'collecting technical data and preparing reports', then he/she would need specialised language training in these areas.

CONCLUSION

In order to accommodate the full range of the levels, it is axiomatic to recognise the reality of bilingual adults' language competence and to draw up assessment procedures and levels which would reflect this. This does need to be implemented if mobility across Europe is to become a reality.

What is needed is a recognition of some of the best features of each member state's system of education, of training and approach to work-based learning and ultimately for these features to be synthesised into a Euro-framework of good practice. France and Germany both demonstrate features which potentially can be incorporated into the British system and conversely, the versatile and holistic approach to assessment of prior learning within the British system can be adapted for use in other member states.

APPENDIX 7.1

6. AIRCRAFT MECHANIC (M/F) MAINTENANCE AND INSPECTION

SEDOC No. 8–45.50

I	II	III	IV	V	VI	VII
Aircraft mechanic (m/f) maintenance and inspection						
	E	844	Aircraft mainte-nance mechanic (m/f)	Certificate of First-Level Vocational Education (Título de técnico auxiliar). Area: vehicle trades; occupation: aircraft/mechanic	• College of Vocational Education (IFP) • Polytechnic Colleges of Vocational Education (IPFP) • Private centres of vocational education	Ministry of Education and Science
		849	Maintenance fitter (m/f)	Job Training Diploma (Diploma de Cursos Ocupacionales): preparer of machine tools	• Job Training Centres of the National Employ-ment Office (INEM) • Job Training Centres (public and private) taking part in the National Training and Employment Plan (Plan FIP)	Ministry of Labour and Social Security (INEM)
	F	50.1095	Aircraft mechanic (maintenance and inspection) (m/f)	Vocational training (CAP) air-frame system mechanic Vocational training certificate (CAP) aircraft maintenance mechanic Specialised in: 1. Piston motors 2. Turbo aero engines 3. Electromechanical and electronic aircraft systems Vocational training certificate (CPP) air-frame systems mechanical fitter	a. Training in a Vocational school (LEP) b. Apprentice training centre (CFA) c. Training in a Private technical school	Ministry of National Education (Administration of the schools and colleges)
		50.1093 50.1094 50.1127			Adult vocational training centre	Ministry of Social Affairs and Employment
	GR		Aircraft Mechanic, Maintenance and Inspector (m/f)	TES (Technical Vocational Schools) Specialist Aircraft Fitter's Diploma	TES	YPEPTH (Ministry of National Education and Religion)

APPENDIX 7.1 cont.

II	III	IV	V	VI	VII
IRL	743.10	Aircraft Mechanic (m/f)	National Craft Certificate	Vocational Education College The Employer	Joint Certifying Body comprising FAS – The Training and Employment Authority and Department of Education incorporating Department of tourism and transport or Air Corps Apprentice School
I		Aircraft mechanic (m/f)	Statement of vocational skills	Businesses	Local Employment Sections
L		Aircraft mechanic (m/f)	a) Vocational training certificate (CAP) b) Vocational and technical training certificate (CATP)	In-company and colleges of technology	Ministry of National Education and Professional Chambers
NL	603	Aircraft mechanic (m/f)	Elementary apprenticeship certificate	In-firm and off-the-job training	Metal Industries Training Board (Stichting Opleiding Metaal, SOM)
P	8.44.01 8.73.70 8.45.50	Aircraft Mechanic (m/f) Aircraft Structure Mechanic (m/f) Aircraft Hydraulic Systems Mechanic (m/f)	Certificate of proficiency	Vocational Training Centre at civil and military aeronautics enterprises	Institute of Employment and Vocational Training; Ministry of Employment and Social Security
UK	SOC 516	Aircraft mechanic (m/f)	1. a minimum of 3 years on-the-job training and Experience Log-book 2. Licence without type and 3. Type rated Licences (various)	1. + 2. + 3. The Employer	1. The Employer 2. Civil Aviation Authority 3. Civil Aviation Authority for M1 operations or The Employer, for M3 operations (CAA approved)

APPENDIX 7.1 *cont.*

ANNEX B
DESCRIPTION OF THE MUTUALLY AGREED PRACTICAL OCCUPATIONAL REQUIRE-
MENTS

I. OCCUPATION: Aircraft mechanic (m/f) maintenance and inspection   SEDOC: 8–45.50

II. DUTIES: The aircraft mechanic is a skilled worker capable of duly performing in an
    autonomous and responsible manner the work involved in the inspection and mainte-
    nance of aircraft.

III. TASKS: On the basis of technical documentation, through rational use of tools and with
     due regard to ecological, health and safety regulations, he/she performs mainly the fol-
     lowing tasks according to job instructions:

1. Organizing his/her workplace.
2. Reading and applying technical documentation.
3. Determining work stages, tools and methods in compliance with manuals.
4. Selecting and applying tools, measuring and auxiliary instruments in compliance with
   manuals.
5. Carrying out regular inspection and maintenance work on aircraft and flight systems in
   accordance with relevant specifications issued by manufacturers and monitoring authorities respectively.
6. Performing maintenance work on the the following sub-systems:
   –   propulsion systems
   –   air-frame systems
   –   undercarriage systems
   –   steering and control systems
7. Checking the work and making the respective sub-systems ready for operation.
8. Preparing reports and notifying those responsible of defective operational parts.
9. Servicing and maintaining relevant equipment, machines and tools and performing
   simple repair work.
10. Collecting technical data on work processes and results.

Source: Journal of the European Communities, No.C 196/54 25/7/91. (Title of an occupational profile table.)

Chapter 8

Partnerships in APL

INTRODUCTION

This chapter looks at systems in Germany and France, which are of direct relevance to the system of APL in Britain. Furthermore, there will be an appraisal of the benefits of partnerships between employers/TECs and colleges of FE for the delivery of training and assessment to bilingual learners and others.

FEATURES OF EUROPEAN EDUCATIONAL AND WORK-BASED PRACTICE

What follows are summary findings of features of European education and training lifted from Germany and France. The proposal is that some of these systems' inherently positive features may be combined with those of a British APL system to strengthen the overall framework of Euro-education and training.

'Dual' system of education and training in Germany

The European Institute of Education and Social Policy Project, *Strategies for VET in Europe*, is a study of vocational education and training (VET) developments in a quartet of major employment sectors in four of Europe's leading economies: France, Germany, Italy and the Netherlands. Four sectors have been selected:

- construction;
- electrical and electronic engineering in the context of multi-skilling;
- motor vehicle maintenance; and
- travel and tourism.

In its report following a visit to Germany 1992, VET in Europe Construction Group identified the following key points for the apparent success of the 'dual system' in Germany as outlined above. The features of the dual system are as follows: two-thirds of 16–18-year-olds combine on-the-job training in the workplace or at a training centre with part-time theoretical studies at a vocational school (*berufschule*). Courses under this system last from two to three and a half years and lead to skilled worker qualifications. Working through local chambers of commerce, employers control and fund most of this training. The chambers are responsible both for the quality of on-the-job training and the assessment of practical skills for the final award. The key points were as follows:

- compulsion – all firms have to pay a registration fee with the chamber; all pay a levy based on payroll regardless of whether they train or not;
- culture – 'a good firm undertakes training' and sees it as part of long-term development; firms with a poor training record are identified in government statistics;
- separation from jobs – employers and trade unions agree that training is distinct from employment; apprentices receive training contracts; firms are encouraged to take on more than they need and there is no stigma in not employing someone at the end of a training period;
- standards – firms wanting to provide training are vetted to make sure programmes meet regulations; trainers must hold *'meister'* qualifications in their skill and be trained as trainers.

The strength of the system is its duration, employer commitment and emphasis on quality; it can be criticised for its old-fashioned and rigid structure because qualifications have application within a narrow occupational field and is characterised by the absence of *accreditation of prior learning*. It is not conducive to the development of new courses and qualifications in 'emergent occupations', for example, in the leisure industry.

The Group's report and recommendations focused on what lessons there might be in the German experience for the UK, in particular for the Training and Enterprise Councils (TECs). One strong recommendation was as follows: 'A change of attitude is needed so that the focus is upon the future long-term benefits to the firm of having a highly skilled and competent work-force, as opposed to the short-term costs of training. Many firms need encouragement to invest in training, with particular assistance directed towards small firms.'

The Group further suggests that TECs have a pro-active role rather like the local chambers of commerce in defining the role of employers through ensuring employer control of training in the following ways:

- registration of all firms and all training contracts;
- monitoring training via log books;
- direct involvement in assessment; and

- finally, setting up co-operative training facilities and providing advocacy and supporting training, whereby larger firms provide training facilities for skills and experience which the smaller firms are not able to provide.

The recommendations put forward by the Group concerning colleges include:

- a review to determine the theoretical and practical components of training, with a view to giving employers greater responsibility over the latter;
- closer links between college curricula and company in-house training; and
- development of a systematic method of recording the practical experience that should be submitted as part of a college's final award.

A logical conclusion of these recommendations is that TECs, in conjunction with colleges of FE and other training providers, should have a vital role in setting up systems of *assessing and accrediting prior experience* of employees wishing to undertake further training and that employees develop a portfolio of their work experience and learner achievements.

It is timely that these recommendations are being made in view of the current, national government-led initiative *Investors in People Awards* (IIP). This is a standard or award given to employers in recognition of their approach to investment in training and skills. It is gained when a company achieves particular targets set for industry as a whole.

In terms of encouraging more companies to invest in training of its staff, IIP is not rigorous enough in its emphasis on an ethos of employer commitment and the long-term benefits of having a high-quality and competent work-force. A more directed interventionist approach is needed which links investment in training with long term economic benefits to the work-force and the unemployed. Plagiarising mandatory elements of the German system, i.e. the key points, and marrying them to the educationally sound practice of APL within an accreditation framework is one way of achieving a radical breakthrough in education, training and work-based learning in Britain.

APL in France

The French experience of APL is worth outlining here as it is possible to graft some of its good points on to the British designed system. The philosophy behind the French experience is the need for the individual:

- to manage personal resources;
- to have a capacity for negotiation; and
- to be able to respond to changes.

The equivalent 'APL' process in France is referred to as the '*bilan de competence*'. The official definition is 'A global process which brings a person to "take stock" of the range of his/her competences, both personal and professional, and also of his/her potential'.

The process can be situated somewhere between a skills or competence audit and an 'APL' device as it shows areas of strength and also of weakness, which need to be addressed. Dr Armina Barkatoolah of AIESE, who has carried out extensive research in this field, has outlined the different stages of appraisal and assessment of competences in '*Le Bilan*', which can be summed up as follows:

- a 'snapshot' of important life experiences and events related with hindsight;
- pinpointing and analysing relevant experiences (training, both social, professional and for personal development); and
- action planning/ '*entremise synthèse*'.

The principal differences between the French and the British systems can be assessed as follows: the French bilan process focuses on the individual and his/her capabilities in the area of core skills and transferable skills. The '*portefeuille*' (portfolio) is devised for the individual to keep as a personal record of achievement and as an awareness-raising exercise; a reminder of his/her *key transversal abilities*, whereas the British APL system places great emphasis on assessing skills and occupational competences which can be accredited. The portfolio that results from the APL process is for individuals to show to providers of training, colleges of FE, institutions of HE, employers and so on.

These *key transversal abilities* as drawn up by the OECD symposium in November 1988 mirror in many ways the skills list outlined by Euro Tech Net:

- efficiency of leadership and organisation;
- ability to:
  (a) negotiate;
  (b) communicate; and
  (c) work in a team;
- self-esteem and the ability to win;
- creative thought and problem-solving ability;
- communication – oral and written;
- literacy and numeracy; and
- learning to learn.

The 15 'soft-skills' concerning the 'worker of the future' cover, by and large, those skills recognised in the GNVQ Core Skills Units. The Euro Tec Net list is as follows:

- flexibility;
- adaptability;
- ability to learn;
- ability to ask questions;
- autonomy;
- responsibility;
- creativity;
- initiative;
- receptiveness to new ideas;
- ability to work in a team;
- ability to communicate;
- analytical ability;
- leadership;
- motivation; and
- an open mind to internal and external influences.

Within the French framework it is recognised that knowing *how* to learn is a vital competence and an indicator for success in the constant process of adaptation and change. The British APL system would benefit greatly from acknowledging this fact and for giving due recognition within the structures of assessment, as has been suggested within the previous chapters.

One of the major advantages of this system of *bilan* in France is that it is mandatory through legislation. Since January 1992, every employee has the right to have his/her *bilan* paid for by the employer. French employers need to integrate the rights of their employees in relation to the *bilan* into their 'Human Resource Strategic' Plan. The problem is that training leave is cash-limited within organisations, so it is not very realistic for an employer to pay for an employee's right to a *bilan* every five years. Throughout France there are about 100 *Centres de bilan de competence.*

These centres are self-funded, charitable, non-profit making organisations with a minimum of three permanent staff. The centres are usually situated in educational or vocational training Institutions and exercise a certain degree of autonomy. Consultants from various organisations can be brought in to help the team on a seconded basis and are paid for by the government.

Employers may refer employees to centres particularly if they fall into the following categories:

- possibility of being made redundant;
- change of employment requiring reorientation or up-skilling;
- technological innovations requiring reskilling; and
- external factors requiring the individual to be more mobile and thus in need of reorientation or mid-career orientation.

A *bilan* uses a guidance and advocacy framework but does not convert knowledge into a qualifications grid as with the APL process. Instead, it is a much broader based process which requires a fair amount of reflection and exploration. There is no standardised prescribed procedure for carrying out the *bilan*, which in itself begs the question of setting quality standards and markers. There are two main processes which can be mutually exclusive in the assessment. The first process involves a more diagnostic and prognostic approach through psychometric testing and interviews. The second process is more of a developmental and evaluative one which enables the individual to review his/her education, work experience, skills knowledge and attitudes. The end result could be like a record of achievement with biographical data and evidence of learning accreditation and so on, with an appropriate action plan for the individual.

A criticism of this system is that it does not offer anything more radical than a conventional British approach to formulating a career action plan and employs more or less the same principles and methodology for achieving, broadly speaking, the same aims of self-assessment, evaluation and possible new directions, i.e. reorientation with an action plan.

Trained counsellors in schools/colleges are available in France but are not as systematically widespread or institutionalised as in Britain. So this system of *bilan* is possibly a means of redress for '*droit d'orientation*' (entitlement to careers advice and guidance) for young adults and mature adults later in life.

Advantages of the 'Bilan' system for APL

One of the best features of this system as mentioned previously, is its emphasis on diagnosing the strengths and areas of improvements of an employee's core skills. Another feature of good practice which could be adopted by British employers is the pro-active role of employers in initiating wholesale '*bilans*' for substantial numbers of their employers. An example of this involved the *National Employers Electricité de France (EDF)* who carried out a survey of a potentially threatened area where employees could be made redundant and were in need of reskilling. The objective was for the individual employees to make a draft for a career plan with their supervisor and head of section. Facilitators were then brought in to carry out a *bilan* with the individual employees which focused on their strengths, areas of improvement and outlined areas for reskilling which could then be implemented through the company. Although in some ways this resembles the British IIP scheme, the difference is that, first, the French scheme has much more legitimate currency because, like the German 'dual' scheme, it is validated through legislation and upheld by its government's pro-active pursuit of excellence in training of its work-force. Second, the *bilan* is a holistic approach to assessing an employee's needs and can therefore pinpoint specific training needs for an individual and so on for a cohort of employees. Under the British IIP, it is very much a case of the employer responding to a specifically perceived need for training among the work-force, i.e. basic skills.

Recent research by the Adult Literacy and Basic Skills Unit (ALBSU) revealed concerns around the area of an insufficiently skilled work-force, particularly as technological advances raise the level of skills now required for jobs. One recent study by a unit of 400 companies found that a quarter of employees were judged to have difficulties at work because of poor literacy and numeracy. However, it is very possible that in excluding a formative diagnostic element as part of APL, other equally urgent training needs such as in the area of Information Technology, which could emerge at a later stage, remain undetected. The IIP programme is an optional one and very responsive in its remit, whereas the French system of *bilan* has more potential for being pro-active by contrast.

A second example is that of a shipbuilding company who needed to make 300 employees redundant. Forty per cent chose to go through the *bilan* process with an audit of their competences, followed by job searches and interviews. Employers in the region of south-west France created a *bourse de competences* (Databank of Competences needed for jobs). Prospective employees could then apply for jobs on the basis of the competences they possessed. The idea of a databank of competences is akin to the notion of a framework of occupational profiles, with 'transparency' for the skills and competences inherent in each occupational field.

Outcomes such as positive confidence building skills and awareness-raising of individuals capabilities are noteworthy. Nevertheless, an outcome which linked into accrediting individual's competences and experiences of work-based learning gives greater currency and empowerment and could be instrumental as a passport to further training and employment.

COMMITMENT FROM EMPLOYERS

The British experience of APL has much more to offer in this way as a potential process of empowerment for the individual in the face of career reorientation, adaptation to new work environments and retraining for skills shortages. However, it is essential for employers to appreciate the benefits of holistic assessment of their work-force and to invest in long-term training.

A recent joint survey carried out by the Institute of Management and the employment company Manpower found that while awareness of the NVQ was high, at 80 per cent among managers, half the managers were not familiar with the details of the qualifications and did not bother to find out how they could help their organisations. Awareness of the Investors in People project stood at 60 per cent but under a third of managers were familiar with the details. In a newspaper article entitled 'Managers ignorant over the nuts and bolts of training' (*Daily Telegraph*, 5 July 1993), Roger Young, Director General of the Institute of Management, said the survey made 'alarming reading' and was quoted as saying 'Our members are professional managers who should need no convincing of their role in encouraging employees to undertake work-based training. Yet this survey reveals widespread ignorance about critical elements of the training revolution.' Maureen Mifling, managing director of Manpower, was quoted as saying 'Skill shortages are a major concern for four in ten employers, but part of the remedy lies in managers' own hands.'

Schemes such as GATEWAY (assessment and guidance initiative – also known as REPLAN) through TECs working with employers, have great potential nationally to include 'APL' centres in the workplace or links with local colleges offering APL services. There needs to be a real commitment from government, employers, TECs and providers of training such as colleges to entitlement of training for the work-force. Implementation of the training would only take place systematically if commitment becomes mandatory and not optional.

'THE APL TRIPARTITE LINK': BENEFITS FOR BILINGUAL LEARNERS

In response to current demographic, social and economic changes, industry, business and Training and Enterprise Councils need to work in partnership much more closely with colleges in promoting and implementing an APL Tripartite Link. The inter-agency partnership needs to focus on developing training which is relevant to the needs of companies and their present and future employees. Colleges have to market their capabilities more rigorously and effectively in order to make businesses and training agencies aware of what services they can offer. This is a two-way process, with constant monitoring, evaluation and feedback. A joint project (RP 321), carried out in 1986–8 by Further Education Unit and REPLAN in Avon LEA, focused on the process of developing and piloting of portfolio preparation for unemployed people, interviewed employers and found that 'concern was expressed at the lack of liaison between FE and industry'. Moreover, employers focused on the value of work experience placements as being particularly valued in the selection process. Business training agencies and industry need to make colleges aware of their requirements particularly in relation to the training and updating of vocational and linguistic skills.

An educational toys supplier based in East London with established links in Paris for the retail and distribution of its merchandise in French nurseries and kindergartens approached a local college of FE for in-service language training for the administrative staff. In doing so, they were asked by the college lecturer in the business administration department to take on two Zairean, French-speaking students with considerable business administration work experience in Zaire, following an NVQ Level II in College for their work placements in the company. The arrangement was very successful as the French-speaking students were able to practise both English and French in the work environment and acted as role models for the English-speaking employees, who were able to practise French in addition to the French language training they gained at the college.

One recommended outcome would be the establishment of a national database of firms needing bilingual/multilingual workers which is available to colleges and other training institutions. This would prove to be very effective in harnessing the talents of bilingual learners for work placement purposes.

Specific areas of potential expertise within the bilingual student population may then be identified and matched to need within specific organisations, i.e. businesses, industry for work-based learning and/or employment. Within this tripartite partnership, colleges, industry and training agencies need to develop a pro-active strategy for delivery of the service based on local priorities and must adjust to situations that are, and will continue to be, constantly changing.

The LASER (London and South East Region, Advisory Council for Education and Training) guidelines put forward a diagrammatic view of College and Company partnership (shown in Appendix 8.1).

The importance of life-long continuous education and training as a cyclical pattern needs to be recognised as an entitlement for all adults, by all. The partnership needs to develop links and collaborative work with community organisations, educational outreach workers and other projects working in the field, as well as with courses designed to enable adults to identify their learning needs, such as Return to Learning and Access to Higher Education courses. By and large, in most colleges and 'partnerships', if links across college provision have been established to integrate vocational and academic provision with adult and community provision, not much emphasis is placed on links with local employers and training agencies to provide a work-based learning collaborative approach.

NATIONAL EDUCATION AND TRAINING TARGETS: HOW 'PARTNERSHIPS' CAN HELP MEET THEM

National Education and Training Targets have been agreed following an initiative launched by the CBI in association with other key partners.

The National Training Task Force has agreed to oversee and review progress at national level, and TECs and local enterprise companies are ideally placed to take the lead locally in achieving the targets. The National Targets for Lifetime Learning concern all mature adults, and in particular, bilingual adults who may be in employment as they are at a disadvantage in the job market.

Within their existing resources, TECs have considerable flexibility to tailor both employment training and employment action in cost-effective ways that could meet the differing needs of the unemployed and existing employees who need retraining or up-skilling.

The Government's six priorities for the 1990s are at the centre of the national strategy and emphasise that 'employers must invest more effectively in the skills their business need'. Moreover, greater emphasis is placed on individuals 'to be persuaded that training pays and that they should take more responsibility for their own development'.

Nevertheless, although the rhetoric is laudatory, what is of concern is that no visible penalties are to be imposed on employers not meeting national targets and unlike the French and German systems of training, there is no statutory obligation on employers to contribute a percentage of their income towards the training of their employees. Consequently, British employers risk becoming reactive rather than pro-active in this context. The French experience has outlined the potential usefulness of an APL process in situations where employers wish to cut back on staffing levels or to redeploy existing staff. Employers could be made aware of their employees' core skills, communication skills and levels of occupational competence, through utilising APL as an integral part of initial assessment and as a diagnostic process which would help guide the individual employee towards the most relevant training course and appropriate vocational qualification for him/her. It could be integrated into an appraisal system and be part of an employee's entitlement at work. It is feasible for medium-sized to larger organisations to 'buy in' skilled assessors from local colleges or training providers to carry out an APL 'audit' of their employees. Smaller companies who are unable to afford the costs should be in a position to work on a co-operative basis with the larger companies by sharing the costs of 'buying in' the skilled assessors. Thus, forming co-operatives and sharing the costs in partnership with the TECs, companies would be able to carry out an APL of their staff at point of entry, and at appropriate points in an employee's working life as part of a continuous process. It would be possible to identify gaps in an employee's skills profile and to identify previously unidentified areas of expertise or competence, perhaps gained from voluntary or unpaid work experience. Employees could then attend appropriate training programmes in colleges or with local training providers for reskilling or up-skilling purposes.

A co-operative of locally based employers or employers within a specific occupational sector could set up a local APL centre which would specialise in assessing and accrediting employees within specific occupational sectors whilst using the work-based facilities of companies and colleges for assessment purposes.

Setting up an assessment option for unemployed adults and mature adult employees is expensive in terms of time and requires experienced and accredited staff. Investment in these services is needed by employers in partnership with TECs and colleges and the Employment Service and would result in employers being much more pro-active. All these initiatives would eventually work towards implementing the CBI's National Targets of Lifetime learning in a more realistic way and much more extensively at local level.

Work-based Assessment: a British Example

A recent report 'Matching Skills: The Project Findings' (June 1993) initiated by British Telecom Education Services focuses on the skills BT expects future recruits to possess. The study centres on BT but raises issues that are clearly of interest to companies in other sectors of British industry. Definitions of the qualities required by individuals in the workplace are developed as follows:

- *Knowledge*: the range of information and nature of understanding gained from experience and study;
- *Skills*: the degree of expertise demonstrated in the undertaking of tasks; and
- *Capability*: the outlook, understanding and way of working that promote innovation and adaptability.

What is of particular relevance here is the profile of the desirable recruit with the potential for added value who is computer-literate, can offer a modern language or bring knowledge gained from previous experience in employment: 'Such people are considered more likely to take immediate advantage of in-house training and prove a quick return on BT's investment in them' (BT 1993). Such an ethos would appear to favour a cohort of bilingual learners with European languages and relevant prior employment expertise and experience.

APL CREDIT VOUCHERS/ADULT COMPACT

A plausible way forward is a system of compacts between employers, TECs and colleges which aims to deliver customised training to existing employees and work-based learning programmes to young adults 16–19 and unemployed mature adults. The ethos of training needs to undergo a radical transformation in Britain so that nationally a system of training vouchers may be implemented along the lines of training credits which enables an individual to purchase guidance and appropriate training. The underlying aim of training credits is to empower learners to purchase training appropriate to their needs, thereby stimulating a competitive and responsive training market. The scheme will be available to all 16- and 17-year-olds leaving full-time education or training, funded by the transfer of resources which would otherwise be paid to college for part-time provision for 16- and 17-year-olds.

In keeping with the idea of unitising the curriculum, 'training credits' provide greater flexibility as colleges deliver a qualification (or unit thereof) rather than enrolling learners on a course. The extension of the scheme of training credits to unemployed mature adults and existing employees and making available to this group of learners adult guidance vouchers and 'APL' vouchers would revolutionise vocational training. In keeping with European developments, an implementation of these schemes within member states would add a fillip to developments in those countries, and could help turn into a reality the recommendations proposed in the Memorandum on Higher Education in the EC – i.e. mobility and credit transfer through modular systems and harmonisation of professional and vocational qualifications, and points for action inherent within the Memorandum on Vocational Training – 'access to and continuous availability of lifelong training to all social groups with improvements in the quality of training.'

One of the criticisms of the German 'dual system' is its very narrow vocational training base. *Adult compacts* are unique in the sense that the trainee is offered broad-based training which prepares him or her for a range of opportunities, while at the same time providing the right kind of quality training to meet the employers' requirements.

There is a clear consensus that individuals must be helped to prepare for a working life which will demand flexibility, initiative and self-reliance; therefore more broad-based skills are needed. There is an expectation that employees should be able to cope with increased responsibility and rapid change in the work environment and to develop transferable skills.

Although the system of adult compacts has been designed initially as an arrangement between an employer and a potential adult employee that employment may be available provided certain conditions are met, it would be feasible to run such a scheme for employees in order to enhance their chances of promotion, to realise untapped potential and in the case of bilingual adults to offer them work experience in a context where they are able to utilise their linguistic skills more fully. It could be that such schemes are Euro-funded, furthermore that companies are paired with their European counterparts so that appropriate work

placements can be provided for existing or potential employees. Once
again, this pro-active focus on the linguistic abilities of employees would
create a radical shift away from the traditional deficit model of bilingual
adults entering colleges of FE for further study. Other generic objectives
covered by the adult compact programme include:

• the acquisition of vocationally specific skills;
• the development of more general skills, habits and attitudes which are
  vital for an effective working life;
• the achievement of nationally recognised vocational qualifications
  wherever possible; and
• the development of a Learner Profile integrated into a record of
  achievement as part of a commitment to life-long learning.

ADULT VOUCHERS FOR BILINGUAL LEARNERS

The concept of an adult voucher scheme has originated from the White
Paper 'People Jobs and Opportunity', which advanced the notion of
giving adults a voucher with which to purchase assessment and guidance
services. It has been pioneered successfully by certain TECs. In relation
to this, TECs and local education authorities have also been invited
to pilot schemes offering credit to unemployed adults for purchasing
Open Learning materials and support.

In terms of APL credit vouchers, the amount of time needed for assessment as part of the APL system would be cross-matched with the vouchers.
If vouchers are being bought by learners, it would be clearly discriminatory towards bilingual learners to expect them to pay more. However,
an ideal option would be for employers and TECs to sponsor and pay
for the APL vouchers, to encourage and enable bilingual learners to
access systems of education and training. The APL vouchers could be
implemented by companies and other organisations as part of initiatives
under Investors in People Awards.

It is envisaged that closer relations between colleges and employers
could be based on an exchange of services:

• College staff could train and assess workplace supervisors as trainers
  and assessors of NVQs;
• College staff could provide APL for workplace staff; and
• Employers could provide work placements for 'unemployed' Adult
  Compact trainees possibly leading to work.

These initiatives can be implemented nationally so that the uniformity
and the quality of the assessment of prior language, learning and work
experience services are monitored and sustained at local level. They would
have the impact of recognising and releasing the potential of bilingual

learners and employees. A European-wide network which implemented these services and allows bilingual candidates to have wider options, would ultimately fulfil the spirit and ethos of the Euro Directives and Memoranda.

GUIDELINES FOR IMPLEMENTING QUALITY CONTROL

The APL service, as as part of Threshold Services, would need to pursue a pro-active strategy for service delivery. For this, the college of FE needs to:

1 have clearly defined aims and priorities in attracting to the service bilingual learners as individuals and as groups from within the local community and local businesses. Feedback should be a priority in the strategy;
2 develop links and collaborative work with voluntary groups, communication organisations, educational outreach workers, local TECs, local authority Economic Development Units;
3 ensure that the service is seen by bilingual unemployed and unwaged adults and bilingual adults with overseas qualifications as relevant to their needs and is accessible and attractive in terms of costing;
4 give sufficient emphasis to counselling as the key activity in enabling bilingual adults to identify and articulate their learning needs; and
5 encourage users to evaluate the service.

In order to provide and store evidence for feedback, the APL service would require a computerised information system which is simple to use, and:

(a) is capable of producing quantifiable information feedback on:
   • the characteristics of bilingual users;
   • patterns of demand;
   • patterns of referral; and
   • unmet/inappropriately met needs and barriers to access;
(b) is capable of correlating different categories of information;
(c) is able to store qualitative information for feedback (i.e. users' experiences of the college and the Threshold Service, in particular cost, etc.);
(d) provides a means of relating the quantifiable to qualitative information which can be used as feedback in the form of statistics; and
(e) protects the confidentiality of users.

In order for the feedback to have maximum impact on the Institution, it would be necessary for the APL workers to have access to formal mechanisms, so that the feedback can effectively reach the key decision-making processes of the Institution whereupon necessary changes can be made to ensure quality control.

CONCLUSION

The development of APL alongside the use of Records of Achievement and the development of portfolios for assessment heralds a radically new approach to assessment and the embedding of alternative, individual routes through education, in particular for bilingual learners in Britain.

To increase participation, there is a need to break down the traditional barriers between academic and vocational education, formal and informal learning and for institutions to recognise formally the parity of value of transnational qualifications and prior experience:

> There should not just be two routes but a multiplicity of inter-related pathways, all of which can lead to higher education and/or a good job, but which recognise that different people want and need different things as they develop.
>
> (Sir Christopher Ball, 'Papering Over the Cracks', *Guardian*, 28 May 1991)

APL is pivotal to a guidance admissions process which widens access to opportunities in Further and Higher Education. By concentrating on the process of skills recognition, it has the potential to build confidence and self-awareness in the areas of language and occupational competence. Consequently, bilingual learners benefit from increased opportunity. Pump-priming inter-agency resources both nationally and internationally into this area ensures a financially viable and quality APL framework. Such a flexible framework can be used as a model of good working practice in Institutions in Britain and Europe. This, in turn, contributes to rich dividends in terms of increased client satisfaction, increased learner motivation and higher recruitment and retention rates.

APPENDIX 8.1 ASSESSMENT AND ACCREDITATION OF LEARNING IN THE WORKPLACE
PROJECT 1988–1990

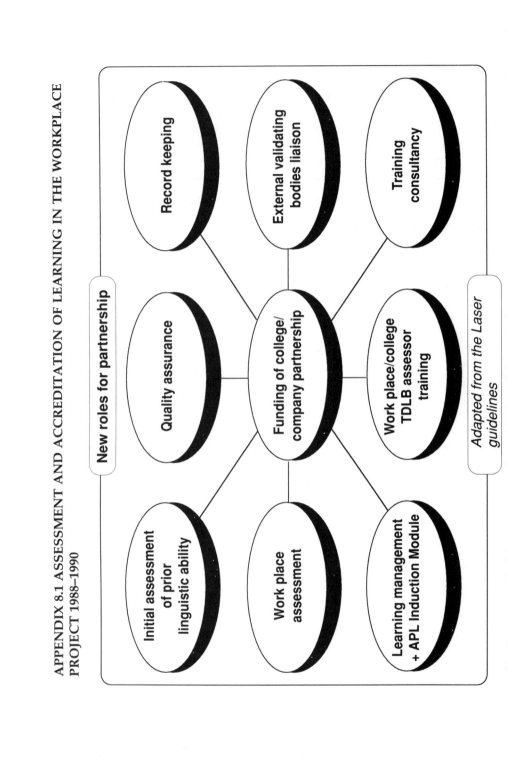

New roles for partnership

Record keeping

External validating bodies liaison

Training consultancy

Quality assurance

Funding of college/ company partnership

Work place/college TDLB assessor training

Initial assessment of prior linguistic ability

Work place assessment

Learning management + APL Induction Module

Adapted from the Laser guidelines

References

ALBSU (1991) 'Basic Skills Screening Assessment', London.
ALBSU/Equality at Work (1992) 'Inside English', Blackburn College.
BBC Education/ALBSU (1992) *Inside English* (video).
Bourneville Project (1993) 'Accreditation and Recognition of Refugees' Professional Qualifications', Birmingham: Bourneville College.
CBI (1991) 'National Education and Training Targets', London.
Cheshire LEA (1989) 'Framework of Adequacy for the Education of Adults', Chester.
City and Guilds (undated) 'Guidelines Booklet (Appendix B): Design and Marketing Schedule for Integrated Assignments (324–1–01)'.
CNAA (1989) *Regulations, Credit Accumulation and Transfer Scheme*, 2nd edn, London.
Croydon LEA (1990) 'Strategic Plan 1990–1993'.
Dadzie, Stella (1993) 'Survey of Numbers of Black Adults with Professional Qualifications Gained Overseas', NIACE/TEED.
Department of Educational Science, Department of Employment, Welsh Office (1991) 'Education and Training for the 21st Century' (Government White Paper), London.
Department of Employment Group (Roberts, C., Garnett, C., Kapoor, S. and Sarangi, S.) (1992) '"Quality in Teaching and Learning": Four multicultural classrooms in Further Education', London: Work-Related Development Fund, TEED, Department of Employment.
Erikson, Frederick and Shultz, Jeffrey (1982) *The Counsellor as Gatekeeper: Social Interaction in Interviews*, London: Academic Press.
European Institute of Education and Social Policy Project (1992) 'Strategies for VET in Europe 1992'.
Euroqualifications Project (DALI) (undated), London.
Evans, Norman (1989) *Experiential Learning: Accreditation and Assessment*, London: Routledge.
FEFC (1992) 'Funding Methodology' and 'Assessing Achievement' (Circulars), London.
FEU (1989) 'The Provision of Foreign Language Training in Industry', London.
—— (1990–1) 'Flexible Colleges' and 'Access to Learning and Qualifications in F.E. [TEED] Project', London.
—— (1992) 'Supporting Learning – Promoting Equity and Participation' and 'A Model for Colleges', London.
—— (1993) 'Working with Europe', London: Focus Consultancy.
FEU Project R321 (1985) 'Staff Development in a Multicultural Society', London.
FEU Project RP594 (1992) 'Achievement Led Resourcing', London.

FEU Project RP693 (forthcoming) 'Cultural Bias in Assessment: Cultural and Linguistic Factors Affecting Assessment', London.

FEU/REPLAN Project RP321 (1986–8), London/Avon LEA.

Further Education Staff College (1989) 'A Guide to Work-based Learning Terms', Bristol.

GNVQ (1993) 'Core Skills Units', NCVQ (April).

Gumperz, John (1982a) Discourse Strategies, Cambridge: Cambridge University Press.

—— (ed.) (1982b) Language and Social Identity, Cambridge: Cambridge University Press.

HMI (1990) 'Measuring Up: Performance Indicators in Further Education', London: HMSO.

—— (1990–1) 'Bilingual Adults in Education and Training' (Ref 7/92/NS), DES.

Honey, P. and Mumford, A. (1986) Using Your Learning Styles, Maidenhead.

Journal of the European Communities (1991) No C196 (25/7/91).

Kidd, Jennifer (1988) 'Assessment in Action', London: UDACE/NIACE.

Kolb, D. A. (1984) Experiential Learning – Experience as the Source of Learning and Development, New Jersey: Prentice-Hall.

Languages Lead Body (1992) 'National Standards for Modern Foreign Languages', November.

LASER (1988–90) 'Assessment and Accreditation of Learning in the Workplace Project', London.

Leach, Robert (1992) 'Go to Work on Your English', NEC.

Liston, David and Reeves, Nigel (1985) Business Studies, Languages and Overseas Trade – A Study of Education and Training, London: MacDonald & Evans, Institute of Export.

McKeown, Neil (1990) Case Studies and Projects in Communication, London: Routledge.

Marshall, Tony (1992) Careers Guidance with Refugees, Refugee Training and Employment Centre.

Nansell, Jack (1990) Assessment of Prior Learning and Achievement: The Role of Expert Systems, London: FEU.

NARIC (National Academic Recognition Information Centre) (1991) The International Guide to Qualifications in Education, London.

NCC National Council (1990) 'Core Skills' (March).

NCVQ (1990) Report No 6: 'Common Learning outcomes: Core Skills in A/AS levels and NVQs', London.

—— (1988) 'Access and Equal Opportunities in Relation to National Vocational Qualifications', London.

Roberts, Celia (1985) The Interview Game and How It's Played, London: BBC Books.

Simoko, S. (1990) APL: A Practical Guide for Professionals, London: Kogan Page.

Smithers, Professor Alan (1993) 'All Our Futures', Channel Four Dispatches (16 December).

South Bank Polytechnic (1992) 'The Assessment of Prior Learning, Progression and Skills for Science', London: Report of the BP Access Project.

Training Agency (1990) 'PIs for WRFE' July, London.

UDACE (1987) 'The Seven Activities of Guidance' and 'Building a Guidance Service', London.

Wilson, Amrit (1985) Asian Women Speak Out, National Extension College.

Wolfe, Alison (1993) Assessment Issues and Problems in a Criterion Based System, London: FEU.

Wolfe, A. and Silver, R. (1986) Work-based Learning: Training Assessment by Supervisors, Sheffield: MSC Series.

Index

The following abbreviations have been used in the index:
APL   Accreditation of Prior Learning Systems
FE   further education
GA   guidance advocate